Nebraska
An Illustrated History

The Great Plains Photography Series

This volume in the Great Plains Photography Series is made possible by a grant from the University of Nebraska Foundation to extend the work of the University beyond its campuses.

Frederick C. Luebke

University of Nebraska Press
Lincoln and London

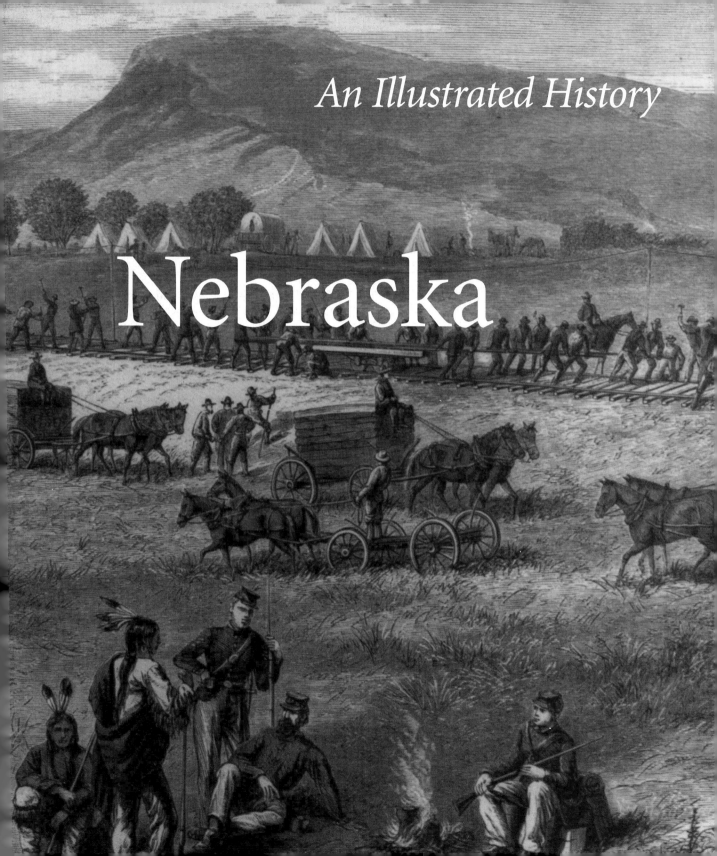

An Illustrated History

Nebraska

© 1995 by the University of Nebraska Press
All rights reserved
Manufactured in the United States of America
⊗ The paper in this book meets the minimum requirements of
American National Standard for Information Sciences—Permanence of
Paper for Printed Library Materials, ANSI Z39.48-1984.
Library of Congress Cataloging-in-Publication Data
Luebke, Frederick C., 1927–
Nebraska: an illustrated history / Frederick C. Luebke.
p.   cm.—(Great Plains photography series)
ISBN 0-8032-2902-X (alk. paper)
1. Nebraska—History.   2. Nebraska—History—Pictorial works.
I. Title.   II. Series.
F666.L83   1995
978.2—dc20   94-47569
                                                              CIP

To the staff of the Nebraska State Historical Society

Contents

Illustrations

Part 2. *A Fledgling State*

Preface and Acknowledgments

What is unique about the history of Nebraska? What makes it distinctive or different from its neighbors? Do the artificial state boundaries imposed by Congress in the nineteenth century on an area of very low population encompass a place where truly significant historical trends occurred?

The idea of this book grew out of an effort to answer these questions. About ten years ago a friend in the Department of History at Indiana University asked me to contribute an article on Nebraska for a book on twelve Midwestern states—from Ohio in the east to the tier of Great Plains states in the west. It was to be a venture in comparative history. My assignment was to write an article on Nebraska's history that would focus on its unique characteristics. Originally published in *Heartland: Comparative Histories of the Midwestern States* and edited by James H. Madison (Bloomington: Indiana University Press, 1988), the article was subsequently reprinted with the addition of twenty-one maps and illustrations in *Nebraska History* (69 [winter 1988]: 150–68). I have summarized the article's essential ideas in the introduction to this book.

Developing a conceptual framework for the history of a state is one thing, but working out the details is another. That is what has demanded most of the time I reserved for research and writing since 1988. Even though I had been teaching the history of Nebraska for many years, I could not complete the task without a great deal of help. Of the people who lent me their knowledge and expertise, none was more important than John Carter, curator of photographs in the Nebraska State Historical Society (NSHS). This book could not have been produced without his splendid cooperation. Carter emphasized the importance of starting with a concept capable of informing the selection of appropriate visual materials. In other words, the text determines which pictures to use; one may have to resist including a brilliant or familiar photograph if it fails to illuminate the idea developed in the text. Further, Carter never imposed his expertise on the selection process: he used his phenomenal knowledge of the Society's huge photography collection to offer possibilities or alternatives, and we often discussed the advantages of one picture over another, but the final choice was always mine. It is a pleasure to acknowledge his generous assistance and advice, his infectious enthusiasm for photographs as historical artifacts, and his willingness to interrupt his own work for the benefit of mine.

I wish also to acknowledge the assistance of other members of the NSHS staff. James Potter, Gail Potter, Martha Miller, and David Murphy were invariably helpful and considerate. Lawrence Sommer, the director of the Nebraska State Historical Society, and James Hanson, his predecessor in that position, were supportive of this project at all stages. Throughout the three decades that I have studied Nebraska history, I have benefitted from the kind and courteous attention that these and many other persons at NSHS extended to me and my work. I dedicate this book to them.

In the course of writing this book I have drawn upon the knowledge of many historians, sociologists, political scientists, geographers, economists, and agriculturalists for criticism of one or more parts of the text. Each has been generous of time and expertise, and some have critiqued several revisions. I thank them sincerely for their help. Most are (or have been) professors at the University of Nebraska–Lincoln: Miguel Carranza, Learthen Dorsey, Francis Haskins, Leslie Hewes, Robert

Knoll, Gary Moulton, Howard Ottoson, Benjamin Rader, James Rawley, Robert Sittig, Michael Turner, David Wishart, and John Wunder. Other readers include Jim Bert (Strategic Air Command Museum), Lori Cox-Paul (NSHS Foundation), Harl Dalstrom (University of Nebraska at Omaha), R. Douglas Hurt (Iowa State University), Orville Menard (University of Nebraska at Omaha), Dennis Mihelich (Creighton University), David Murphy (NSHS), William Rowley (University of Nevada), Jerold Simmons (University of Nebraska at Omaha), Charles Schroeder (University of Nebraska Foundation), Michael Schuyler (University of Nebraska at Kearney), Donald Snoddy (Union Pacific Museum), Charles Trimble (Red Willow Institute), and Todd White (Offutt Air Force Base). I benefitted especially from the criticism of Carlos Schwantes of the University of Idaho, who is the author of histories of both Washington and Idaho, and of James Potter, editor of *Nebraska History*. I followed the advice offered by all these scholars in virtually every instance, but needless to say, that does not absolve me from the responsibility for the errors of fact or interpretation that may remain.

I wish also acknowledge the assistance of others who helped me in ways too various to list here, but usually in connection with the identification or acquisition of illustrative materials. Charles Flowerday of the University of Nebraska–Lincoln Conservation and Survey Division was especially helpful. Among the many others who responded cheerfully and patiently to my requests were Jay Bailey, Lynn Beideck-Porn, Roger Bruhn, Ann Billesbach, Donal Burns, Deborah O'Donnell, Jodie Fawl, Charles Francis, Robert Gillan, Stanley Haas, William Hansen, Sharon Jefferson, Martha Kennedy, Virginia Knoll, Stephen Lavin, James McKee, James Merchant, Mark Miller, David Murphy, Jon Nelson, Allison Petersen, Joseph Porter, Roger Reeves, Mila Saskova-Pierce, Patricia Sloan, Kevin Spradlin, Joseph Svoboda, E. Arthur Thompson, E. N. "Jack" Thompson, John Weihing, and Todd White. I extend my heartfelt thanks to them all. I could not have completed this book without their assistance. My apologies go to anyone whose name I have inadvertently omitted.

The production of this book with its nearly three hundred illustrations is exceptionally expensive. Because Nebraska is a lightly populated state, there is almost no possibility of recovering production costs through sales, a circumstance that makes subventions and other forms of assistance necessary. The University of Nebraska Foundation provided a generous subsidy. The Nebraska State Historical Society Foundation supported picture acquisition with a small but essential grant. The majority of the photographs reproduced in this book were donated by the Nebraska State Historical Society. Others were provided gratis by the Union Pacific Museum, United States Air Force, Omaha World-Herald, Omaha Public Power District, Loup Power District, the Stuhr Museum of the Prairie Pioneer, Thayer County Museum, John Deere Company, Mutual of Omaha, Iowa Beef Processors, Hispanic Community Center, the Office of the Governor, and the Nebraska Department of Administrative Services. Various units on three campuses of the University of Nebraska provided photographs gratis or at cost. Other agencies and organizations, including the Nebraska Department of Roads, the Western Heritage Museum of Omaha, the Douglas County Historical Society, and the Journal-Star Company of Lincoln, contributed photographs at cost.

I am pleased to recognize two other indispensable sources of help. The first is the University of Nebraska–Lincoln, most especially its Department of History and the Center for Great Plains Studies. Both contributed to this project in ways too numerous to mention. I wish also to recognize specifically the assistance of Joan Curtis and Sandra Pershing, secretary and staff assistant in the Department of History. I deeply appreciate and gratefully acknowledge their efficiency and good cheer.

The second indispensable source are many friends, both personal and professional. In addition to those mentioned above, I wish to acknowledge my debt to Robert Knoll. He has been an unfailing source of encouragement and knowledge, and he has been a willing listener. But my best friend is my wife, Norma Wukasch Luebke. Her support has been invaluable in quality and incalculable in quantity. An editor by profession, she gave generously of her time to enhance clarity of thought and cogency of expression. Her organizational skills were central to the coordination of the text, illustrations, and captions, as well as the acquisition of the images and the acknowledgment of sources.

Nebraska
An Illustrated History

Introduction
The Place and the People

That small part of North America occupied by Nebraska is much like its neighboring states. Although the history of Nebraska bears many similarities to that of its neighbors, Nebraska has its own unique character. It is warmer than the Dakotas, colder than Kansas, drier than Iowa, and wetter than Wyoming. It is a grassland, not naturally forested like much of Minnesota. Its topography is more varied than that of Illinois, but it has nothing like the Black Hills of South Dakota or the Ozarks of Missouri. Like Kansas and Iowa, Nebraska has great beauty, but little of the kind that appeals to modern romantics who idealize mountains and seashores. One of Nebraska's illustrious sons, Alvin Johnson, wrote in *Pioneer's Progress: An Autobiography* that the state's magnificent plains would have delighted the classical Romans, who detested the Alps as "horrid and miserable" but loved verdant fields that bordered "sluggish streams exuberant with harvests."

Nebraska straddles much of the Great Plains from east to west. Part of the Midwest, it encompasses 77,355 square miles in a roughly rectangular shape. Stretching westward from the Missouri River at Omaha for 430 miles to Wyoming, it separates Kansas from South Dakota by 210 miles. It occupies a broad plain that slopes gradually upward from the southeastern corner near Falls City, where the elevation is 840 feet above sea level, to the far southwestern corner near Kimball, where it rises to 5,426 feet.

Patterns of rainfall, temperature, soils, and topography in the eastern third of the state, where two-thirds of the people live, resemble those of Iowa. But again, as one travels westward across the state, the physical environment gradually changes. Rainfall decreases from thirty-six inches per year in the southeast to fifteen in the northwest. The quality of the soil also changes. In the east, deep and rich soils are common, but much of the central part consists of the grass-covered Sand Hills, an area of about twenty thousand square miles roughly equivalent to the state of West Virginia. Inhabited by fewer than one person per square mile, this region is ideal cattle country. West of the Sand Hills is the Panhandle, a lightly populated area with strong affinities for Wyoming, which it resembles as much as eastern Nebraska resembles Iowa.

Rivers are crucial to an understanding of Nebraska history. Lying entirely within the drainage basin of the Missouri River, the state is threaded by several secondary streams—the Republican, the Platte, the Loup, the Elkhorn, and the Niobrara—that form a ladder of rivers flowing eastward toward the Missouri, Nebraska's eastern boundary. But only the Platte rises in the Rocky Mountains and has the plenteous flow such origins afford, and it alone runs the length of the state from west to east. Its broad valley provides a ribbon of fertile soil and a spinal cord of transportation and communication. The wide and shallow Platte River has even provided the state with its name, for in the Omaha and Oto languages Nebraska means "flat water."

The Platte River valley has always been central to Nebraska history. It was America's first great highway to the West. In the mid-nineteenth century it funneled several hundred thousand people westward across the Great Plains to new homes in Oregon, California, and Utah. It was the natural route for the first transcontinental railroad. Later, after the advent of the automobile, the first band of concrete to stretch across America paralleled the Platte, as does much of Interstate 80 today. Even the airlines seem to trace this natural highway as they leave contrails high in the sky, six miles above its shallow and interwoven channels.

But physical characteristics such as topography, rainfall, soils, and rivers merely set the limits for the history of a given place. How a society orders its affairs over time is governed more by the culture its members have brought to the land they inhabit.

The first people who came to the place we now call Nebraska were the Native Americans. Like the Euro-Americans who came later, the various Indian tribes differed in language and culture. The mixture in Nebraska was unique—similar to but certainly not the same as the groups who populated surrounding areas. So it was also with the people who came to Nebraska in the nineteenth century. Most settlers came from states directly east; fewer came from southern states or New England. Other newcomers were immigrants from northern and central Europe. Understanding the cultures of all these people helps explain Nebraska's history.

The uniqueness of Nebraska's history emerges from the interaction between place and people—between environmental and cultural forces. But history is also the study of change over time. The time factor, as it may be called, is an essential ingredient in the recipe for the history of Nebraska. What happened here is intimately connected to the discovery of gold in California or the Civil War, to cycles of drought, and to many technological developments in transportation, communications, and agriculture. To understand and illustrate these historical connections is what this book is all about.

Having Theirs Taken is the title of this image from the Humphrey Collection, Nebraska State Historical Society (NSHS). The place is Lincoln, probably the "North Bottoms," where many German-speaking immigrants from Russia lived. The date is about 1910. Having two cameras focused on the three-generation family was confusing to two of the children: no doubt the group was asked to pose for the photographer in the picture, but the boy confidently posed for the unseen cameraman as his curious sister sneaked a glance. Courtesy NSHS, H926:389.

Before Statehood

Part 1

A Place on the Way to Somewhere Else

*To the Native Americans, the Great Plains were attractive and desirable.
Generally living in harmony with the physical environment, they found
the plains of Nebraska to be productive, even bountiful. The plains were
the center of their universe—the place above all others where they wanted
to be.*

*For many white men in the early nineteenth century, however, Nebraska
was a territory that had to be crossed in order to get somewhere else. For
them the Great Plains often seemed like an obstruction. It was attractive
enough, but it made one's journey longer or more difficult than it would
otherwise be. Fur traders—usually French-Canadians in the eighteenth
century—were the first. Exploring the Missouri River basin, they and their
American successors in the nineteenth century found some fur-bearing animals in Nebraska, but they were more interested in the resources located
farther west and north on the northern plains and later in the Rocky
Mountains. Military explorers, beginning with the famous Lewis and
Clark Expedition of 1804–6 and continuing with Zebulon Pike, Stephen
Long, and others, usually pursued objectives that lay beyond Nebraska.*

Scientists and artists among these and other explorers sought and recorded much valuable information about the plains and its inhabitants.

Nebraska was also a transit area for the several hundred thousand Americans who crossed the plains in covered wagons headed for Oregon, California, Utah, Colorado, and other mountain states in the West. In their diaries and reminiscences they sometimes commented on the fact that land in Nebraska, particularly the eastern portions, was attractive as potential farming country. But Nebraska was not open for settlement until 1854. Besides, they left home for farms in Oregon, gold in California, or the Mormon Zion in Utah, not treeless prairies, rich though the soil was. A few travelers returned later to settle in Nebraska, but their number was small.

For the builders of the first transcontinental railroad, Nebraska was also a place to be crossed. Working west from Omaha in 1865 along the Platte, their first goal was to connect with the West Coast, not to develop Nebraska, even though that quickly became an important objective, too. Railroads transformed the Nebraska Territory and stimulated large-scale settlement, as did the Homestead Act passed by Congress in 1862, which made rich farmland available to settlers at almost no cost. Along with the farmers came thousands of merchants, professional persons, craftsmen, and common laborers. Led especially by town-builders and speculators, these people created Nebraska's first government.

But Nebraska has never entirely lost its character as a transit area. In the twentieth century, when American society was transformed by the automobile, the nation's first transcontinental highway—the Lincoln Highway—generally followed the railroad route across Nebraska, as does Interstate 80, which permits Americans to cross the plains in safety and comfort unimaginable to the overlanders of the 1850s. Contrails left by transcontinental airliners are fleeting evidence of still other travelers across the plains. Flying in pressurized cabins at altitudes exceeding thirty thousand feet, passengers are scarcely aware of Nebraska as a place along their way.

The key to Nebraska history is the Platte River, shown here in a photo by J. Carbutt as it appeared near Cozad in October 1866, a time when it carried much more water than it does today. Running the length of the state, the Platte fixes the state's east-west orientation. Its valley provides a ribbon of fertile soil and a spinal cord of transportation—America's first great highway to the West. Courtesy Union Pacific Museum Collection. H7-190.

The First Nebraskans *1*

People have lived within the present borders of Nebraska for more than twelve thousand years. Archaeological research shows that through the centuries, groups entered and abandoned the area as its climate fluctuated between long periods of drought and times of plentiful moisture. Each group modified its way of life to survive under prevailing conditions in the plains environment. The most ancient inhabitants were nomadic hunters, but centuries later others came to the grasslands from wooded environments. Here they hunted, fished, and farmed.

Such migration in and out of the plains continued until recent times. Constant movement created a highly diverse mixture of Indian languages and cultures. The Pawnees and their northern relatives, the Arikaras, lived here the longest. They came from the south at least four or five centuries ago and established villages along the Platte, Loup, Republican, and other streams in central Nebraska. In the eighteenth century several small tribes of Siouan linguistic stock, including the Omahas, Poncas, and Otoes, entered eastern Nebraska and lived near the Missouri River. Other tribes, such as the Teton Sioux (Lakotas), Arapahos, and Cheyennes, migrated westward from forested areas north and east of the Missouri River, some of them less than two hundred years ago. Altogether, the various groups living in what is now Nebraska may have numbered about forty thousand in 1800.

The Indians understood their world to have a unity or coherence that was incomprehensible to Euro-American intruders. Unlike the whites, they made no distinction between practical and religious activities. Among the Pawnees, for example, sacred ceremonies were as essential as hoeing was to make corn grow. Nor could buffalo hunting be separated from agriculture: crops could not grow without rituals in which offerings of buffalo meat were made.

Beginning in the seventeenth century, plains Indian cultures were profoundly influenced when Spanish intruders introduced horses, which were not native to America. When sedentary, horticultural peoples such as the Pawnees and Omahas who had entered the area early acquired horses in the eighteenth century, they quickly adapted them for use on their long seasonal bison hunts into western Nebraska and central Kansas. But feeding large herds of horses created severe shortages of grass in fall and winter near their villages. The Pawnees solved this problem by burning the tall-grass prairies, which stimulated earlier and heavier yields of grass but also destroyed scarce timber stands.

Late-arriving tribes such as the Lakotas, finding their woodland ways of limited use in the semiarid grasslands, adapted to the plains environment by evolving a culture in which the horse played a central role. Completely nomadic, they lived in tepees yearround, in contrast to the Pawnees and Omahas, who inhabited earth lodges except when on the hunt. Disdaining agriculture, the nomadic tribes became dependent on the bison for food, clothing, tools, and scores of other household items.

Although some tribes regarded others as enemies, they also engaged in intertribal trade and shared the resources offered by the plains. Some tribes raided each other for horses. When European explorers and fur traders began to penetrate the area, the Native Americans usually welcomed them and eagerly exchanged furs for guns and ammunition, metal utensils, kettles, blankets, clothing, and ornaments, as well as alcoholic drink. Unhappily, such contacts also spread diseases, such as measles, smallpox, influenza, and mumps, for which they had no natural immunity. Epidemics devastated the Indians, and in some cases more than half the population was swept away.

Still, traditional Indian culture thrived in Nebraska until the 1830s. In that decade the Omahas, buffeted by disease and skirmishes with other tribes, desperately shifted from one camp to another on the Missouri and Elkhorn rivers before settling in a village west of Bellevue in 1844. Similarly, the Pawnees suffered devastating losses from smallpox and later from cholera, and thus weakened, were vulnerable to attacks from the Lakotas. As the Brulé and Oglala bands of the Lakota nation moved southward into western Nebraska, they successfully evicted Pawnees from territory that lay astride the white man's trail to Oregon, California, and Utah. The Brulés and Oglalas thus had frequent contacts with whites trekking westward, which meant exposure to disease and intermittent fighting with the U.S. Army.

As white penetration of Nebraska increased in the 1840s and 1850s, the traditional cultures of the several tribes were permanently changed. In the 1820's, the U.S. government began negotiating with various tribes for cessions of Indian lands in Nebraska. These negotiations were not yet completed in the 1850s when Nebraska became a territory and, for the first time, land was made available to whites for ownership.

1.1. The Pawnees and the several Siouan groups in eastern Nebraska preferred to live in villages of circular earth lodges that generally faced east. Supported by a framework of joined posts and lintels, the exterior consisted of sod layers resting on branches of trees woven in a basketlike pattern. The windowless lodges were vented at the top to admit light and allow smoke to escape. This photograph was taken by William Henry Jackson near Genoa in 1871. Courtesy NSHS, 1396:1–2.

1.2. George Catlin, *Catching the Wild Horse.* Horses arrived in Nebraska early in the eighteenth century, transforming the culture of the plains people. Some tribes, such as the Lakotas, became completely nomadic. Others, such as the Omahas and Pawnees, remained horticultural but ordinarily went on extended bison hunts twice each year. George Catlin executed a sketch for this lithographic image in 1834 when he visited the Comanches. In his journal Catlin described in detail how the Comanches captured and tamed these mustangs. From the Catlin portfolio in the Christlieb Collection, Love Library. Courtesy Great Plains Collection, University of Nebraska–Lincoln.

1.3. In 1859, Albert Bierstadt, the famous painter of the American West, photographed this Sioux standing by his tepee with the North Platte River in the distance. The bison-hunting Lakotas, Cheyennes, and Arapahoes developed the tepee as an ideal dwelling. Easily collapsed and readily transported, tepees were also used by the horticultural tribes while on the hunt. Courtesy NSHS, B588.5:1.

Indian Record
of a
Battle
between the Pawnees
and Konzas, being a
Fac Simile of a delinea-
tion upon a Bison Robe

1.4. Titian Ramsay Peale, *Indian Record of a Battle Between the Pawnees and Kanzas, being a Facsimile of a Delineation upon a Bison robe.* Titian Ramsay Peale, who accompanied the Stephen Long Expedition in 1819, copied this depiction of intertribal conflict from an Indian painting. Few Indian paintings from this early period, which were frequently limned on bison robes, have been preserved. Courtesy Yale Collection of Western Americana, Beinecke Rare Book and Manuscript Library.

The Fur Trade in Nebraska 2

The first Europeans to enter the land that would be called Nebraska were French and Spanish fur traders of the eighteenth century. Pushing up the Missouri and its tributaries, they mingled freely with the Indians and were readily accepted by them. Most of these traders were illiterate and left no record other than their progeny. The explorer Etienne Veniard, Sieur de Bourgmont, in his account of a trip to the mouth of the Platte River in 1714, made the first recorded use of the word *Nebraska* when he identified the Platte River as the *Nibraskier*.

The traders, whether French, Spanish, or the Americans of the early nineteenth century, were not themselves trappers. The Indians were the producers: they caught the animals, skinned them, and prepared the pelts for the traders, who offered knives, guns, ammunition, kettles, blankets, beads, and other manufactured goods, including whiskey, for the furs.

Systematic exploitation of the animal resources of the Platte River region began with the establishment in 1812 of Fort Lisa, a fur trading post on the Missouri north of present-day Omaha. It was built by Manuel Lisa, a Spanish trader originally from New Orleans who had led a successful expedition up the Missouri to the Yellowstone River and beyond in the preceding year. This post became the focal point of fur trading in the area for the next decade. Traders often took up residence in Indian villages far from the post, collecting furs through the winter months.

The traders were mostly interested in beaver pelts, although there was a brisk trade in muskrat, fox, and deer, and later in bison robes. Beaver, which were used to create the felt for a popular style of hat in the early nineteenth century, soon disappeared from the plains, though they continued to survive in the mountains. Monogamous, not prolific, almost sedentary in their habits, the beaver were highly vulnerable to uncontrolled harvesting.

In the 1820s the hostility of Indian tribes in the upper Missouri basin, especially the Arikara, forced a reorganization of the fur trade and shifted the center of activity to the Rocky Mountains. Under the new system, Euro-Americans became trappers themselves instead of depending on the Indians. Living in the Rockies throughout the year, the mountain men, as they were called, gathered furs and prepared them for shipment to market in early summer, when they would rendezvous at a prearranged site for trade and revelry. The success of this commerce, which reached its fullest development in the 1830s, depended on a safe and direct trade route to markets in the eastern states, a route that bypassed the hostile Arikaras. The Platte River valley provided that essential transportation link. The fur traders' caravan of 1830 was the first to demonstrate the valley's feasibility as a wagon route.

Curiously, the first American to traverse Nebraska along the Platte River, Robert Stuart, traveled from west to east. Stuart had been a member of the expedition led by the fur trader and merchant Wilson Price Hunt in 1810–12 up the Missouri River and across the mountains to Astoria at the mouth of the Columbia River on the Pacific Ocean. Sent to deliver dispatches to John Jacob Astor in New York, Stuart sought out a more direct overland route between Astoria and St. Louis in 1812–13. He came upon South Pass in Wyoming, followed the Sweetwater to the North Platte, and traveled downstream across Nebraska to the Missouri. A dozen years passed, however, before the trail he blazed would be put to use.

Although most Native Americans of the plains eagerly welcomed the advent of the fur trade and the goods it brought, they also suffered because of it. Their culture was subjected to severe stress, and the introduction of the white man's diseases was devastating—thousands died of smallpox, measles, and venereal diseases. The population of the Pawnees was cut in half by smallpox in the winter of 1831–32; the Mandans, a sedentary tribe located near present-day Bismarck, North Dakota, were virtually wiped out in 1837–38. Later, whiskey became a staple of the fur trade and worked further destruction on Indian society and culture. Important though fur traders were for the history of the plains, they were both despoilers of Indian culture and thoughtless exploiters of the environment.

BELLVUE.

Mr DOUGHERTY'S AGENCY
on the Missouri

Agentschaft des H. Dougherty
am Missouri

Agence de Mr Dougherty
sur le Missouri

London, published by Ackermann & Cᵒ 96 Strand September 1ᵗʰ 1841.

2.1. Karl Bodmer, *Bellvue, Mr. Dougherty's Agency on the Missouri,* 1833. In 1822 the Missouri Fur Company established a fur trading post at Bellevue, which became the earliest permanent settlement in Nebraska. Located on the Missouri River north of the mouth of the Platte, it also became the headquarters of Major John Dougherty, the Indian agent for the United States government. Courtesy Joslyn Art Museum, Omaha, gift of the Enron Art Foundation.

MISSOURI INDIANER.

Indien Missouri

MISSOURI INDIAN.

OTO INDIANER.

Indien Oto

OTO INDIAN.

CHEF DER PUNCAS.

Chef des Puncas

CHIEF OF THE PUNCAS.

2.2. Karl Bodmer, *Missouri Indian, Oto Indian, Chief of the Puncas,* 1834. These three portraits of Nebraska Indians were sketched separately by Karl Bodmer when he returned down the Missouri River with Prince Maximilian of Wied-Neuwied in 1834. Later he combined them in this engraving. Each man displays evidence of the fur trade: a commercial blanket, a padlock worn as an ornament, and a peace medal. Courtesy Joslyn Art Museum, Omaha, gift of the Enron Art Foundation.

3 Exploration on the Plains
Soldiers, Scientists, and Artists

Most of the early American explorers of the Great Plains traveled *through* rather than *to* Nebraska. President Thomas Jefferson, who in 1803 had negotiated the acquisition of the Louisiana Purchase from France (which doubled the size of the United States and included all of present-day Nebraska), dispatched the first expedition into the newly acquired territory. Led by army officers Meriwether Lewis and William Clark in 1804–6, the expedition sought to discover an overland route to the mouth of the Columbia River on the Pacific Ocean and ultimately to the treasurers of the Orient. Jefferson's instructions also required them to make systematic scientific observations of the flora, fauna, topography, and inhabitants of the territory they passed through.

Traveling laboriously up the Missouri River in a keelboat and two dugout canoes, the Lewis and Clark party skirted the edge of Nebraska in the summer of 1804. The mouth of the Platte was an early goal, but their most famous stop in Nebraska was on a bluff north of Omaha where they held a council with Oto and Missouria Indians. Called Council Bluff, this meeting ground later became the site of Fort Atkinson.

The next expedition to the West only touched Nebraska. In 1806, Lieutenant Zebulon Pike was ordered by General James Wilkinson to venture onto the plains and eventually into Spanish territory for what was essentially a spying mission. On his way from St. Louis to the Rockies, he marched through Kansas to return some Osage travelers to their villages and briefly visited a Pawnee village on the Republican River in what is today Nebraska, where he sought to negotiate peace. Pike then headed south to the Arkansas River, which he followed to the Rockies.

Five years later a natural scientist ventured into the region. John Bradbury, a distinguished Scottish botanist, accompanied the John Jacob Astor fur-trading expedition hundreds of miles up the Missouri River. Like Lewis and Clark, Bradbury experienced only Nebraska's eastern border, but he broadened his view beyond botany to include valuable observations on the entire plains environment.

The Platte River valley came into its own as the highway to the West with the next military expedition, which was led by Major Stephen H. Long in 1820. Striking westward from their winter cantonment on the Missouri near Fort Lisa, Long and a party of twenty men traveled up the Platte on horseback. Long's party included Edwin James, botanist and surgeon, the painters Samuel Seymour and Titian Peale (the latter classified as a naturalist), a topographer, a hunter, interpreters, and soldiers. They visited a Pawnee village on the Loup River, rode south to the Platte at Grand Island, crossed the river to the south side near the present-day city of North Platte, and followed the south fork to the Colorado Rockies.

Long and his scientist companions perceived the semiarid high plains as a bleak region unfit for agriculture. In the report of the expedition written mostly by James and published in 1823, they announced that the plains should forever remain "the unmolested haunt of the native hunter, the bison, and the jackall" and act as "a barrier to prevent too great an extension of our population westward." On their map of the region they inscribed in large, bold letters the words "Great American Desert."

During the next three decades the Great Plains region was crisscrossed by a variety of persons, each with his own purpose. Commerce dominated in the southern plains as the Santa Fe Trail was developed in the early 1820s. Adventure stimulated some excursions and the pursuit of science motivated others. In 1832, Captain Benjamin Bonneville, on leave from the army and leading a troop of 110 men and twenty wagons, headed west from Fort Osage (near Independence, Missouri) on a route that approximated the later Oregon Trail. In the same year the amateur painter and anthropologist George Catlin, intending to capture the character of Indian life before it vanished, ascended the Missouri on the maiden voyage of the steamboat *Yellow Stone.* Prince Maximilian of Wied-Neuwied, accompanied by the gifted artist Karl Bodmer, pushed up the Missouri on his scientific expedition in 1833. In 1837, another painter, Alfred Jacob Miller, engaged by the British sportsman William Drummond Stewart, accompanied a caravan of American Fur Company wagons along the Platte through Nebraska to Fort William (later called Fort Laramie) in present-day Wyoming and on to the annual rendezvous with the mountain men.

Military excursions were not unusual. Among the most significant for Nebraska was an expedition led in 1835 by Colonel Henry Dodge from Fort Leavenworth in Kansas overland to the vicinity of present-day Lincoln. After visiting an Otoe village on the Platte, Dodge followed the south fork of the river to the present-day Denver area and returned to Fort Leavenworth via the Arkansas Valley and the Santa Fe Trail. Intended to impress the Indians with the military might of the U.S. Army, the Dodge excursion resembled a later expedition led by Colonel Stephen Watts Kearny up the North Platte to South Pass in 1845. By that time emigrants to Oregon had begun to use the Platte River valley as the highway to the West and earnestly desired military protection.

3.1. Meriwether Lewis (1774–1809), shown here in a portrait by Charles Willson Peale, was President Jefferson's choice to command an expedition through the newly acquired Louisiana Purchase to the mouth of the Columbia River in 1804–6. A captain in the U.S. Army, Lewis had been Jefferson's private secretary since 1801. Later he served briefly as governor of Louisiana Territory before his tragic death at age thirty-five. Courtesy Independence National Historical Park.

3.2. William Clark (1779–1838) was chosen by Meriwether Lewis to share the leadership of the Corps of Discovery, as the expedition to the Pacific Northwest was officially called. Formerly a captain of militia, Clark was a genial complement to the mercurial Lewis. Clark enjoyed a long career of public service, most notably as the first superintendent of Indian affairs. Portrait by Charles Willson Peale. Courtesy Independence National Historical Park.

3.3. Stephen H. Long (1784–1864) was brevet major in the U.S. Army Engineers in 1820 when he commanded an expedition to ascend the Platte River to its source and discover the headwaters of the Red River. Although neither goal was realized, Long's was the first government-sponsored expedition to traverse the future state of Nebraska. Portrait by Charles Willson Peale. Courtesy Independence National Historical Park.

3.4. Samuel Seymour, *Pawnee Council* 1820. Samuel Seymour, who created a visual record of the Long Expedition in 1820, rendered this view of Major Long's meeting with the leaders of the Pawnees near what soon became Fort Atkinson on the banks of the Missouri. His sketch emphasizes American military authority. Army officers are at the center of the composition; a Pawnee chief, not clearly delineated, stands before them. Other Indians appear in muted colors, their backs to the viewer. Courtesy Yale Collection of Western Americana, Beinecke Rare Book and Manuscript Library.

Fort Atkinson *4*
Army Outpost on the Missouri

Significant numbers of Euro-Americans first lived in present-day Nebraska from 1819 to 1827, when the U.S. Army maintained an outpost at Council Bluff, the place upstream from Omaha where Lewis and Clark had held council in 1804 with Oto and Missouria Indians. Intended to protect the fur trade in the upper Missouri basin, the fort was built on high ground in 1820, and the garrison occupied a temporary cantonment on the floodplain.

Named after Colonel Henry Atkinson, the commander of the Yellowstone Expedition of 1819, the fort became the largest in the West. It was surrounded by a stockade and had two bastions, one of which commanded the main channel of the Missouri River as it existed in 1819. Fort Atkinson was a major element in a strategy devised by Secretary of War John C. Calhoun to stabilize the northern boundary of the United States against British intrusions from Canada. During most of its brief existence, Fort Atkinson was garrisoned by about five hundred soldiers. Outside the stockade were a variety of buildings, such as storehouses, mills, a dairy, and a distillery, as well as cabins for a small civilian population who provided a variety of services for the military. Women and children were present—laundresses attached to the regiments and the families of officers who dared to live in such a remote and isolated post.

Fort Atkinson thus had the characteristics of a permanent settlement. For a time the federal government's Indian agent resided there, small businesses served both military personnel and fur traders, a post school for the children was maintained, and agriculture was practiced on a surprisingly grand scale. The post commanders readily recognized that the soldiers, many of whom had fled arduous farm labor, would have to produce their own food—corn, wheat, potatoes, and vegetables, plus oats, corn, and hay for the livestock, including cattle and hogs—if an adequate diet was to be maintained at a place so far from a source of supplies.

Life at the fort was characterized by monotonous drudgery and boredom. Military drill and discipline seemed excessive and pointless to the soldiers. Drunkenness was endemic, disease a constant menace, and desertion frequent. The Indians of the region were peaceful and the British in Canada were no longer a threat to the fur trade or national security. Only in 1823, when the Arikaras far upstream attacked a fur-trading party, did the soldiers engage in any fighting.

In 1827 the federal government decided to abandon Fort Atkinson, by that time in a state of disrepair. The garrison was removed to Fort Leavenworth, which had just been established to provide military protection for the Santa Fe Trail, and to Jefferson Barracks near St. Louis. The buildings of Fort Atkinson quickly deteriorated and were stripped of anything of value by the local Indians. More than a quarter century passed before any pioneers settled in the vicinity.

4.1. Fort Atkinson was a major military installation of the 1820s with a square stockade enclosing a space the size of two football fields. Most buildings inside the stockade were living quarters for the soldiers, and at least fifty buildings were clustered outside the fort. The gateway to the western fur trade, Fort Atkinson also served as the headquarters for the U.S. Indian agent and was the jumping-off point for several trading expeditions to the southwest. This photograph shows a view from the southeast of the scale model on display at the Ft. Atkinson State Historical Park. Courtesy NEBRASKAland Magazine/Nebraska Game and Parks Commission.

5 Steamboats on the Missouri

Without the transportation link afforded by the Missouri River, the development of Nebraska and other plains states would have come later and taken a different form. As it was, fur traders, like most explorers and the military, depended on water transportation to their sources of supplies and markets. This relationship remained unchanged until Nebraska was connected with the East by rail in 1867.

Before the development of the steamboat, access to Nebraska by water was very difficult. Pirogues, bateaux, and mackinaws were used, but most of the freight was carried on keelboats during the early decades of the nineteenth century. These long and narrow vessels with rounded bow and stern had long runways along the sides. In effect, the crew pushed the boat upstream by thrusting long poles to the bottom of the river, walking as on a treadmill to the stern, and then hurrying back to the bow to start another run. In swift currents the crews had to go ashore and use a towline to pull the vessel along the riverbank. Often seventy or eighty feet long and twelve feet wide, keelboats were equipped with roofed cabins and cargo spaces. A mast and sail made it possible to take advantage of favorable winds.

The invention of the steamboat and its use on the Missouri River dramatically improved transportation and communication. The first successful application of steam power to commercial water transportation came in 1807. By 1819 the use of steamboats had developed sufficiently and spread far enough for Major Stephen H. Long to transport his expedition to Fort Lisa aboard the *Western Engineer,* which was specially designed for shallow-water navigation. But this effort to use the latest technological advancement was hindered by mechanical breakdowns, inadequate power against the swift Missouri current, and ignorance of the river's ever-changing channels.

More than a decade passed before the Missouri River was successfully opened to commercial steamboat navigation. Regular packet service from St. Louis to Independence, Missouri, was a reality by 1829. In 1831 the American Fur Company dispatched its steamboat *Yellow Stone* up the Missouri River beyond Nebraska to Fort Pierre. A year later, with the artist George Catlin as a passenger, the *Yellow Stone* pushed all the way to Fort Union at the mouth of the Yellowstone River. These two voyages established the practicality of steamboating on the upper Missouri, and soon Fort Union became the focal point of the fur trade on the upper reaches of the river. Regular traffic patterns developed as supplies were shipped upstream and baled furs back down.

By the mid-1840s the traffic stimulated by the fur trade was augmented by overland travelers bound for Oregon, Utah, and later California. After 1854, when the Nebraska Territory was organized, steamboats frequently docked on the west side of the river at infant settlements such as Brownville, Nebraska City, and Omaha. Traffic increased greatly at the end of the decade after gold was discovered in Colorado and before the Civil War upset normal patterns of trade and transportation. Plying the treacherous channels of the Missouri were scores of vessels—fifty-nine in all, according to a newspaper report in 1858—and more were to come, especially in 1864 and 1865 as the war drew to a close.

The largest of the Missouri steamboats, which were as much as 250 feet long and 40 feet wide, were capable of carrying three hundred passengers in addition to several hundred tons of cargo. Some boats offered pleasant accommodations, but the passengers of others often complained about overcrowding, filthy conditions, and bad food. It was also a dangerous business. By the end of the nineteenth century, at least 273 vessels had suffered some catastrophe and sunk on the Missouri River, 58 of them along Nebraska's eastern boundary. Even so, steamboat transportation was much preferred to travel by stagecoach or wagon.

By 1860 the agricultural production under way in Nebraska contributed to the steamboat business as shipments of corn, oats, and potatoes were carried to eastern markets. Soon, however, railroads would replace steamboats as the main mode of transportation to Nebraska, even though steamboats continued to be used on the upper Missouri for two more decades.

5.1. Titian Peale, *Western Engineer*, 1820.
The earliest attempt to navigate the
Missouri River with a steamboat occurred in 1819 when the Stephen Long
Expedition used the *Western Engineer* to
advance upstream to Engineer Cantonment, near Fort Atkinson, then under
construction. Titian Peale, a son of the
distinguished American painter Charles
Willson Peale, produced this sketch in
1820. Courtesy American Philosophical
Society.

DAS DAMPFBOOT YELLOW-STONE.
am 19ten April 1833.

LE BATEAU A VAPEUR YELLOW-STONE.
le 19 Avril 1833.

THE STEAMER YELLOW-STONE.
on the 19th April 1833.

5.2. Karl Bodmer, *The Steamer* Yellow-Stone *on the 19th April 1833.* By the 1830s steamboats on the Missouri reached far beyond Nebraska. Like George Catlin in 1832, the Maximilian expedition traveled on the American Fur Company's *Yellow-Stone.* When the steamboat stranded on a sandbar in April 1833, Karl Bodmer recorded the event with this watercolor. Courtesy Joslyn Art Museum, Omaha, gift of the Enron Art Foundation.

5.3. Alfred Matthews, *Nebraska City River Front, 1865.* Steamboats were the essential transportation link for the Missouri River settlements in Nebraska, most of which sprang to life in 1854 when Congress created the Nebraska Territory. A major port of call, Nebraska City received enormous shipments of goods for transfer to westbound wagons. This image of the Nebraska City riverfront was painted by Alfred Matthews. Courtesy NSHS Museum of Nebraska History, N361:13.

5.4. During the 1870s and 1880s, hundreds of steamboats like the *Red Cloud* plied the dangerous, shifting channels of the Missouri. Regular service was standard by 1860, and steamboats soon ascended the river to Fort Benton in Montana, then the head of navigation. Courtesy NSHS, W724:69.

6 The Overlanders

The Platte River valley, which forms the natural highway to the American West, was used by nearly half a million people in the nineteenth century on their way to the farms of Oregon, the gold mines of California, and the Mormon Zion in Utah. For them, as for the fur traders, Nebraska was a vast land to be crossed, but it was not a worthless place. Some of the overlanders, as they were called to distinguish them from those who risked the journey to California by sea around Cape Horn, remembered Nebraska's verdant prairies and later returned to settle there after experiencing disappointments farther west.

Most travelers arrived at one of the "jumping-off" points—towns on the Missouri River such as Independence, Westport, Atchison, St. Joseph, Nebraska City, and Omaha—by steamboat, which was entering its golden age in the 1840s. Although some drove their own wagons across Missouri or Iowa to the river towns, most preferred the relative ease of travel on the Missouri River. They would go as far upstream as possible to a town where they could outfit themselves with wagons, oxen or mules, food, and other necessary supplies for their transcontinental adventure. This pattern continued until railroad connections rendered long-distance travel by wagon across the plains obsolescent.

The optimal time to leave the Missouri River was about 15 April. By then the possibility of a late winter storm had faded and there was sufficient grass to feed the draft animals. The goal was to cross the Sierra Nevada in California before October, when winter snows rendered the mountains impassable. A typical wagon train would have to travel an average of about 15 miles per day to cover the distance, a task easy enough for mules but more challenging for the slower but stronger oxen.

In the 1840s, towns in Missouri and Kansas were the most frequently used jumping-off points, but by the mid-1850s Council Bluffs and Omaha were more important. The Mormons, however, usually left from northern towns because they preferred to cross Iowa with their own wagons from Nauvoo, their settlement in Illinois. Like most emigrants who ventured onto the plains from Omaha, they traveled on the north side of the Platte, while the majority of overlanders remained on the south side. Each of the feeder trails converged at Fort Kearny, which had been established on the south side of the Platte by the army in 1848 to protect the overlanders.

Travel was comparatively easy west of Fort Kearny. The valley was flat and broad, grass was usually in ample supply, and there were no rivers to cross for many miles. But overlanders on the south side had to ford the Platte somewhere west of the fork—a hazardous business in late spring when the waters were swollen with snowmelt from the Rockies. Many travelers met with disaster at one of the several crossings between the present-day cities of North Platte and Julesburg, Colorado. Those who succeeded crossed the high plain to Ash Hollow, where a narrow and steep defile to the North Platte River again caused many difficulties. The last segment of the journey across the Great Plains took the overlanders past famous landmarks—Court House Rock, Chimney Rock, and Scott's Bluff—to Fort Laramie, a fur-trading post near the junction of the Laramie and North Platte Rivers. Established in 1834, Fort Laramie had been taken over by the army in 1849 to protect travelers on their way to California.

The threats to safety posed by hostile Indians were often exaggerated in the emigrant guides and newspapers of the time. But Indians did frighten overlanders by their begging, stealing, and threatening behavior. Certain years, such as 1857, 1862, and 1864, were particularly troublesome, but there were relatively few skirmishes resulting in the loss of life during the quarter century that the trail was in frequent use.

Diseases were a much greater threat. Cholera was the most devastating. Spread chiefly by polluted water, cholera raged intermittently but was catastrophic in 1850 and again in 1852, when at least two thousand overlanders were stricken before they reached Fort Laramie. Mortality on the trail was approximately 5 percent; disease was the cause in 90 percent of the cases.

6.1. This company of Mormons moving to Utah in 1866 is the only group of travelers on the Platte River road known to have been photographed. Their camp, struck in preparation for the long trek to Utah, was located near the Missouri River a few miles north of Nebraska City. Courtesy NSHS, E54:31.

6.2. Nebraska City, like Omaha, was a major jumping-off point for travelers on the Overland Trail. Here a train of wagons waits in front of Hawke & Nuckolls, a Nebraska City outfitting firm, before heading westward. Courtesy NSHS, F863:2.

6.3. Rarely photographed, Fort Kearny was established in 1848 by the U.S. Army to protect travelers on the Overland Trail. Fort Kearny was the focal point for several streams of emigrants from jumping-off points on the Missouri River. This view of barracks at the fort was taken in 1858. Courtesy NSHS, K24:55.

6.4. Crossing the Platte was always hazardous, especially in May and June, when the flow was swelled with water from melting snow in the Rocky Mountains. Here the Mormon train of 1866 fords the South Platte River near present-day Hershey in early August, showing that a century ago the Platte carried much more water than it does today. Courtesy NSHS, E54:32.

6.5. Travelers on the Oregon Trail often used their wagons to create a corral for oxen, mules, and horses. Here freighters headed for Utah are lassoing oxen in preparation for a day's journey. Courtesy NSHS, F863:11.

6.6. Overlanders eagerly looked for landmarks in western Nebraska. The most famous was Chimney Rock, shown here from the north in a sketch by William Quesenbury, who crossed Nebraska in 1851 on his return from the goldfields of California. Since then erosion has changed the shape and reduced the height of Chimney Rock considerably, probably by more than fifty feet. From the Omaha World-Herald's William Quesenbury Overland Trail Sketchbook. Courtesy Omaha World-Herald Company and NSHS Foundation (1850–51).

7 The Creation of Nebraska Territory

The creation of Nebraska as a governmental unit by Congress in 1854 is connected to the perception of the territory as a place to be crossed, not because a large population clamored for some sort of government. In the months preceding its founding, Nebraska had no more than a few hundred Euro-Americans. The impetus for the creation of Nebraska obviously lay elsewhere.

After the end of the Mexican War, the discovery of gold in California in 1848, and the rapid growth of population on the West Coast, there was much agitation in Congress and elsewhere in the nation to bind East and West together with a transcontinental railroad. The application of the enormous power of steam to a wagon fitted to iron rails laid over long distances and the development of a nationwide network of railroads was a recent, spectacular advance of technology. After the admission of California to statehood in 1850 there was much debate over which route a railroad across the continent should follow. United States Senator Stephen A. Douglas of Illinois favored a route that led west from Chicago to the Platte River valley and from thence to San Francisco. He understood that at least a modicum of government would be necessary wherever the railroad would be built. In his capacity as chairman of the Senate Committee on Territories, he sponsored a bill in Congress to create two territorial governments—Nebraska and Kansas—in the Great Plains region.

Heretofore the plains had been thought of as a vast frontier of little value permanently reserved for the Indians, but now the region moved to the center of national attention. An intense debate ensued over the Kansas-Nebraska Bill, as Douglas's proposed legislation was called, that welded the creation of western territories to the debate over the legal status of slavery. One of the bill's provisions specifically repealed the Missouri Compromise of 1820, which had forbidden slavery in the territories north of what is today Oklahoma. It went on to incorporate the principle of "popular sovereignty," which permitted the people of the territories to decide whether or not to legalize slavery within their borders. The issue was finally resolved in 1854 when Congress passed the Kansas-Nebraska Act, a momentous action that led to the demise of the Whig Party, the emergence of the strongly antislavery Republican Party, and ultimately to the Civil War.

By the terms of this legislation the Territory of Nebraska embraced a vast space west from the Missouri River to the continental divide and north from the Kansas boundary to Canada. According to a census taken hastily and prematurely in autumn 1854, the population of the territory was 2,732. Two-thirds lived south of the Platte, most within a few miles of the Missouri River, and all but a few had come to Nebraska from somewhere else within a few months.

President Franklin Pierce appointed the first territorial governor, a politician from South Carolina named Francis Burt who apparently intended that Bellevue should become the capital. Two days after he had taken his oath of office, Burt died from an illness contracted while en route to Nebraska. Burt's death was an event of enormous consequence for Nebraska, for into his place strode the territorial secretary, Thomas Cuming, a young, aggressive journalist from Iowa who, as acting governor, was determined to make Omaha the capital. A mere twenty-five years old, Cuming was associated with several Council Bluffs speculators who hoped to make their town the terminus of the transcontinental railroad—a road to certain wealth.

As a major step in that direction, these entrepreneurs, organized as the Council Bluffs and Nebraska Ferry Company, built a two-story brick structure in Omaha and offered it to the territory as its first capitol. Acting Governor Cuming announced in an official proclamation that the territorial assembly would meet in Omaha, not Bellevue, and happily accepted the offer of the Council Bluffs company. Omaha thus benefited directly from Cuming's schemes. In order to assure that the capital would not be removed from Omaha, Cuming had earlier created legislative districts that grossly overrepresented the population north of the Platte River, and he gerrymandered Bellevue into a district dominated by Omaha.

As a consequence of Cuming's connivance, Omaha was destined to become the metropolis of Nebraska, bearing a relationship to the rest of Nebraska not unlike that of Chicago to Illinois. Possessing a favorable location that gave access to the hinterland tapped by the Platte, Omaha became the major industrial and transportation center of Nebraska.

Within a few years the huge size of Nebraska Territory as determined by the act of 1854 was greatly reduced. In 1861 Congress created Dakota Territory and thereby established (with a minor exception) the present northern and western boundaries of Nebraska.

NEBRASKA BILL

CONSTITUTIONAL

PRINCIPLES TRIUMPHANT

7.1. Representative William A. Richardson, a Democratic congressman from Illinois, introduced a "Nebraska Bill" in 1853 that would have created a Territory of Nebraska encompassing all of present-day Kansas and Nebraska and stretching westward to the continental divide. The bill was defeated in the U.S. Senate. Richardson served as territorial governor of Nebraska in 1858. Courtesy NSHS, P853, from an original in the Yale University Art Gallery.

7.2. George Simons, *View of Belleview*, 1854. Bellevue began in the 1820s as a trading post of the Missouri Fur Company. It was the only continuously inhabited place in Nebraska during the preterritorial years and would probably have become the capital if Governor Burt had not died two days after taking office. Courtesy Center for Great Plains Studies Art Collection, University of Nebraska–Lincoln.

7.3. Nebraska's first territorial governor, Francis Burt, was a forty-seven-year-old politician from Pendleton, South Carolina. Staunchly pro-slavery, Burt was an auditor in the U.S. Treasury at the time of his appointment. He died two days after assuming office. Courtesy NSHS, B973:1.

7.4. When Governor Burt died, Thomas Cuming, as territorial secretary, assumed the role of acting governor from 18 October 1854 to 20 February 1855. During that brief time, he made momentous decisions that strongly influenced the kind of place Nebraska would become. Courtesy NSHS, P853.

8 Nebraska's Founders
Speculators and Politicians

Nebraska's founders were not distinguished statesmen. Compared to the illustrious company who gathered in Philadelphia in July 1776 to create the United States of America, Nebraska's first political leaders were a rude, self-serving lot. All had come from someplace else, and very recently at that—a matter of weeks or a few months. Having no sense of loyalty or commitment to this new, raw place, they were interested in economic success and little else. Nebraska was a place in which to get rich if you could and get out if you could not.

A correspondent of the *New York Times* reported in January 1856 that Omaha was populated by people hoping to find a fortune on the frontier. Many sported phony titles and questionable credentials. There were, he said scornfully, "four generals, three majors, thirty captains, colonels, and squires, fifty gentlemen around town—respectable loafers—seven doctors, . . . a plenty of speculators without a dollar to speculate on; a goodly array of 'have beens'; a merry sprinkling of old broken-down party hacks from the States who refer in majesty to bygone glorious exploits in the political arena, and expect to be rewarded here." These plus twenty-five lawyers and "a small invoice of absconding debtors."

Most of the men elected to the first territorial legislature, which convened early in 1855, were connected in one way or another with townsite speculation. Other citizens, especially farmers, had no time for politics or public service. But politics was mother's milk for the would-be founders of frontier cities. Everywhere pushing and promoting the place that attracted their time and energy, they inundated the legislature with private bills of incorporation for towns, ferries, bridges, banks, and land companies, as well as railroads and universities. They understood that the survival of the town they promoted was intimately linked to their ability to attract the capital, a railroad, county government, a federal land office, or some other guarantee of economic stability and growth.

Most of these fledgling towns—Omaha, Nebraska City, Brownville, and others—were sited on high ground near the Missouri River or one of its tributaries. Except for Bellevue, all sprang forth in 1854 or soon thereafter. Some disappeared within a decade, leaving few traces other than numbers in the federal census reports of 1860. Others were "paper towns" only that were never built even though speculators drew plats and filed them with the legislature.

Newspapers in such new towns were sometimes controlled by the local land company and amounted to little more than advertising sheets designed to sell residential and commercial lots. Such ventures in journalism gave the appearance of prosperity, progress, and permanence. The first such newspaper to appear in Nebraska, the *Nebraska Palladium* of Bellevue, was dated 15 July 1854, less than two months after Congress had created the territory. It was in fact printed in Iowa. Its front page offered no news at all, but consisted entirely of filler material—essays, poetry, and incidental articles pirated from other published sources.

The members of the first territorial legislature, all young and politically inexperienced, were generally innocent of the niceties of parliamentary procedure. They conducted the affairs of government amidst disorder and acrimony, which included frequent denunciations of Acting Governor Thomas Cuming as a consummate scoundrel and manipulator. A few of the earliest lawmakers were not even residents of the territory at the time. Yet somehow laws were enacted. In addition to bills of incorporation, the first legislature passed at least some of the laws required to establish an orderly society in a frontier environment.

8.1. The first territorial capitol, erected in Omaha in 1854, was the most impressive structure in the infant city. Located on 9th Street between Farnam and Douglas Streets, the capitol measured seventy-five feet by thirty-five. The assembly met on the first floor, the council on the second. Courtesy NSHS, C244:1.

8.2. The second territorial capitol was erected in 1857–58 on a commanding site west of the business district. This image of the west front was taken about 1868 by a well-known Western photographer, William Henry Jackson. Courtesy Great Plains Art Collection, University of Nebraska–Lincoln.

8.3. This view of Omaha, photographed in 1864 from 17th and Farnam Streets, reveals a thriving town of more than 2,000. Omaha was not yet connected by bridge with Iowa, but its growth was guaranteed by its status as the territorial capital and its selection in 1863 as the eastern terminus of the Union Pacific Railroad. Courtesy Great Plains Art Collection, University of Nebraska–Lincoln Center for Great Plains Studies.

8.4. *A Nebraska Legislative Scene.* From Sorenson, *Story of Omaha.* On several occasions, deliberations in the Nebraska territorial legislature degenerated into chaos, as this engraving suggests. All semblance of parliamentary decorum vanished as tempers flared, knives and guns flashed, and physical violence ensued. Courtesy NSHS, PC1371:E712.9.

9 The Territorial Economy

During the territorial period (1854–1867), servicing transportation systems was the foundation of economic activity in Nebraska. Steamboat connections on the Missouri River at first provided the essential link to the settled East. All the significant towns in the territory were river towns. Many were important as "jumping-off" points where overlanders could buy supplies, wagons, and teams. In the late 1850s, the overland ox-and-wagon freighting businesses, headquartered in Omaha and Nebraska City, supplied the U.S. Army in the West and the mining camps in Colorado. Stage coaches and for a short time the Pony Express were also important parts of the transportation business. The climax of transportation in this period came with the construction of the transcontinental railroad west from Omaha, beginning in 1865.

Without these transportation systems to and through Nebraska, there was little incentive for storekeepers, lawyers, artisans, laborers, and farmers to settle in the raw territory. Even though the population of the territory increased tenfold between 1854 and 1860 to nearly thirty thousand, most gainfully employed people were engaged in nonagricultural pursuits according to the census of that year. Of these, un-skilled workers and servants made up the largest number, but there were many merchants, bankers, traders, innkeepers, and craftsmen. The building trades were in great demand, since every structure in sight had been erected in the past six years. Manufacturing was limited mostly to sawmills and gristmills. Because the steamboat crews were not residents, they do not appear on the census manuscripts, but team-sters, drivers, blacksmiths, and whipmakers were much in evidence.

Still, farmers constituted the largest single occupational category in 1860—nearly 40 percent of the work force. But the farms were very small, averaging about fifty acres of improved land, and many of the farmers were engaged in other activities at the same time. Most farms were located within a day's journey of the Missouri River, usually along such tributaries as the Big and Little Nemaha Rivers, the Platte, the Elkhorn, and lesser streams. They were usually marginal operations producing for subsistence and the local market, including grain and livestock for freighters and emigrants. By 1858 Nebraska farmers began to export corn, oats, and potatoes on a modest scale downriver to mar-kets in St. Louis and elsewhere, despite high transportation costs.

The late 1850s were a difficult time for Nebraskans, as for other Americans. The territorial economy was stricken with a severe depres-sion following a general financial panic in the East. The many "wildcat" banks in the territory came tumbling down as fast as they had been cre-ated. Real estate values collapsed, interest rates soared, and "hard" money disappeared. Circumstances were made worse by drought and grasshopper plagues in 1859 and 1860. But with the discovery of gold in Colorado, the freighting industry regained prosperity as thousands of hopeful adventurers streamed westward through the land of the Platte.

ARMY OF THE WEST!

16,000 YOKE

OF

GOOD WORKING CATTLE,

From Four to 7 years of age, wanted at

NEBRASKA CITY,

for hauling freight from this point to Utah, for which SEVENTY-FIVE DOLLARS per Yoke will be paid. Notice will be given through the newspapers of the time they are to be delivered, but suppose they will be wanted about the first of May.

FIFTEEN HUNDRED MEN

Wanted for teamsters who will be found and paid Twenty-five dollars per month out and back.

None but men of good habits need apply; as drinking intoxicating liquors, card playing, and profane language will not be permitted while in employment. Each man will be presented with a Bible and hymn book. Forty Wagon Masters wanted who must come well recommended and who will be paid the usual wages.

A number of houses will be rented in Nebraska City, and one large store room. Apply to
RUSSELL, MAJORS & WADDEL.
by KINNEY & HOLLY, Agents.   Mr 20-t

9.1. In 1857 the firm Russell, Majors, & Waddell advertised for oxen and teamsters for its thriving freighting business. The firm virtually monopolized military freighting on the plains and transformed Nebraska City into a major river port. Courtesy NSHS.

9.2. Nebraska City was a major center for hauling commercial freight in ox-drawn wagons between the Missouri River and army posts in the West. This engraving shows buildings of Russell, Majors, & Waddell in 1859. Freighting companies employed hundreds of Nebraskans as teamsters, drivers, whipmakers, and blacksmiths. Courtesy NSHS, F863:13.

9.3. Pony Express rider. Carrying mail by "pony express" across the continent from St. Joseph, Missouri, to California was a romantic but financially unsound enterprise that began in April 1860 and lasted a mere eighteen months. In Nebraska the route followed the Overland Trail from Fairbury to Scottsbluff along the Little Blue, Platte, and North Platte Rivers. Service ended with the completion of the transcontinental telegraph in October 1861, shown under construction in this engraving from *Harper's Weekly*, 2 November 1867. Courtesy NSHS, P818:5.

9.4. When the Union Pacific railroad was built west from Omaha, all equipment and supplies had to be brought in by steamboat. Here the *Colorado* unloads railroad supplies at Omaha in 1865. Courtesy NSHS, R152:26.

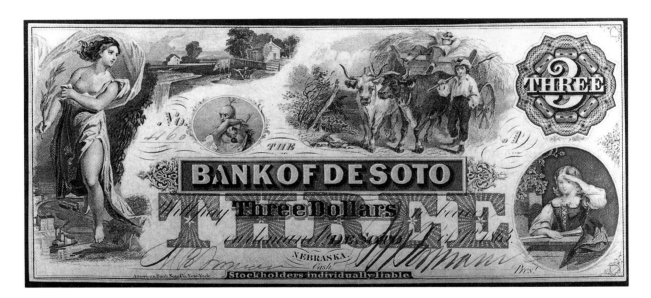

9.5. Before the passage of the National Banking Act by Congress in 1862, banks throughout the United States printed their own money. This three-dollar note issued by the Bank of DeSoto (a community near Blair that disappeared long ago) became worthless after the Panic of 1857. Courtesy NSHS, Museum of Nebraska History.

Building the Transcontinental Railroad *10*

Building a railroad across the continent through seventeen hundred miles of virtually uninhabited and inhospitable territory—vast interior plains, forbidding mountains, and threatening deserts—was a herculean task that stirred the imagination of many Americans. But such an enterprise also had to be economically viable. For a railway to be flung across this distance, government subsidies on a grand scale were required. Land grants, a free right-of-way, and construction loans were prerequisites to construction.

The organization of Nebraska Territory in 1854 was part of this grand plan. Yet for several years no progress was made toward a transcontinental railroad because Southerners in the U.S. Senate, determined to get a southern route, blocked enabling legislation. But once the southern states seceded from the Union in 1861 and their senators walked out of Congress, the railroad acts of 1862 and 1864 were passed and construction could proceed.

The first act passed by Congress for this purpose failed to sweeten the pot sufficiently to attract private investment capital. But the second one did, as it doubled the land grant to ten square miles per mile in a checkerboard pattern on both sides of a free right-of-way. The sale of land was intended to be substitute income for the railroad companies until the resident population increased enough to support such a transportation system. The immediate costs of construction were partially met by government loans amounting to sixteen thousand dollars per mile on the plains. The loans were doubled and tripled in plateau and mountainous regions.

With such incentives, private investment capital poured in, and construction of the Union Pacific Railroad began in 1865, one mile per day at first but more rapidly as methods were perfected. The route struck westward from Omaha to the Platte River and followed the north side of the river to the fork near the city of North Platte. It continued along the South Platte River to Julesburg, Colorado, before reentering Nebraska and following Lodgepole Creek into Wyoming. In November 1867 rails reached Cheyenne; the continent was finally spanned in May 1869.

The force of construction workers, which at its peak numbered ten thousand men, consisted mostly of Civil War veterans and immigrant laborers, chiefly Irish. Grading crews lived in temporary camps at the end of construction. Track-laying workers often lived in train cars that functioned crudely as dormitories. Still other workers, together with storekeepers, bartenders, hunters, cooks, and a full quota of male and female adventurers, lived in portable villages that were established every one hundred miles or so to serve as temporary supply terminals. Known as "Hell on Wheels," these camps were rough and rowdy and amply supplied with facilities for sin—saloons, gambling dens, and brothels.

In 1870 Congress authorized another railroad in Nebraska. The law authorized the Burlington and Missouri Pacific Railroad to construct a line from the Missouri River to the Union Pacific at Kearney. The railroad chose a route from Plattsmouth to Lincoln, the new state capital, and west to Kearney. Much like the Union Pacific, the Burlington received a substantial land grant. Soon other railways and branch lines spread across the state and profoundly influenced the development and quality of life in Nebraska.

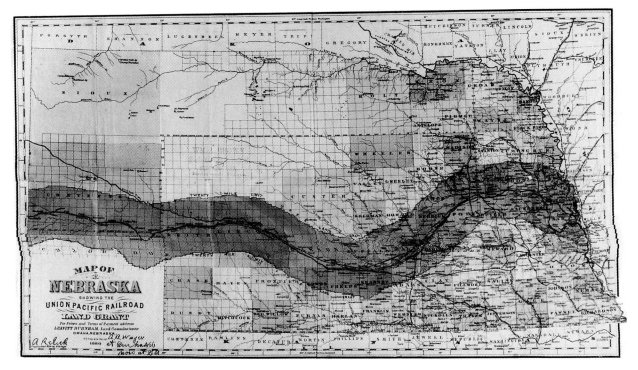

10.1. The Railroad Act of 1864 gave the Union Pacific half of all the land in a grant forty miles wide across Nebraska. Awarded to the railroad in a checker-board pattern, the land was then sold to settlers. The income served as a sub-stitute for railroad fares and freight charges until the land was settled and crops produced. Courtesy Union Pacific Museum Collection.

10.2. Until Omaha was connected in 1867 by rail to Iowa across the Missouri River, all supplies, including steam engines, train cars, rails, spikes, ties, and firewood, were brought by steamboats owned by the Union Pacific to this supply base, photographed in 1869. Courtesy Union Pacific Museum Collection.

10.3. Thomas Durant, vice president and general manager of the Union Pacific, examines the track bed near Cozad on the north side of the Platte River in October 1866. Grading has been completed and railroad ties have been dropped off, but rails have not been laid. At that time crews were laying two to three miles of track per day. Courtesy Union Pacific Museum Collection.

10.4. This drawing by A. R. Waud illustrates the buzz of railroad construction activity. A locomotive at the far left pushes train cars, including some that served as housing for workers, to the end of the track, where workers lay rails and drive spikes to hold them in place. In the foreground soldiers fraternize with Indians, and covered wagons drawn by mules transport supplies to grading crews working some miles ahead. Horse-drawn wagons carry loads of ties as empty wagons return for additional loads. A temporary camp of tents for workers has been pitched in the background. Courtesy NSHS, R152:106x.

10.5. This carefully posed image can only suggest the machine-like coordination that track-laying required: three strokes to the spike, ten spikes to the rail, four hundred rails to the mile. The divided labor system was developed by General Jack Casement, the supervisor of track-laying for the Union Pacific. It anticipated the assembly line methods adopted later in meat-packing plants and automobile factories. Courtesy Union Pacific Museum Collection, JC-209.

10.6. When construction reached the 100th meridian at Cozad, 247 miles west of Omaha, in October 1866, the Union Pacific sent an excursion train to the site and celebrated with a three-day-long party. In this photograph by John Carbutt, the railroad's directors pose beneath a signpost erected for the occasion. The celebration was a publicity event staged by Thomas Durant to focus nationwide attention on the Union Pacific and the transcontinental railroad. Courtesy Union Pacific Museum Collection.

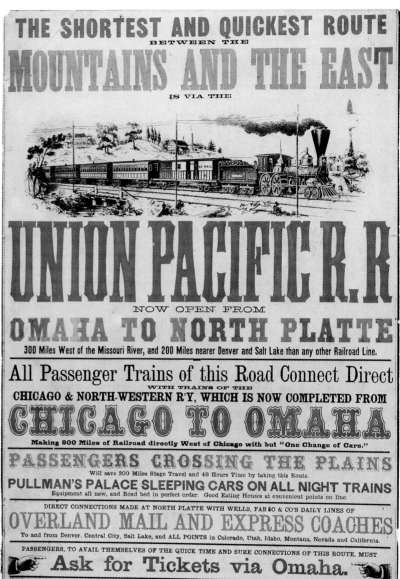

10.7. In 1867, two years before the transcontinental railway was completed in Utah, the Union Pacific issued this advertisement for passenger travel to North Platte. Thereafter, most settlers in Nebraska arrived by train rather than covered wagon. Courtesy Union Pacific Museum Collection, 501960.

11 Getting Land

The Farmers' Frontier

By the mid-1850s it was clear to many people that Nebraska had a great potential for agriculture. But before any land could be acquired by settlers, the claims of the various Indian nations had to be satisfied. The Indians were the legal occupants of the land and they held the title to it. The United States therefore negotiated a series of treaties and agreements, beginning in 1825 and continuing into the 1880s, that transferred ownership to the federal government a piece at a time at bargain rates. Sadly, the average price paid for land in Nebraska was ridiculously low—less than ten cents per acre, usually not in cash, but calculated in terms of merchandise or services.

Although cessions were made in most of the areas where Euro-American farmers wanted to settle by 1854, pioneers could not acquire land until government surveyors had completed their work. Farmers could buy land from the government under the terms of several laws. Most important was the Pre-emption Act of 1841, which permitted a "squatter," a settler who had moved onto public land before it was surveyed, to buy a maximum of 160 acres at $1.25 per acre. Land could also be purchased from the federal government at auction sales, and it often went in large tracts. There were several other ways to acquire government land, including military bounty land warrants, a veterans benefit of that time.

In 1862 Congress passed the momentous Homestead Act. This law permitted a citizen (male or female) who was at least twenty-one years old and had not borne arms against the United States to claim 160 acres of government land. After five years of residence, the homesteader had to "prove up" his claim, demonstrating that the land had been improved, if he or she wished to become the legal owner. So generous was the law that even aliens who had taken out their first naturalization papers were eligible. Eventually about 30 percent of public land in Nebraska passed into private ownership by means of the Homestead Act, which attracted many immigrants to Nebraska and other plains states. To their dismay, however, they often found that the best land had already gone to the railroads or had passed into the hands of speculators. There was also much dishonesty and fraud involved in filing, proving up, and contesting claims, as well as maladministration especially in connection with later amendatory laws such as the Timber Culture Act and the Desert Land Act.

Despite its shortcomings and disappointments, the Homestead Act was enormously important for the settlement of Nebraska. It brought thousands of settlers to the territory and hastened the pace toward statehood. Most especially, it helped change the perception of Nebraska from "a place on the way" to a place in which to stay.

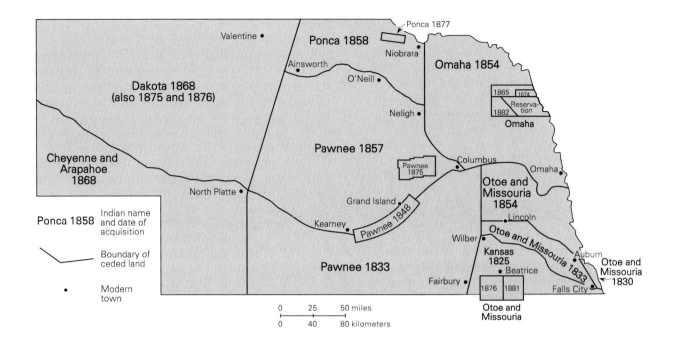

Valentine •

Ponca 1858

Ponca 1877

Niobrara

Omaha 1854

Ainsworth

O'Neill •

Dakota 1868
(also 1875 and 1876)

1865 | 1874

Reserva-
tion

1882

Omaha

Neligh •

Pawnee 1857

Columbus •

Omaha •

Cheyenne and
Arapahoe
1868

Pawnee
1875

Otoe and
Missouria
1854

North Platte •

Ponca 1858   Indian name
              and date of
              acquisition

Grand Island •

Pawnee 1848

Lincoln •

Boundary of
ceded land

Kearney •

Otoe and Missouria 1833

Wilber •

Auburn •

Otoe and
Missouria
1830

•   Modern
     town

Pawnee 1833

Kansas
1825

• Beatrice

Fairbury •

1876 | 1881

Falls City •

Otoe and
Missouria

0   25   50 miles

0   40   80 kilometers

11.1. When the United States acquired Nebraska as part of the Louisiana Purchase from France in 1803, it recognized that the ownership of land remained with the several Indian nations. Through a series of fifteen treaties and other legal agreements from 1825 to 1882, the federal government bought the land and opened it to settlers. On average, the Indians received ten cents per acre, far below what was then a fair price. Sometimes payment was made in the form of guns, ammunition, tobacco, and blankets. The Native Americans rarely understood the full implications of the treaties, most of which they signed reluctantly and under pressure. Map by The Map Press, Lincoln, Nebraska.

11.2. Allegedly the first person in the United States to acquire land under the provisions of the Homestead Act of 1862, Daniel Freeman filed a claim on a tract a few miles northwest of Beatrice, Nebraska, moments after midnight on January 1, 1863, the day on which the law went into effect. This calotype of his homestead was taken about 1865. Homestead National Monument near Beatrice commemorates Freeman's claim, but the log cabin there is not the original. Courtesy NSHS, R811.9:1.

11.3. During the first ten years of the Homestead Act, approximately twenty-eight thousand claims were filed in Nebraska, of which sixteen thousand were "proved up" after five years. Here a family of homesteaders, with their livestock and wagons full of belongings, approach their destination in Custer County in 1886. Courtesy NSHS Butcher Collection, B983:2938a.

12 Nebraska in the Civil War

Although the Civil War (1861–65) affected Nebraska in many ways, the state suffered little compared to Kansas, where guerrilla warfare caused much devastation, injury, and death. For a short time at the beginning of the war, southeastern Nebraska near the Kansas border was terrorized by "Jayhawkers" who were allegedly pro-Union but in fact were lawless bandits bent on stealing horses and robbing stores and homesteads. Unlike Kansas, Nebraska was far from slave-holding areas in Missouri, and large-scale slavery did not exist. The Census of 1860 revealed a total of fifteen slaves in Nebraska, all household servants and their children, but there were few defenders of that pernicious institution in the state.

Nebraska supplied more than its share of soldiers for the Union army. About 3,300 claimed Nebraska as their home, a remarkably high proportion of the approximately 9,000 males between the ages of twenty and fifty who resided in the territory in 1860. In all, 239 Nebraskans died in the war, mostly from disease or accidents.

Shortly after the outbreak of war in April 1861, territorial Governor

Alvin Saunders called for the formation of the First Nebraska Volunteer Infantry regiment. John M. Thayer, who had been brigadier general of the territorial militia, was appointed colonel. He and his troops boarded steamboats at Omaha in July and left for Missouri, where they participated in a few skirmishes before seeing action in major engagements in February and April 1862 in the battles of Fort Donelson and Shiloh, Tennessee. In 1863 the First Nebraska Infantry was reconstituted as a cavalry regiment and subsequently furloughed to Omaha.

In 1863 a second Nebraska cavalry regiment was recruited for nine months' service in response to fears of Indian warriors who had fled to Dakota Territory after the Santee uprising in southern Minnesota. Commanded by Colonel Robert Furnas, this regiment participated in the slaughter of a large Sioux camp at White Stone Hill north of Fort Pierre in Dakota Territory on 3 September 1863.

The Civil War had important consequences for the history of Nebraska. Guerrilla warfare in Kansas interfered with overland freighting and diverted much traffic from St. Joseph, Missouri, northward to Nebraska City and Omaha. It also disrupted steamboat transportation on the Missouri River—Nebraska's indispensable link with the outside world—and led to shortages of many goods. Nebraska City became a haven for Civil War refugees, especially Missourians trying to escape the depredations of fighting along the Missouri-Kansas border. This influx intensified housing problems. The loss of young men to the army inevitably created manpower shortages at a time when demands for corn and wheat, especially in Colorado, invigorated agriculture in Nebraska. Wartime taxation was also a problem; as a money-saving measure, the territorial legislature did not convene in 1862 or 1863. The Civil War transformed partisan politics in Nebraska as the Republican party was greatly strengthened.

The war also stimulated fears that Indians would attack isolated dwellings on the frontier after troops were withdrawn for battlefields in the South. The army established Fort Cottonwood east of present-day North Platte (later renamed Fort McPherson) in September 1863 and Fort Mitchell west of present-day Scottsbluff in August 1864 to protect transportation on the Overland Trail.

From the Native American point of view, increased traffic on the Overland Trail divided the dwindling bison herds that were central to their subsistence. They felt threatened by the emerging reservation policy of the federal government that promised to confine certain tribes to inadequate and undesirable tracts in Colorado and elsewhere. In August 1864, responding to troubles in Colorado, the Cheyenne, Arapaho, and Brulé Sioux began a series of coordinated raids on ranches along the Platte River and attacked freight wagons and stage coaches between Fort Kearny and Denver. Depredations extended as far east as settlements along the Little Blue River west of Fairbury, where the loss of life and destruction of property caused many frontier settlers to panic and flee eastward. The army recalled the First Nebraska Cavalry from furlough and assigned it to Fort Kearny to escort travelers and freighters and to protect stagecoach stations and road ranches on the Oregon Trail.

In November 1864, Colorado cavalry under the command of Colonel J. M. Chivington, a former Nebraskan, brutally massacred an unsuspecting band of Cheyennes, mostly old men, women, and children, at the Sand Creek Reservation in southeastern Colorado. In retaliation, Julesburg, located in Colorado close to the Nebraska border, was sacked twice. As the Civil War drew to a close, relations between whites and plains Indians degenerated to their lowest point up to that time.

12.1. Among the many political leaders in Nebraska who had prominent records of military service, Colonel John M. Thayer, commander of the First Nebraska Infantry, was the most distinguished. He attained the rank of major general shortly before the end of the Civil War and a year later was elected as one of Nebraska's first U.S. senators. In 1886 he was elected governor, a post he held until 1892. Courtesy NSHS, T371:1.

12.2. This image of Private James R. Hutton of Sarpy County, age nineteen, is one of the few photographs extant of Nebraska volunteers in the Civil War. A soldier in Company E, First Nebraska Infantry, Hutton was killed accidentally while on picket duty near Jacksonport, Arkansas, on 7 May 1864. Courtesy NSHS, H984:40.

12.3. Robert W. Furnas of Brownville was appointed colonel of the short-lived Second Nebraska Cavalry regiment in 1863. An influential politician, journalist, and horticulturalist, Furnas later served as governor of Nebraska (1873–75) and was a founder of the Nebraska State Historical Society. Courtesy NSHS, F987:2.

12.4. This studio portrait of Private Jacob Coffman taken in 1863 was probably intended to stimulate patriotism and devotion to the Union cause. Coffman, who came from Falls City, enlisted in Company L, Second Nebraska Cavalry, and attained the rank of corporal. Courtesy NSHS, P853.

12.5. Fort Cottonwood, located on the Overland Trail east of the forks of the Platte River, was established in September 1863 to keep the transportation link with western territories open and to prevent Indians from fording the Platte River at that point. This 1864 drawing by Major George M. O'Brien shows the position of the fort on the south bank of the Platte. In 1866 the fort was renamed to commemorate General J. B. McPherson, killed in the Battle of Atlanta. Courtesy NSHS, M171:1a.

12.6. Nancy Jane Fletcher Morton was nineteen years old on 9 August 1864 when she was captured by a large band of Indians who attacked a train of freight wagons owned by her husband, Thomas Morton, near present-day Lexington. Most members of the party—at least a dozen—were killed in this incident, known as the Plum Creek Massacre. Mrs. Morton was held prisoner until her release was negotiated in December 1864. Courtesy NSHS, C337.5:54.

A Fledgling State *Part 2*

Nebraska's First Quarter Century

Nebraska became a state in 1867. By that time, after a dozen years as a territory, fundamental transformations were already underway. Because of the railroad, Nebraska was changing from a transit area to a place where people settled permanently on farms and in small towns formed to serve the needs of the nearby agricultural population. During the 1860s Nebraska's population quadrupled to 123,000. Thousands of settlers were drawn by the prospect of farm ownership under the terms of the Homestead Act and other land laws. At the same time, railroad connections gradually replaced steamboat transportation as the main link to markets in the East. Inevitably, people began to talk about statehood for Nebraska.

Statehood was a highly partisan issue. Republican politicians, strongly in the majority in that era of civil strife, favored statehood because they believed it would be to their advantage, both locally and nationally. Democrats were opposed, arguing that it would only increase taxes.

In 1864, the Republican-dominated Congress, with an eye on presidential elections to come, passed an enabling act that authorized Nebraskans to proceed with the formation of a state government. This effort ultimately met defeat in a popular election. In 1866, Republican leaders in Nebraska tried again. Aware that there was no strong popular sentiment in support of statehood, they hastily drew up a woefully inadequate constitution and bulldozed it through the legislature. It was then submitted to the voters, who narrowly approved it in an election that did no honor to democratic principles, even in that permissive era.

Congressional approval was opposed by Radical Republican senators who objected to a clause in the proposed state constitution that limited the right to vote to free white males, thereby deliberately disenfranchising black citizens. They successfully amended the bill in a way that required the Nebraska legislature to remove the offensive restriction if statehood was to be granted. This action was of great importance to the Radicals because it affirmed the right of Congress to impose conditions on the state-making process and, by extension, on former slave states that had seceded and were then seeking readmission to the Union. President Andrew Johnson, who bitterly opposed the Radical Republicans, vetoed the measure, but Congress responded by overriding his veto.

In accordance with this act of Congress, the Nebraska legislature, technically still a territorial body but in fact elected as a branch of state government, convened in a special session on 20 February 1967 and removed the provision that restricted the franchise to free white males. On 1 March 1867 President Johnson reluctantly signed a proclamation that admitted Nebraska as the thirty-seventh state.

During the next quarter century, people spread across the state. Settlers from eastern states and many European countries acquired farms; towns and villages popped up along the railroads as if by magic. The range-cattle industry emerged in the west as dispirited Indians were herded onto reservations. Schools, churches, and courthouses were erected as Nebraskans built a society that was as similar as possible to the one they had left behind.

President Andrew Johnson's proclamation, dated 1 March 1867, clearly states that the Nebraska legislature was required by Congress to extend the right to vote to African Americans—former slaves—as a condition for admission into the union as a state.

By the President of the United States of America

A Proclamation

Whereas the Congress of the United States did by an act approved on the nineteenth day of April, one thousand eight hundred and sixty four, authorize the people of the Territory of Nebraska to form a Constitution and State Government and for the admission of such State into the Union on an equal footing with the original States, upon certain conditions in said act specified; and whereas said people did adopt a Constitution conforming to the provisions and conditions of said act and ask admission into the Union, and whereas the Congress of the United States did on the eighth and ninth days of February, one thousand eight hundred and sixty seven, in mode prescribed by the Constitution, pass a further act for the admission of the State of Nebraska into the Union, in which last named act it was provided that it should not take effect except upon the fundamental condition that within the State of Nebraska there should be no denial of the elective franchise or of any other right to any person by reason of race or color, excepting Indians not taxed, and upon the further fundamental condition that the Legislature of said State, by a solemn public act, should declare the assent of said State to the said fundamental conditions and should transmit to the President of the United States as authenticated copy of said act of the legislature of said State, upon receipt whereof the President by proclamation should forthwith announce the fact, whereupon said fundamental conditions should be held as a part of the organic law of the State, and thereupon and without any further proceedings on the part of Congress, the admission of said State into the Union should be considered as complete, and whereas within the time prescribed by said act of Congress, of the eighth and ninth of February, one thousand eight hundred and sixty seven, and declaring that the aforenamed provisions of the third section of said last named act of Congress should be a part of the organic law of the State of Nebraska; and whereas a duly authenticated copy of said act of the legislature of the State of Nebraska has been received by me.

Now therefore, I, Andrew Johnson, President of the United States of America do, in accordance with the provisions of the act of Congress last herein named, declare and proclaim the fact that the fundamental conditions imposed by Congress on the State of Nebraska to entitle that State to admission to the Union have been ratified and accepted, and that the admission of the said State into the Union is now complete,

In testimony whereof, I have hereto set my hand, and have caused the Seal of the United States to be affixed

Done at the City of Washington, this first day of March in the year of our Lord, one thousand, eight hundred and sixty seven, and of the Independence of the United States of America, the ninety first

Andrew Johnson

By the President

William H. Seward
Secretary of State

A Capital Controversy 13

The location of the capital was the hottest political issue in territorial
Nebraska. Having the capital would guarantee the survival of the town
in which it was located—growth would be assured and business ventures of many kinds would succeed. Carpenters, masons, storekeepers,
hotelkeepers, and many other craftsmen and tradesmen would find
employment; printers would secure government contracts; and lawyers
would be attracted like bees to honey. The capital was a prize well
worth fighting for in those uncertain times.

Resentment ran deep over the manipulation by Omaha partisans to
get and keep the seat of government in 1854. Bellevue, which had been
passed over by Acting Governor Thomas Cuming, joined with the
more populous towns south of the Platte River in repeated but unsuccessful efforts to remove the capital from Omaha to another place—any
place—as long as it was south of the Platte.

Omaha partisans generally understood that once statehood had been
achieved it would no longer be possible to fend off the "South Platters."
By the mid-1860s, Omaha was more willing than before to accept the

inevitable because by then it had already won the race for economic superiority. As the eastern terminus of the transcontinental railroad, its future was assured and its ability to tap the resources of the Platte valley unquestioned.

Legislators from the South Platte country were determined to take the capital away from Omaha. One of the first bills passed by the new state legislature created a commission consisting of the governor, the secretary of state, and the state auditor to select a new site for the capital on state-owned land south of the Platte River. The capital was to be placed somewhere in a tract consisting of Seward County, the northern two-thirds of Lancaster County, and the southern portions of Saunders and Butler Counties. The lawmakers also specified that the state university and agricultural college be combined as one institution and located in the new capital, which was to be named for the recently martyred Abraham Lincoln. Even the state penitentiary was to be located in or near it. This decision, which ran counter to the typical nineteenth-century pattern of distributing the institutional functions of state government among competing cities, placed them all on neutral ground.

The commissioners acted quickly. They selected a site on land donated by the residents of a hamlet named Lancaster. Renamed Lincoln, it was replatted and lots were put up for sale at auction. Sales were disappointing at first, but after conniving with a group of investors from Nebraska City, the commissioners saved the capital for Lincoln by raising enough money to proceed with the construction of a statehouse on land set aside for that purpose.

The first state capitol was an ungainly structure hastily erected by an undependable contractor. In December 1868 it was ready for occupancy, but its inadequacies were apparent almost immediately. Politicians from communities farther west in the state began to agitate for the removal of the capital from Lincoln to Columbus, Kearney, or elsewhere. The best way to fend off such threats was to repair, expand, or replace the existing structure, a task that was accomplished in stages during the 1880s.

The relocation of the Nebraska state capital from Omaha to its permanent home in Lincoln symbolized the transformation of Nebraska from a transit area to a place for permanent settlement. Despite its rapid and substantial growth, Omaha seemed to mean transportation to somewhere else: it was cosmopolitan, diverse, outward-looking, and seemed dominating and aggressive to other Nebraskans. So Lincoln was created as the new capital city in a place where there was no city. Situated in a promising agricultural area south of the Platte, Lincoln signaled values of local development, permanence, and respectability.

13.1. When this photograph of Omaha was taken in 1867, Nebraska had just been admitted as a state. Omaha was still the capital, and the territorial capitol building (on the horizon) functioned as Nebraska's first statehouse. Courtesy NSHS, 054:787.

13.2. In accordance with the state law that the capital be removed from Omaha to a site south of the Platte River, the capital commissioners announced their selection of Lincoln on 14 August 1867. Courtesy NSHS.

13.3. Lancaster scarcely existed as a village when it was selected as the site of the new state capital. This view, photographed in 1868, looks westward toward Salt Creek from present-day 9th and O Streets. Courtesy NSHS, L741:38b.

13.4. Built of limestone quarried near Beatrice, the first capitol in Lincoln was funded by the sale of lots on land donated to the state. The ineptly designed building was so poorly constructed that it began to crumble soon after construction. Courtesy NSHS, L244:20.

13.5. Lincoln boomed during its first five years, as this 1874 image reveals. The capitol, located at the southeastern edge of town, dominates the horizon. Courtesy NSHS, L741:79a.

13.6. The treeless Nebraska prairie is revealed in this view from the capitol dome in 1872. The two mansions on the right were erected in 1870 by capital commissioners Thomas Kennard and John Gillespie to demonstrate their confidence in Lincoln as a city that would succeed. The Kennard House still stands. Courtesy NSHS, L741:11.

14 A Network of Rails

Constructing a transcontinental railroad across Nebraska from east to west was quite different from building a network of branch lines to serve the needs of a local agricultural population. The filling-in process began in 1870 when the Burlington and Missouri River Railroad received a land grant from Congress to begin construction of a line westward from Plattsmouth to Lincoln. Others followed in the next two decades, including the Northwestern, Rock Island, Missouri Pacific, and smaller lines no longer in existence.

During the next twenty years, railroad track mileage in Nebraska expanded to 1,868 in 1880 and 5,148 in 1890, mostly in the eastern and southern parts of the state. The success of the railroad companies, of which the Union Pacific and the Burlington were the most important, depended on the development of local agricultural resources and a large rural population. The railroads did everything possible to advertise Nebraska as a land of abundance and prosperity as they connected existing towns in eastern Nebraska and created scores of new towns in the west.

Many of the first pioneers hoped to acquire farmland under the terms of the Homestead Act of 1862. But when they arrived in the state, they discovered that much of the best agricultural land had been given to the railroads by the federal government in the form of the enormous land grants arranged in a checkerboard pattern (in square-mile blocks) for twenty miles on both sides of the railroad right-of-way. Although homesteading was possible on the alternate sections and on what lay beyond, the value of the land depended on proximity to the railroad. Even high-quality land was limited in value if it was too distant.

The relationship between local transportation and the network of rails determined the location of many towns in central and western Nebraska. Land companies owned or controlled by the railroads usually platted these towns, which were built around sidings and depots. Stations, which became the nuclei of these prairie communities, were placed every six to ten miles. Placement was governed by the distance a farmer could drive his horse-drawn wagon to town, conduct his business, and return home the same day, a maximum round trip of fifteen to twenty miles. If the farming population was to be served effectively, no more than twenty miles could separate one railroad line from another. To be closer usually meant that there would not be enough business to support a line.

Thus farmers who settled Nebraska were linked to the local market centers by horse-and-wagon transportation, and the towns were connected to the national economy by the railroads. The national railroad network was unified by the adoption of a standard gauge (the size of the space separating the rails). In the 1860s, the federal government decided that if a railroad was to get a land grant it would have to adopt the standard gauge of four feet, eight and one-half inches.

14.1. The process of filling in branch lines was greatly stimulated when the Burlington and Missouri River Railroad developed the area north of the Platte with a branch line leading through the Sand Hills. Local farmers with their teams of horses or mules provided much of the labor. In 1886, Solomon Butcher photographed a few workers with their wives and children in a construction camp near Sargent. Courtesy NSHS Butcher Collection, B983:3496a.

14.2. Custer County was connected with the world in 1886 when this first passenger train steamed into Broken Bow. The railroad stimulated a spurt of growth for the town and county in the late 1880s. Courtesy NSHS Butcher Collection, B983:2217a.

Cheap Farms! Free Homes!!

ON THE LINE OF THE

Union Pacific

RAILROAD.

The Great Trans-Continental Route from

Omaha to the Pacific Ocean.

A Land Grant Direct from the Government of

12,000,000 ACRES

Of the best Farming and Mineral Lands in America.

3,000,000 ACRES CHOICE FARMING LANDS

On the Line of this Great Highway in the

STATE OF NEBRASKA

In the great Platte Valley, now for Sale, for Cash or long credit at low rates of interest. These Lands are near the 41st Parallel of North Latitude, and for salubrity of climate and fertility of soil are unsurpassed by any in the United States.

Convenient to Market both East and West. Prices range from Two to Ten Dollars per Acre.

COLONIES

Can find more desirable locations on these lands than elsewhere, as they can settle on the line of the road, secure the Government Lands under the Homestead Laws and purchase the Railroad Lands on very favorable terms.

GREAT INDUCEMENTS to SETTLERS with LIMITED MEANS

2,500,000 Acres Rich Government Lands

Along the Road between Omaha and North Platte, surveyed and open for entry under the Homestead and Pre-emption Laws, and can be taken by actual settlers only. An opportunity never before presented for securing homes near a great rail road with all the conveniences of an old settled country.

ATTENTION SOLDIERS !

Under the amended Homestead Law, Soldiers who served three months or more in the war of the Rebellion, can secure a Homestead of 160 Acres of Government land within the Railroad limits, equal to a direct bounty of $400.

Descriptive Pamphlets, with Maps, now ready and sent free to all parts of the United States, Canada and Europe. Address,

O. F. DAVIS, Land Commissioner, U.P.R.R.Co., Omaha, Nebraska.

14.3. The Union Pacific and other railroad companies widely advertised the sale of their federal land grants. In this example from the late 1860s, the Union Pacific linked the sale of "cheap farms," land acquired from the federal government, with "free homes," 160-acre homesteads available under the Homestead Act. Courtesy Union Pacific Museum Collection.

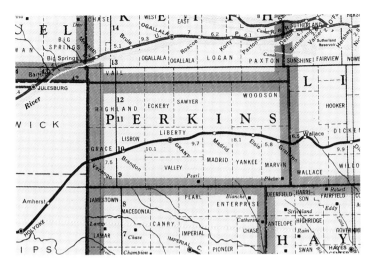

14.4. The Burlington railroad sent a branch line through Perkins County, 20 miles south of the main line of the Union Pacific. The small numbers near the railroad lines indicate the miles between stations. In this county the railroad determined the location of all towns. Courtesy NSHS, M782:1953-R13.

14.5. This photograph of an unidentified hamlet in central Nebraska conveys the bleak and raw character of prairie towns that grew up around railroad stations and sidings. The depot is situated at left on the main line of the Union Pacific. Telegraph poles parallel the tracks. A grain elevator snuggles up to the siding, where a short train fueled by wood goes about its tasks. A street crosses the tracks from the left (where the largest part of town evidently was) to a cluster of buildings on the right. The Platte River and a grove of trees lie in the distance. Photograph by Mitchell and McGowan. Courtesy Union Pacific Museum Collection.

Towns on the Plains *15*

Towns were prominent in pioneer Nebraska and as essential then as they are now. The earliest ones, including Omaha, Nebraska City, and Brownville, were villages strung along the west bank of the Missouri River, where they served as river ports and as trading centers for nearby farmers. Founded within days or weeks of each other in the summer of 1854 after the enactment by Congress of the Kansas-Nebraska Act, they resembled hundreds of other towns in the Midwest. Throughout the 1850s and 1860s, other towns and villages were created in the eastern third of state, usually along the rivers.

Typically, early Nebraska towns were hastily built with cheap materials. Homes lacked the amenities of central heating, electricity, running water, and indoor plumbing. There was no such thing as a paved street. Because of the absence of trees on the plains, these villages were at first barren, windswept places—statements of hope rather than artifacts of accomplishment. Residences were usually surrounded by open space, but false-fronted buildings in the commercial districts were crowded on narrow lots, each businessman eager to harvest a share of the trade with farmers from the surrounding countryside. In the 1870s and 1880s, when the railroad network was cast across the state, many of these towns were bypassed. Such villages were destined to atrophy and die.

Most of the towns that survived were joined with the national economy by a railroad, whose local station was the symbol of enormous power for good or ill in the community. Many, especially the county seats, became what geographers call "central places." They were not primarily residential communities; instead, they performed marketing functions and provided a variety of services. Their main customers were the families who lived on farms in the surrounding countryside.

Most such towns were very much alike. Besides the general store and specialty shops, they provided livery stables, blacksmith shops, hotels, saloons, warehouses, grain elevators, churches, and a school. Most also offered the services of a bank, a real estate agency, and a lumberyard that sold not only building materials but also coal for heating and cooking. Larger towns also supported lawyers, doctors, and a weekly newspaper publisher who also served as a job printer. If the town was the seat of county government, there would be a courthouse, judge, sheriff, clerk, treasurer, and assessor. Railroad division towns usually had boarding houses for unmarried males. Brothels were not uncommon, although tolerance for them waned significantly in the 1890s.

In eastern Nebraska, most of the county seats were platted before the network of railroads was built. Following the typical Midwestern pattern, the courthouses were customarily placed in a square surrounded on all sides by a variety of business enterprises. The railroad depot was located as close to the heart of town as its late arrival permitted. But farther west, the transportation system determined the location and the layout of the towns. The depot, normally placed on land granted to the railroad by the federal government, displaced the courthouse square as the center of activity. In this arrangement of urban space, the courthouse usually was built on cheap land donated by the railroad on the edge of town. Commercial ventures would then line one street running parallel to the railroad tracks and another that linked the depot and the courthouse.

By modern standards, the cities and towns of the nineteenth century were unattractive, unpleasant places. Not even the larger cities—Omaha, Lincoln, Hastings, and Kearney—had made any significant adaptations to the plains environment. Instead, they reflected the standards and customs that prevailed in eastern cities, including the monotonous rectangular grid of streets.

Problems of sanitation were often ignored. Because streets were unpaved, animal excrement often converted them into cesspools. Since there was no collection of garbage and rubbish, rats multiplied. Unpenned hogs and chickens foraged garbage, and packs of semiwild dogs roamed freely. Human waste from overfilled privy vaults sometimes contaminated well water. Diseases such as typhoid fever and dysentery were common, and sewage systems scarcely existed. Omaha began construction of its sewage system in 1878, but it was not completed until 1895. In 1880, Lincoln had a twelve-inch line that serviced three buildings in the business district. Omaha got its first water system in 1881, when its population exceeded thirty thousand. Parks were rare, though Lincoln had a largely neglected ten-acre tract and Omaha was progressive enough to hire professional engineers to design its Hanscom Park.

By the end of the 1880s, the frontier phase of most Nebraska towns had passed. Balloon-frame wooden structures with false fronts in the commercial districts were replaced by substantial buildings called "business blocks," usually constructed of brick or stone. Some streets were paved with bricks, and a few were even illuminated at night. Trees lined the avenues in residential areas. Public transportation systems had been introduced in the largest cities and utilities were in place, including systems for water, electricity, gas, and telephones, though they were neither extensive nor efficient. Nebraska's cities had begun to take on the appearance that we would recognize today.

15.1. Plattsmouth in 1872. The internal spatial relationships of the oldest
towns in Nebraska such as Plattsmouth,
shown here about 1872, were shaped by
their relationship to the Missouri River.
This photograph shows the linkage at
the water's edge between river traffic
and the Burlington railroad tracks,
which had been built only a year or two
earlier. Courtesy NSHS, C334:10–24.

15.2. Grant, a railroad town and the seat of Perkins County, was typical of many western Nebraska towns. In this 1890 image, stores with false fronts huddle together on a broad unpaved street in a vast, windswept, treeless plain. Courtesy NSHS, H992:1.

15.3. In 1887, Ansley, located in Custer County near the center of the state, was still a very new town. Main Street was crowded with stores, including a coal yard, a land office, and a restaurant, that were hastily built on narrow lots. Wagons, reapers, mowers, and other machinery were left in the street, awaiting buyers. Courtesy NSHS Butcher Collection, B983:3437.

15.4. The power of the railroad in central and western Nebraska is suggested by this panoramic image of McCook taken in the mid-1890s. The railroad tracks and sidings, passenger station, and workshops dominate the foreground. Lumberyards and various commercial enterprises parallel the tracks, and other businesses stretch away from the noisy and dirty railroad to the treeless residential district on the high ground. The horizon is punctuated by church spires, windmills, and water tanks. Courtesy NSHS, C689:3–4.

15.5. This map of Tecumseh, the seat of
Johnson County in the southeastern
part of the state, illustrates the spatial
relationships typical of many Midwestern towns. The courthouse square
is near the middle of town at the center
of the business district. The railroad was
built later and came as close to the
square as possible. From the *Official
State Atlas of Nebraska* (1885), courtesy
NSHS.

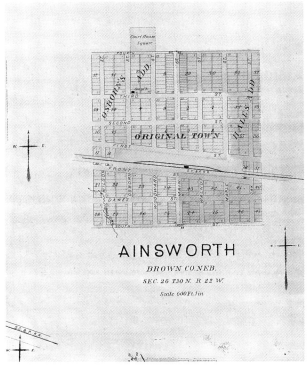

15.6. Ainsworth, the seat of Brown
County, illustrates the railroad-
dominated type of urban geography.
The courthouse square is located beyond the business district on the edge of
town where land was cheap. From the
Official State Atlas of Nebraska (1885),
courtesy NSHS.

15.7. Nothing contributed more to the appearance of permanent prosperity in Nebraska towns than the many substantial "blocks" erected in the booming 1880s before the depression of the mid-1890s. Pictured here is the Norris Block in Beaver City, built by future U.S. Senator George Norris when he was a young lawyer practicing in Furnas County. Courtesy NSHS, N855:249.

15.8. At some time or another, every Nebraskan must feel like this lonely figure battling the wind in Alliance. By the 1890s, when this photograph was probably taken, most western Nebraska towns were still raw and unfinished. But Omaha, Lincoln, and other eastern cities appeared more settled, permanent, and inviting. Courtesy NSHS, A436:25.

16 Hard Times in the 1870s

Despite the transforming effect of railroad transportation, the first decade of Nebraska's history as a state was not easy. The greatest growth was in the eastern third, where the railroad network was functioning and expanding. Agriculture was becoming the foundation of the state's economy. The capital had been transferred from Omaha to Lincoln, railroad lands were being taken up, and agricultural settlement was expanding up the Platte, Republican, and Elkhorn River valleys.

Then a double disaster struck. First, the Panic of 1873 hurled the country into a depression of considerable severity, made worse by the reluctance of governments—national, state, or local—to provide assistance to its citizens. Second, the plains had to endure one of its periodic droughts and, as usual in such times, a plague of grasshoppers. But this national catastrophe, beginning in 1874 and lasting through 1876, was unprecedented in American experience.

Thousands of new Nebraskans faced financial ruin and thousands more were destitute. The threat of starvation was immediate and intimate. It fell with special force on the frontier of settlement, which at that time slanted irregularly in a southwesterly direction from the mouth of the Niobrara River to the Republican River valley.

A distinguished Nebraska historian, Addison Sheldon, describes in *Nebraska: The Land and the People* his personal encounter with the plague of grasshoppers in 1874:

In a clear, hot July day a haze came over the sun. The haze deepened into a gray cloud. Suddenly the cloud resolved itself into billions of gray grasshoppers sweeping down upon the earth. The vibrations of their wings filled the ear with a roaring sound like a rushing storm. As far as the eye could reach in every direction the air was filled with them. Where they lighted they covered the ground like a heavy crawling carpet. Growing crops disappeared in a single day. Trees were stripped of leaves. Potatoes, turnips and onions were pursued into the earth. Clothing and harness was cut into shreds if left exposed.

Everywhere the earth was covered with a gray mass of struggling, biting grasshoppers. Turkeys and chickens feasted on them. Dogs and swine learned to eat them—the latter making them their chief food for days. . . . Many settlers had nothing to live on during the winter but their sod corn and garden. These were gone. It looked like starvation. The future held no hope, for the very soil was filled with eggs which would hatch a hundred times as many grasshoppers the next spring.

At first the state government, fearing negative publicity that would slow immigration into the state, tried to minimize the danger. But when the full magnitude of the disaster became apparent, both the state government and private agencies organized relief efforts. Units of the U.S. Army also provided important aid by distributing, without governmental authorization, surplus food and clothing. Only belatedly did the U.S. Congress appropriate funds to relieve the suffering of afflicted citizens on the plains from Montana to Kansas. Thousands had no choice but to flee the region for the security offered by more friendly environments farther east.

Cities were also affected, but less directly. Many experienced sharp decreases in population. By the late 1870s, however, the rains returned, the grasshoppers disappeared, and the economy rebounded. Nebraska, like its neighbors north and south, was on the verge of an extraordinary boom.

16.1. Grasshoppers where so numerous in 1874 that they could stop trains. Wheels of steam engines would spin on the tracks when the swarming creatures were crushed, as this engraving of a Union Pacific train in Nebraska suggests. Courtesy NSHS, R152:65.

16.2. Grasshopper-catching devices such as this horse-powered machine were recommended in the *Report of the Commissioner of Agriculture* in 1877, the last year of the plague. Courtesy NSHS, F233:139A.

16.3. A cloud of grasshoppers could destroy a cornfield in a matter of hours. The damage was worst in recently settled areas of central Nebraska, where many farmers lost their first year's crops. Courtesy NSHS, s653:94-9.

17 Beef Bonanza
The Range Cattle Industry

Cattle ranching in central and western Nebraska generally preceded agricultural settlement. Its origins were closely connected to two developments in the American West: travel on the Overland Trail and the discovery of gold and silver in the Rocky Mountains of Colorado in 1858. The development of ranching depended on transportation technology and the elimination of the great herds of bison as competitors for the grassland resources of the Great Plains.

Travelers on the Overland Trail unintentionally contributed to an early form of cattle ranching in Nebraska. Eager to reach their distant destinations, they sometimes pushed their oxen to the limits of endurance. Their footsore and exhausted animals could not continue without extended rest, a luxury few travelers could afford. Frontier entrepreneurs known as "road ranchers" provided the solution to the problem. Willing to exploit any opportunities that came their way, they sometimes accepted trail-worn beasts in payment for goods sold or in exchange for fresh, rested oxen. In this way they developed small cattle herds. But their market was limited and few road ranchers ever made the transition to cattle-raising on a large scale.

Most of the big cattle ranches in the state had origins that were closely connected to the development of transportation technology. In the late 1860s, when railroad lines extended onto the Great Plains in Nebraska and Kansas, Texas cattlemen began to drive great herds of longhorns from the southern plains to the closest railheads. These drives brought into existence famous cattle towns such as Abilene, Wichita, and Dodge City in Kansas and Ogallala in Nebraska, from where steers were shipped in cattle cars equipped with provisions for feed and water to the recently developed meat-packing plants of Chicago, Omaha, and elsewhere. Ogallala received more than one hundred thousand cattle from Texas each year in the late 1870s and early 1880s.

Other cattlemen decided that it made more sense to avoid the "Long Drive" from Texas by grazing their cattle on government-owned land in Colorado, Wyoming, and western Nebraska along the branches of the Platte or other streams. Several of these operations entered Nebraska in the mid-1870s from the West and dominated much of the Panhandle until a consolidation movement began in the 1880s. Organized into corporations, many cattle companies attracted investments of eastern and European capital.

Thus began the decade of the "Beef Bonanza," as it was called by James S. Brisbin in *Beef Bonanza, or How to Get Rich on the Plains,* published in 1881. Great riches presumably awaited the entrepreneur daring enough to purchase a herd of Texas cattle, acquire a small tract of land to serve as a headquarters, make dubious use of federal land laws to secure water rights along a nearby creek, and let nature take its course. The herd could be expected to increase naturally as it grazed on the open range, the huge tracts of grass-rich land that were still in the public domain.

The range-cattle industry developed first in the southwestern and Panhandle regions of Nebraska and in the upper reaches of the Elkhorn River valley in the north. In the 1880s, many small operators began to move into the vast, grass-covered Sand Hills country closer to the center of the state. After the Burlington railroad penetrated the area in the late 1880s, the Sand Hills became and has remained Nebraska's most important cattle-grazing region.

The development of ranching in the Sand Hills came just as the old open-range system was ending. As cattlemen expanded operations throughout the West and saturated the world market with their product, beef prices began to drop. Many ranchers understood that if they were to compete effectively they would have to improve the quality of their stock by importing Hereford, Angus, or Shorthorn bulls and ending indiscriminate breeding by fencing their herds. In the late 1880s a series of blizzards destroyed countless cattle; droughty summers followed. Throughout the West many of the largest and best-known land and cattle companies went bankrupt.

At the same time, homesteaders were venturing into cattle country, building sod houses and fencing their land. In 1887 Nebraska amended its Herd Law of 1870, which made ranchers liable for damage done by their stock to farmers' crops, to make enforcement a matter of county option. Since the farmers, or grangers, easily outnumbered the ranchers in most Nebraska counties, they quickly brought an end to the open range. Surviving ranchers introduced improved management techniques, used fences to enclose natural meadows, and harvested hay, both natural and cultivated. A new era had begun.

17.1. The McDonald Ranch, located near Cottonwood Springs on the Platte River, was one of many "road ranches" on the Overland Trail where travelers could buy supplies and exchange foot-sore oxen for fresh animals. Usually crude and dirty, road ranches combined the functions of trading posts, hotels, and blacksmith shops. They were especially numerous west of Fort Kearny on the south side of the river. Courtesy NSHS, R629:1.

17.2. Ranchers moved into Nebraska's Panhandle before they occupied the Sand Hills. The headquarters of the Hat Creek Ranch, located in the northwestern corner of the state, is pictured here about 1890. The haymows reveal that the owners no longer depended solely on the open range for cattle feed. Courtesy NSHS, s618:3–18.

17.3. A lad on a white horse posed with cowboys on the Cal Snyder ranch in Custer County for this branding scene captured by Solomon Butcher in 1888. A woman in a sunbonnet observes the action from the right. Courtesy NSHS Butcher Collection, B983:1830.

17.4. In 1902, cowhands employed by the Spring Lake Ranch near Gordon held still for this group portrait in front of a tent mounted on a cook wagon. A woman holding a baby sits inside the tent. Courtesy NSHS, M327:5.

17.5. This photograph suggests that by 1900, cowboy mythology was well-developed in Nebraska. Sadie Austin, described as a "typical Nebraska cow-girl," holds a shotgun in her right hand and sports a six-gun at her left. How she could ride her horse so saddled while wearing a full skirt can only be imagined. Courtesy NSHS Butcher Collection, B983:2436.

17.6. Following the disastrous winters of the late 1880s, Bartlett Richards developed the Spade Ranch—the largest in Nebraska—in the Sand Hills of Sheridan and Cherry Counties by adopting new methods of management. Pictured here are the original buildings as they appeared in the 1890s. They included, left to right, the manager's house, the log-cabin cook house, the ranch headquarters, and the barn. Courtesy NSHS, R513.9:182.

17.7. Cattle graze by a Sand Hills lake in this bucolic landscape photographed about 1900 on the Lee Brothers Ranch near Brownlee in Cherry County. Three well-dressed mounted figures, including a boy, pose with the herd. Courtesy NSHS Butcher Collection, B983:1837.

The Boom before the Bust *18*

After Nebraska was linked by rail to the East, its population exploded. By 1870 it had reached 123,000; twenty years later it topped one million. All through these two decades, "boomers"—mainly real estate speculators, town promoters, and railroad propagandists—extolled the unlimited potential of Nebraska as a prairie paradise. In the 1870s the boomers were joined by others with excellent reputations as scientists who proclaimed that plowing up the plains had the effect of increasing rainfall—that rain follows the plow.

Trying to dispel the image of the Great Plains as a vast desert rivaling Africa's Sahara, boomers declared that the time had come for farmers to settle the plains. According to Professor Samuel Aughey of the recently founded University of Nebraska, the increase in rain in the late 1870s following several years of severe drought was due to cultivated fields having absorbed and stored rainwater. He argued that grasslands merely shed rainfall into creeks and rivers. But agricultural success, Aughey predicted, would lead to more farms and still more rain, which in turn would produce more trees that would transpire more moisture into the air to form moisture-laden clouds. In the inflated words of Charles Wilber, a notable Nebraska town builder, in the 1878–79 annual report to the Nebraska State Horticultural Society: "the agencies of civilization now in action are such as will secure a complete victory over wilderness and waste places of western territory." The plow, he cried, was the instrument that would convert the desert into a garden.

This utterly false notion was vigorously espoused and eagerly accepted by the gullible just as the state was recovering from the consequences of the Panic of 1873, drought, and grasshopper invasions. Boomer propaganda, a return of national prosperity, and an increase in rainfall stimulated heavy settlement in central and western Nebraska during the 1880s.

By 1890 farmers had penetrated every fertile valley or tableland that offered promise of successful farming. Even the population of the Panhandle, which in 1880 was 2,257 (few of whom were farmers), increased to more than 40,000 a decade later. Prosperity seemed assured. Instead, drought and depression during the early 1890s, as in the 1870s, drove a substantial part of the farming population out of the region.

18.1. Local citizens and a band of musicians celebrated the departure of a thirty-five-car "boom train" from Hebron in 1887. The train made a five-day trip through Missouri, Iowa, and Illinois to declare the wonders of Nebraska and encourage prospective settlers to settle in Thayer County. Courtesy Thayer County Museum, Hebron.

18.2–3. Two bird's-eye views of Grand Island from the same vantage point in 1879 and 1890 reveal the enormous growth that took place there during the boom decade of the 1880s. The views look eastward down Second Street at Elm Street. *Courtesy Stuhr Museum of the Prairie Pioneer.*

Farming on the Plains *19*
The Role of Technology

Farming was limited in Nebraska during the territorial period. Farms were small, averaging only about fifty acres under cultivation. Tools and implements were crude and simple. Markets for agricultural products were few, and capital for investment was in short supply. But after Nebraska was linked by rail to the East, farming was transformed into the state's basic producer of wealth—the foundation of its economy.

The key to this transformation was technological development. Railroads were the prime example of the new technology, and a national transportation network depended on the ability to mass-produce steel. Blast furnaces that converted molten pig iron into steel were operating in the United States by 1864, just as the construction of the transcontinental railroad through Nebraska was about to begin.

Other developments in agricultural production also depended on the mass production of steel. By the 1870s, Nebraska farmers could buy a variety of new and improved plows, harrows, seed drills, corn planters, cultivators, and, by the end of the decade, endgate manure spreaders—all having important parts made of steel and all brought to

Nebraska on steel rails. Steam-powered threshing machines and combines were not far behind.

The ability to mass-produce steel was also central to solving the question of fencing. In eastern states an ample supply of timber made it possible to build fences out of wood. In the treeless plains, no satisfactory substitute was found until 1873, when a practical barbed wire was invented. Soon millions of pounds of steel were processed into barbed wire and transported to the enormous market in the plains states, where without adequate fencing homesteaders had been unable to protect their fields of corn and wheat from grazing herds of cattle.

Steel was also connected to the problem of water. Nebraska farm families typically depended on wells that were extremely difficult and dangerous to dig by hand. This problem was solved later in the century by the application of steam power to drilling equipment made of steel. In the meantime water had to be brought up from the ground by other methods. Although windmills were common in Euro-American culture, the 1850s saw the development of self-governing windmills that adjusted to changes in speed and direction of the wind. Nebraska farmers began to build or buy such windmills in the late 1870s.

Dairy farming was important in Nebraska in the nineteenth century. The use of silage as cattle feed was a part of this development. The first silo was built in 1873, and by 1890 most dairy farmers in Nebraska had one. Cream separators, which were available by 1884, were especially important for the many Nebraskans who produced cream for the butter market. Thus, cream typically went to the local creamery and the skim milk went to the hogs.

Far from eastern centers of population, Nebraska could never expect to become a major producer of dairy products. But beef on the hoof was another matter. Again, Nebraska benefited from a confluence of technological developments. Extensive pens to receive and load steers for shipment to slaughterhouses were invented by Joseph McCoy in 1867, and special train cars were built to supply animals with food and water during the long trip to the stockyards in Omaha, Chicago, and elsewhere. To create facilities in those cities to receive the shipments, Philip Armour invented the meat-packing plant in 1868. But the problem of transporting dressed beef from the packing houses to the great cities of the East remained. Even though the preservation of meat by canning was well developed by the 1860s, the greatest success of the industry awaited the invention of the refrigerator car in 1868.

Transportation and marketing were also important for other products of Nebraska agriculture, notably wheat. Railroad connections were as important for wheat growers as for cattle ranchers. Storing wheat in grain elevators at the railroad was crucial to processing wheat into flour. As wheat became a major crop in the Great Plains, most of the problems connected with grain elevators were solved and Nebraska farmers gained easy access to national markets; more distant markets opened as transatlantic steamships became common in the 1870s. Soon Nebraska had captured a share of the world grain market.

Farming in Nebraska was different from farming in eastern states. It was not merely a matter of a different physical environment—a flat grassland with a semiarid climate of temperature extremes—agriculture developed later in a period of exceptionally rapid technological change.

19.1. Nebraska was settled at a time when a variety of farm machinery was available for purchase. In 1888, William Sullivan of Sargent proudly posed for Solomon Butcher, displaying his team and wagon, cultivator, harrow, mower, and butter churn, along with his family, sod house, and livestock. Courtesy NSHS Butcher Collection, B983:1023.

19.2. Threshing machines were well developed by the 1870s, but rigs equipped with a blower to stack the straw evenly were first manufactured in the mid-1880s. This steam-powered rig was photographed in Custer County about 1905. Courtesy NSHS, C984:16-10.

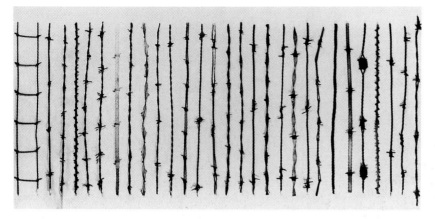

19.3. Barbed wire was essential to the development of Nebraska as a farming and ranching state. This photograph illustrates the varieties that were developed in the 1870s and 1880s. Courtesy NSHS, C984:16-9.

19.4. The installation of a new self-regulating windmill in 1887 was a major event for this Custer County household. The man on the wooden framework below the fan emphasizes the importance of the windmill for these pioneer farmers. Courtesy NSHS Butcher Collection, B983:3208.

19.5. Grain-elevator technology was developing rapidly as Nebraska was being settled. Elevators provided storage for grain awaiting delivery to distant markets. Here farmers are lined up with loaded wagons at an elevator in Wausa in 1904. Courtesy NSHS, W354:60.

Log Cabins and Sod Houses *20*

Among Nebraska's most important contributions to American folk culture is the sod house, a structure built of layers of sod (dirt bonded by intertwined grass roots) called "Nebraska marble" by cheerful pioneers. It was a practical response to the treeless environment of the Great Plains. Nebraska was not the only place where sod houses were built, but they were especially numerous in this state and it was here that they attained their fullest development.

The earliest rural inhabitants of Nebraska did not build sod houses. Like their predecessors in eastern states, they built log cabins. The banks of the Missouri River and its tributaries were wooded (as 97 percent of Nebraska was not), and it was there that the earliest pioneers lived. As settlement moved westward, the supply of suitable trees diminished until few trees could be found other than cottonwoods. Although hardwood was always preferred, logs from cottonwood trees were often used, even though they were soft and would warp dreadfully when dried. Log cabins were built in much of the eastern quarter of the state, normally along river bottoms. They were common as far west as

Grand Island and Kearney on the Platte and could be found along the Republican, Elkhorn, and Niobrara Rivers as well. A few were even built near wooded areas in the western part of the state.

Given the shortage of trees, Nebraska pioneers turned to sod as a substitute. The techniques of sod-house construction were learned gradually by experience during the 1850s and 1860s. Most "soddies" were small, dark, dirty, and infested with vermin, but they were also relatively cool in summer, warm in winter, and impervious to the ravages of prairie fires. Later, when manufactured doors and windows could be purchased at lumberyards and a hipped roof could be made of boards and shingles instead of tree branches, grasses, and sod, many pioneers began to think of sod houses as permanent dwellings instead of temporary structures to be inhabited until a frame house could be built.

The sod itself was sliced out of the ground with a specially designed plow. A typical piece was three feet long, one and one-half feet wide, and several inches thick. The sods were quickly laid grass side down in double rows on a prepared site before they could dry out. They were placed in alternate patterns, like bricks, and every third layer would be laid crosswise in order to bond the two parallel rows. Because the walls were so thick, a house with external dimensions of eighteen by twenty-four feet thus would enclose an interior space of only twelve by eighteen feet. The sides of the wall would then be dressed with a spade, cracks daubed with mortar, and interiors plastered with clay.

Structural problems remained. Because of their great weight, walls tended to settle or sag, so that doors and windows would be thrust out of kilter and sometimes broken. Even the best sod roof was leaky and dirty. But as railroads penetrated the sod-house country and brought lumberyards to the frontier, the worst problems could be solved. Still, most farmers considered a frame house to be a symbol of success and superior to a soddie; the sod structures were often converted to barns or storage sheds when the farmer could afford something better. But some soddies were so well planned, constructed, and cared for that a few—perhaps two dozen—remain in use today.

20.1. Log cabins were common in eastern Nebraska along wooded rivers but relatively rare in central Nebraska, where this substantial dwelling was constructed. Located in a wooded area on the South Loup River near Callaway, it was built of cottonwood logs by Al Wise, pictured here with his family in 1892. Courtesy NSHS Butcher Collection, B983:710.

20.2. Dwellings dug out of a hillside were sometimes built as temporary housing. This example in Custer County, photographed by Solomon Butcher in 1892, shows the thickness of the sod walls, often thirty-six inches, and how bricks of sod were laid alternately to bond the wall together. The wagon behind the dugout is loaded with sod to repair the roof. Courtesy NSHS Butcher Collection, B983:1653.

20.3. Here two settlers near the Dismal River in Thomas County load sod onto a wagon. Bricks of uniform width and thickness have been cut with a specially designed "grasshopper" plow. Freshly cut bricks were loaded onto a wagon laid grass side down before they could dry out. Courtesy NSHS, s679:8.

20.4. This small sod house built by John Curry in Custer County in 1887 illustrates a gable-end construction, which placed enormous weight on the side walls. Uneven settling of sod walls often caused windows to buckle and break. Curry and his wife prominently display prized possessions. To the right is the family's well with a bucket attached to a pully. Courtesy NSHS Butcher Collection, B983:1048.

20.5. Intended as a permanent dwelling, this substantial structure in Custer County (photographed by Solomon Butcher in about 1888) boasts a hipped roof that evenly distributes the weight of the roof. Double-hung windows, purchased in town, are placed at the outer edge of the sod wall to create more interior space. Courtesy NSHS Butcher Collection, B983:1552.

20.6. The extraordinary Haumont
House, one of the few two-story sod
houses ever built, was constructed by
Belgian immigrants near Broken Bow in
1884. It stood for nearly ninety years until it was bulldozed in 1973 as a hazard to
curious tourists. Imitative of a French
provincial chateau style, the rounded
corners were purely decorative. Courtesy NSHS Butcher Collection,
B983:1004a.

20.7. For many pioneers, replacing a soddie with a frame house was a symbol of success. Here Anton Smock, a prosperous farmer of Oconto, stands proudly before his complex of buildings, which includes a new frame house. He apparently continued to use his original soddie for storage purposes. Courtesy NSHS Butcher Collection, B983:1764a.

21 Making a Home on the Nebraska Frontier

By the standards of our technologically advanced culture, living in a sod house would be simply intolerable, almost incomprehensible, even as a temporary expedient. If we judge on the basis of nineteenth-century culture and expectations, it was neither easy nor attractive but not dire. And by no means did all pioneer farm families in Nebraska live in sod houses.

Whether a family resided in a soddie or a frame house, making a home on the rural frontier meant incessant, arduous work for most women: cooking meals, cleaning the house, washing and ironing, sewing and mending clothing, tending the chickens, working the garden, milking the cows, canning fruits and vegetables, churning butter, baking bread, brining corn and sauerkraut, knitting stockings, making soap, and gathering cow chips for fuel. It meant fighting lice, fleas, and bedbugs. Sometimes it also meant hauling water, hoeing the fields, helping with harvests, mending fences—whatever was necessary for the family to survive in a harsh and demanding environment.

Poverty and deprivation were standard on the rural frontier. Substitution became a way of life: lard for butter, turnips for potatoes, sorghum for sugar, thistle leaves for tea, and parched wheat or barley for coffee. Women, men, and children went barefoot whenever possible, mostly because shoes were expensive.

The frontier was also a threatening environment. For new settlers the extremes of a midcontinental climate with its blizzards and stifling heat waves were especially severe. Grass fires were a threat to crops, livestock, homes, and life itself. An adequate supply of potable water was always a problem. The threat of sickness, malnutrition, serious disease, and debilitating injuries was unrelenting. Some pioneers perceived Indians as menacing—the barriers of culture were too great for mutual understanding and sympathetic contact to develop.

The perils of childbirth in isolated circumstances were naturally recurrent, and women assisting women in childbirth was standard. Doctors were rare, hospitals nonexistent. Birth rates in nineteenth-century America dropped steadily to 4.24 per woman in 1880. On the Nebraska frontier, birth rates were a little higher but so was infant mortality. Although children were cherished for themselves, they were also economic assets, and having more children improved chances that some would survive to maturity. Large families also meant companionship, and young helping hands meant that more acres could be farmed.

Isolation on the pioneer homestead was intolerable for some women. Weeks or months could pass without contact with another woman. The earliest years were the most difficult, for then the monotonous solitude and physical distance from other women was most severe. There were more men than women on the Nebraska frontier, but the difference in numbers was not as great as often thought. Nebraska's agricultural frontier was populated mostly by young families, unlike transportation centers or mining towns that had a disproportionate number of young, unattached males.

Mobility on the Nebraska frontier was high. Families that would stay on the same homestead from one decennial census to the next were only a fraction of the total: the failure rate was very high. Women participated in most decisions to move, even though the nineteenth-century family was strongly patriarchal. Although such moves were often from one homestead to another farther west, many were to farms or towns back east or to towns on the frontier. For some wives and mothers, the hope of success on the rural frontier was short-lived, but most women learned to adapt and improvise. They coped bravely and well.

21.1. Rural Nebraska offered a life of relentless, arduous labor, as suggested by this photograph of two couples, young and old, living near the mouth of the Niobrara River in Knox County. Their stockade-style log cabin is placed dangerously close to the stream on the left. Courtesy NSHS, K74:9–22.

21.2. This broom-wielding wife and mother seems determined to maintain cleanliness in a difficult setting, captured in this photograph by Solomon Butcher in Custer County in 1886. Her canaries, proudly displayed in two cages on either side of the entrance, helped dispel the silence of rural isolation. Courtesy NSHS Butcher Collection, B983:1162.

21.3. The pride of this Custer County woman led her to deny the photographer, Solomon Butcher, permission to photograph her mean dwelling. Instead, she gathered the family around her most highly prized possession, an ornate reed organ. Similarly, her husband displays his team of mules, wagon, horse, farm implements, and livestock. Hogs run loose to control rattlesnakes near the house. Courtesy NSHS Butcher Collection, B983:3535.

21.4. This elegantly attired woman appears outside her first residence in 1882 near McCook. The single window suggests a dark and dank interior. Like her dwelling, the outhouse is also built of sod. The treeless landscape reveals the unbroken space that isolates her from a distant neighbor, whose house is silhouetted on the horizon. Courtesy NSHS, C689:5.

22 A Flood of European Immigrants

Although European immigrants had been present in Nebraska's population from the earliest times of white settlement, the arrival of the railroad in all agricultural parts of the state permitted an extensive settlement of various immigrant groups. In each of the federal censuses from 1860 to 1900, European immigrants (not including their American-born children) constituted about one-fifth of the total population of the state. In some cases the railroads brought colonies of Germans, Danes, and Swedes to buy and settle on farmland owned by the railroad. Other immigrants took advantage of land available under the Homestead Act. Still others, including many Irish, worked on railroad construction and stayed on, usually in the towns, but sometimes on farms.

Omaha always registered the largest and most diverse population, but in most parts of the state the countryside and its farms attracted more immigrants than the cities and towns. European-born Nebraskans often lived and labored in eastern parts of the United States before settling on the plains.

The mosaic of ethnic settlements established in the 1870s and 1880s has continued to the present time. Throughout the state the descendants of the original settlers continue to occupy the land. Those of German ancestry are by far the most numerous and are found everywhere in the state. A century later, according to the 1980 census, 22.4 percent of all inhabitants in the state were "single-ancestry" descendants of German immigrants. They were most highly concentrated in the northeastern quadrant, where, for example, in Cuming County they were 52.7 percent; in Cedar County, also located in the northeast, 50.9 percent; and in Thayer County, located on the Kansas border, 50.7 percent.

Other European ethnic groups are concentrated in certain areas. Even though their total numbers are small compared to those found in the cities of eastern states, they are remarkably high proportions in many thinly populated rural counties in Nebraska. The Czechs provide the best known example: in 1980 the highest percentages of "single-ancestry" Czechs in the United States by county were found in Butler County (32.3 percent), Colfax County (27.5 percent), and Saline County (24.2 percent). Nebraskans of Polish ancestry are not numerous, yet their highest concentration in the United States is in Sherman County at 26 percent, and third highest in Nance County at 20.3 percent. The county with the second-highest proportion of Swedes in the United States was Polk at 19 percent and the third highest was Phelps at 18 percent.

How does one account for such figures? Each of the groups had strong traditions of agriculture and each felt the pressures of technological change during the 1880s when rich farmland in eastern Nebraska was available for homesteading or purchase. Nebraska also offered a congenial and attractive setting for maintaining ethnocultural forms, including language and religion. As technological change transformed agriculture, many descendants of European immigrants left the farms for the cities, but there have been few in-migrants to take their places. The Swedes, Danes, Czechs, Poles, and Germans from Russia also formed rural colonies, while Irish, English, Scots, and Welsh often preferred urban settings.

In general, European immigrants experienced little discrimination in Nebraska, although it was easier for them to succeed in the economic sphere than the political. They preferred to establish their own religious and cultural worlds when possible—which was often difficult in Nebraska, where the physical environment often dictates a sparse population spread over vast spaces. The ethnic institution that immigrants were most likely to re-create was the church. Hence, the Nebraska countryside continues to be dotted with the churches of Lutheran, Catholic, Mennonite, and other immigrant faiths, buildings that became the focus of immigrant social life. Because of the rural exodus, some churches have been abandoned, others torn down, and a few moved to new locations, but many still serve the rural population of the state. With their spires piercing the Nebraska sky, they continue to enliven the rural landscape.

In the nineteenth century, immigrant Nebraskans were served by many foreign-language newspapers. The German newspapers were the most numerous—more than sixty were founded in the nineteenth century. Most were weeklies with small circulation and brief duration, but the *Omaha Tägliche Tribüne* was an established daily paper. Other ethnic institutions, such as social, fraternal, and cultural organizations, were more difficult to sustain, and most have now disappeared. Many small businesses and insurance companies that originally catered to particular ethnic groups survived by abandoning their ethnic exclusiveness and merging with other firms.

Ethnic consciousness is not a vital matter for the majority of Nebraskans today. Most descendants of nineteenth-century European immigrants have long ago lost all the obvious marks of ethnicity. Yet behaviors and attitudes rooted in ethnicity remain. Unidentified or submerged, they have moved silently into the behaviors and attitudes of the middle class, where they reside today, as American as apple pie. Contemporary demands for public morality and the concomitant emphasis on family values, self-help, and work for its own sake are distilled at least in part from this source.

22.1. Major railroads advertised heavily for immigrant farmers from Europe to come to Nebraska. The Burlington prepared this Czech-language brochure for distribution in Austria-Hungary, New York, and other major ports of entry. The drawings promise bountiful success in six years. The Czech in translation: "600,000 acres of B. & M. Railroad land in eastern Nebraska are for sale at cheap prices and liberal terms." The same brochure was also published in German and other languages. Courtesy NSHS, A245:10.

22.2. Soon after the Burlington arrived in Lincoln in 1870, it built these structures to provide free temporary quarters with cooking and washing facilities for immigrants before they traveled on to lands they had purchased from the railroad. The Union Pacific offered similar arrangements in Omaha. Courtesy NSHS, L741:572.

22.3. Lincoln served as a major destination for German immigrants from Russia, beginning in the mid-1870s and continuing until World War I. Many German farmers from Russia purchased land from the railroads and others hired out as agricultural workers, especially in the sugar-beet fields in the Platte River valley. Courtesy NSHS, W727:143.

22.4. This congregation of Swedish Baptists, dressed in their finest clothes, gathered for a group portrait in the snow outside their sod-house church in rural Sherman County. Their pastor, Bible in hand, is seated second from the left. Courtesy NSHS, N829:32.

22.5. Czech immigrants to Nebraska were unusual in that many, perhaps half, were anticlerical. Instead of joining together in churches, they often organized fraternal societies. This photograph, taken in 1978, shows the brick building that housed the Bila Hora (White Mountain) lodge of the Western Bohemian Fraternal Association (Z.C.B.J.) in Verdigre. Courtesy Roger Bruhn.

23 Strangers in Their Own Land

Long before Congress created Nebraska Territory, Americans thought of the Great Plains as an area far from white settlement that should be reserved for the Indians. Beginning in the 1820s the federal government removed many eastern peoples from their ancestral homes to a "permanent Indian frontier" on the plains. Various groups were assigned to specific tracts, especially in present-day Kansas and Oklahoma, where their isolation was expected to remove them from conflict with white society.

Nebraska Indians were part of this development. In 1833 the Otoes and Missourias ceded their lands to the government, retaining only a tract between the Big and Little Nemaha Rivers. In 1854, the government shifted them to a much smaller strip of land on the Kansas border between the Big and Little Blue Rivers. In the same year the Omahas accepted a tract in what is now Thurston County, where they remain today on Nebraska's best-known reservation. In 1858, the Poncas, a small Siouan tribe that had lived for many generations at the mouth of the Niobrara River, unhappily ceded their lands for a tract between the Niobrara River and Ponca Creek in present-day Boyd County.

Changes in the development of the reservation system accelerated in the 1860s, due in part to events associated with the Civil War. Increased traffic on the emigrant and mail routes across the plains to western mining frontiers often infringed on Indian hunting grounds. Restless plains tribes reacted by disrupting traffic on the Overland Trail, which was Colorado's lifeline to the East. Although the governor of Colorado Territory had made some efforts to resolve the conflict peacefully, he decided in 1864 to force Indians from areas in Colorado recently occupied by whites. This policy, brutally carried out by territorial militia, led in November to the massacre at Sand Creek of Cheyennes and Arapahos—people who at that time were trying to cooperate with the federal government. Most of the victims were old men, women, and children.

Deeply apprehensive of white encroachments on their lands, many Indian leaders reasoned that peace negotiations would be fruitless and that confrontation offered better chances for survival. The Cheyennes, Arapahos, and the Brulé intensified attacks on isolated settlements on the plains and spread terror as far east as Grand Island. Panic swept the Nebraska plains in 1865 and many whites fled eastward, their fear of Indian attacks greatly stimulated.

When the Civil War ended in 1865, the U.S. Army, no longer preoccupied with the Southern insurrection, shifted its attention to the Indians of the plains. The military was prepared to use a policy of force to "pacify" the Indians. Other Americans, stimulated by the startling revelations of a congressional investigation into the Sand Creek massacre, advocated what seemed to be a more humanitarian approach—a policy of peace, education, and assimilation. The federal government finally decided, as a general policy, to force all Indians from the open range and place them on reservations where the peace advocates could educate them, as wards of the federal government, in white ways including religion, language, customs, and values.

Certain military leaders pointed out that such a policy required the extermination of the bison herds that were the foundation of plains Indian culture. Their elimination would force the Indians to rely on government distribution of beef as a substitute, a prospect welcomed by the range cattle industry, then in its infancy.

In 1867 the federal government undertook a new series of negotiations with plains Indians for their removal to reservations. In the same year, Nebraska was admitted into the Union as a state, and most Nebraskans of that time believed that such Indian tracts were fine as long as they were located elsewhere. They frequently petitioned Congress to rid their state of its few remaining reservations and to dispatch the Indians to the Dakotas and Oklahoma, which did not become states until much later.

In 1868 many of the Sioux, though not all, reluctantly accepted the idea of a large reservation in Dakota Territory, and after some indecision the federal government in 1873 established the Red Cloud Agency for the Oglala Sioux near present-day Crawford in the northwestern corner of Nebraska. Nontreaty Indians continued to resist the imposition of the reservation system.

The Pawnees, a confederation of seminomadic horticulturists who had long occupied lands in east-central Nebraska from the Loup River south to the Republican, were reduced in 1857 to a reservation in the Loup valley, a tract coterminous with present-day Nance County. Repeatedly harassed during the next fifteen years by Sioux raiding parties on one side and subjected to encroachment of their lands by white settlers on the other, in 1874 the Pawnees as a matter of survival decided to sell their reservation and leave Nebraska for a reservation in Oklahoma where they hoped to preserve their way of life. Many Nebraskans, eager to exploit the fertile lands and the stands of timber along the Loup River, were delighted.

In 1865, the Omahas ceded the northern half of their lands to the Winnebagos, a displaced Wisconsin tribe who were starving on the lands to which they had been assigned in Dakota Territory. In Knox County a reservation was created for the Santee Sioux from Minnesota.

Also in 1865, the Poncas benefited from a new agreement that restored to them their historic lands at the mouth of the Niobrara, where they sought to transform themselves from bison hunters to farmers. Government officials, in a tragic effort to protect the Poncas from Sioux raids, compelled them in 1877 to move to Indian Territory, where one-quarter of their people died within a year. Standing Bear, a Ponca chief, led a part of the tribe back to Nebraska, where they were welcomed by the Omahas to their reservation. He was arrested and brought to trial. The court battle that ensued led to a celebrated decision declaring that Standing Bear "was a person within the meaning of the law," and that therefore he was being held illegally by the government. He was allowed to remain in Nebraska after the trial.

The Otoes and Missourias, who had merged as one tribe in 1854, were forced off their land and relocated in Oklahoma in 1881. By that time the Southern Cheyenne and Arapaho also had been assigned to reservations in Indian Territory, all with disastrous results.

The discovery of gold in the Black Hills in the mid-1870s complicated matters greatly for the Sioux, who were outraged by the lawless intrusion of prospectors and other frontiersmen onto lands that had been assigned to them by treaty. When the Sioux refused to grant mining rights in the Black Hills, the government ordered them to withdraw from hunting lands in Wyoming and Montana territories and report to their reservation agencies in Dakota Territory and northwestern Nebraska. Because the Sioux were unwilling or unable to comply with this directive, officials declared them to be "hostile" and ordered the army into action. Even though the Sioux inflicted a smashing defeat upon troops commanded by Colonel George Custer at the Little Big Horn in Montana in 1876, they lacked the strength needed to win the war for their homelands. Finally forced onto reservations on the northern plains, they continued the fight by defending their culture from assimilationist pressures.

Nebraska's Native Americans were thus forced to accept reservation life. Shocked by defeat in battle, devastated by the destruction of the great bison herds upon which their culture depended, deprived of their land, weakened by disease and malnutrition, reduced to dependency on government handouts, and badgered by missionaries and government agents to become hybrid Americans, most Indians of the plains sank into destitution on reservations that were mere remnants of their once vast territories. They were strangers in their own land.

23.1. Soon after the Omaha Indians accepted their reservation in 1854 in what is now Thurston County, the Presbyterian church started a mission school in which the children were forced to abandon their traditional clothing, food, customs, and language and learn the white man's ways. In this image, the Indian children, dressed in European clothing with their hair trimmed short, pose with their teachers, including the bearded Reverend William Hamilton, who headed the mission until 1870. Courtesy NSHS, P928:17.

23.2. Representatives of the Pawnee and Ponca tribes from Nebraska, joined by "unauthorized" delegations of the Potawatomi and Sac and Fox tribes, met with government dignitaries and interpretors in Washington DC on 31 December 1857. The Pawnees were there to confirm a treaty negotiated earlier that year in which they surrendered most of their lands in Nebraska. The Poncas were discussing a similar treaty that was signed several months later. This photograph, the earliest known to exist of Indian delegations in the national capital, was taken on land adjacent to the White House. Courtesy NSHS, PC1782:1-1.

23.3. One resolution of conflicts between Indians and travelers across Indian lands was to lure the Indians away from the Overland Trail. To this end, in 1873 the government relocated the Red Cloud Agency from the North Platte valley to a favorable site near present-day Crawford, nearly a hundred miles away, which offered ample supplies of timber, water, and grass. Here the government agent distributed supplies and sought to maintain the peace. As this picture suggests, the agency was a cluster of workshops, corrals, storehouses, and residences enclosed within a stockade. In 1877 the agency was moved to Dakota Territory to what later became the Pine Ridge Reservation. Courtesy NSHS, J82:80.

23.4. Standing Bear posed for this portrait in 1879 after his trial before Judge Elmer Dundy, who ruled in his favor. General George Crook, whose duty it was to arrest Standing Bear, interested Thomas Tibbles of the *Omaha Herald* in the case and the injustice being done to the Poncas. Tibbles in turn brought nationwide publicity to the case, which was tried in Omaha. Courtesy NSHS, R539:2-2.

23.5. For most Indians of the Great Plains, life on the reservations meant unrelieved destitution. These unidentified women, probably members of the Brulé Sioux tribe, illustrate the impact of white culture. They live in rectangular log structures, not round, transportable tepees. Some of their clothes were manufactured in eastern textile factories. In the background are buckets, a grindstone, and other evidence of white technology. Courtesy NSHS, A547:2-76.

23.6. Indians who lived on the reservation were dependent on government distributions of beef and other supplies. The cattle pictured here in 1889 on the Rosebud Reservation in South Dakota were substitutes for the bison that earlier had formed the foundation of Plains Indian culture. Mounted Indians await the release of cattle, which they will "hunt" as they had the buffalo. The Indian families would then skin and dress the carcasses on the prairie where they were killed. Courtesy NSHS, A547:2-63a.

23.7. Despite the corrosive effects of reservation life, many Native Americans sustained their language, customs, costumes, and ceremonies, as shown in this image of Sioux and Omahas in 1893. The American flags suggest the ceremony may have taken place on July Fourth, Independence Day. Courtesy NSHS: J82.47

Forts and Soldiers on the Nebraska Frontier

24

The Indian troubles that flared up during and after the Civil War led to the establishment of a series of forts to keep the peace on the frontier. Some were short-lived. Forts McPherson (1863) and Mitchell (1864) protected travelers on the Oregon Trail. Fort Sidney (1867) defended construction crews working on the Union Pacific railroad. In the early 1870s two forts were established to deal specifically with the problems associated with dislocated Indians. Fort Hartsuff, located near the center of the state, was designed to protect settlers in the North Loup River valley as well as Pawnee Indians on their reservation in Nance County from marauding bands of hungry and impoverished Sioux. Construction of the fort began in 1874, when the Pawnees had already decided to move to Indian Territory. The fort was abandoned in 1881.

The most important nineteenth-century military installation in Nebraska was Fort Robinson. Its origins are tied to the Red Cloud Agency, which was created in 1868 in accordance with a treaty that closed the Bozeman Trail, a road through Indian territory in Wyoming connecting the Oregon Trail with gold and silver mines in Montana. At the agency, the federal government distributed food, clothing, tools, domesticated animals, and other supplies to Indians in exchange for land the Sioux had ceded to the United States. In addition to dispensing rations, the agent's tasks included keeping the peace among several thousand dislocated, impoverished, and restive Indians.

The Red Cloud Agency had a troubled history. Originally placed in the North Platte River valley, it was moved in 1873 to a site near the White River in the Pine Ridge country. Early in 1874, as tension at the agency mounted, military authorities decided that troops must be stationed there if violence was to be prevented. A temporary camp was established near the agency while permanent quarters—barracks, warehouses, and officers' quarters—were constructed one mile to the west. In January 1878, a presidential order granted this encampment official status as Fort Robinson. It became a permanent army post with a military reservation that eventually grew to cover thirty-six square miles and remained an active military post until 1948.

Fort Robinson was closely connected to a series of tragic events in the history of the plains Indians. The first occurred in 1877, after Crazy Horse, a talented leader of the Oglala Sioux who had fought brilliantly at the Little Big Horn, surrendered with his band at Fort Robinson. Some months later, in a misunderstanding of his intentions, Crazy Horse was arrested. As he was taken to the guardhouse, he made a frantic attempt to escape, which resulted in a mortal wound by bayonet.

In 1878, a band of Northern Cheyennes, devastated by disease, malnutrition, and homesickness, broke out of the reservation in Indian Territory where they had been sent some months earlier. They trekked northward on an epic march, intending to reestablish their former life in their home territory. Harassed all the way to Nebraska, one contingent under the leadership of Dull Knife was captured by the army and taken to Fort Robinson. The Cheyennes were then imprisoned pending their willingness to return to Oklahoma. Preferring death to such a fate, they made a desperate but futile effort to escape in January 1879, using guns they had successfully hidden at the time of their surrender. Pursued by troops into the bluffs west of the fort, the Cheyenne suffered more than sixty deaths—a third of the entire company of men, women, and children. Thus ended a remarkable saga of human fortitude and determination.

With the arrival of the railroad in 1887, Fort Robinson increased in importance as it became a regimental cavalry headquarters. Its last involvement in Indian affairs occurred in 1890–91, when it served as the staging area for troops engaged in the Wounded Knee campaign. The climax of that effort was the massacre of more than two hundred people in South Dakota.

Fort Niobrara, the last of the frontier forts, was established in 1880 to protect cattlemen and their herds from the Sioux, who were still feared even though they were confined to their reservation located a few miles north in Dakota Territory. By that time, however, they were a destitute people, their culture broken. Fort Niobrara was abandoned in 1906.

24.1. This fierce-looking, saber-wielding soldier posed while stationed at Fort McPherson, which was established in 1863 on the south side of the Platte River downstream from present-day North Platte. First called Fort Cottonwood, it was abandoned in 1880. Courtesy NSHS, M171:24.

24.2. In 1874 nearly a thousand soldiers were transferred from forts in Wyoming to the Red Cloud and Spotted Tail Agencies in Nebraska. Their camp, pictured here in 1877, eventually grew into Fort Robinson, a permanent installation. Named for a young lieutenant killed in 1874, the fort played a major role in the subjugation of the plains Indians. Courtesy NSHS, R659:4570.

24.3. Daily life at Fort Robinson gradually became routine and the quality of life improved for soldiers and officers. Permanent living quarters were built, including this duplex constructed of adobe bricks in 1887 for officers and their families. Courtesy NSHS, R659:5a.

24.4. Here the "I" troop of the Sixth Cavalry is shown on a training patrol at Fort Robinson in 1897. The fort became the headquarters for four cavalry regiments, including the Ninth and Tenth, which were segregated African-American units. Courtesy NSHS, H216.5:2.

24.5. This 1887 photograph shows Eighth Infantry soldiers drilling at Fort Niobrara. Located near Valentine on the Niobrara River, Fort Niobrara took the place of Fort Hartsuff as one of a circle of posts surrounding Sioux lands in Dakota Territory. It was intended to protect settlers, especially cattle ranchers, in north central Nebraska. Courtesy NSHS, N718:14.

African Americans in 25
Nineteenth-Century Nebraska

Throughout the nineteenth century the total number of African Americans in Nebraska was very small, and yet their role in the state's history was significant. The first federal decennial census taken after the creation of Nebraska Territory revealed about seventy-five blacks in a population of nearly twenty-nine thousand.

In the years just before the Civil War, slavery was permissible in the territories (not states) where legislatures did not forbid it. On several occasions the Nebraska territorial legislature tried to eliminate slavery, but each time the territorial governor or the council refused to concur. The census of 1860 records fifteen slaves in Nebraska, all women or their children. They worked as domestic servants, either in Nebraska City for the freighting magnate Alexander Majors or for army officers stationed at Fort Kearny. Except for a tiny cluster of four families in Omaha, the free African Americans in 1860—about sixty people—were widely dispersed. Some were women married to white men; they and their children formed a major part of the total black population identified by the census takers.

After the issue of slavery had been resolved by the Civil War, the African Americans in Nebraska were often temporary rather than permanent residents. Some were drovers who herded Texas longhorns to the railheads in Nebraska, and a few stayed on as cowboys in western Nebraska. Others were soldiers stationed at Forts Robinson and Niobrara. African American women often were employed as domestic servants in the cities, some as live-in servants by wealthy white families.

Such circumstances worked against family life and permanent residence. African Americans had few opportunities to become integral parts of society, even on a segregated basis. Still, a small community developed in Omaha among families of men who were employed by the Union Pacific railroad as waiters or porters on long-distance passenger trains. Gradually these and other African Americans developed the institutions, especially churches, that help give racial and ethnic groups a sense of identity and community. By no means were all African Americans of the time restricted to menial occupations. For example, the census of 1880 reveals that in Lincoln about one-third of the gainfully employed blacks were skilled workers such as cooks, barbers, and carpenters.

A few African-American rural settlements were founded about 1880, notably in Franklin, Harlan, and Hamilton Counties, but these early efforts to join the ranks of Nebraska farmers failed. As former slaves, most such pioneers lacked the experience and the capital necessary to get started as farmers. The most successful African-American agricultural settlement—Brownlee in the Sand Hills of Cherry County—did not begin until early in the twentieth century.

Homesteading was a difficult challenge for anyone, even for the most experienced farmers. Still, the records reveal examples of successful black homesteaders, and some seem to have been well-integrated into their local communities. The best known and perhaps most successful African-American farmer was Robert Ball Anderson, born a slave in Kentucky in 1843. A Civil War veteran, Anderson was among the earliest settlers in northern Box Butte County near Hemingford. He arrived in the mid-1880s, persisted under difficult circumstances, and eventually expanded his holdings to more than two thousand acres, specializing in breeding horses.

By the end of the century African Americans numbered 6,269—less than one percent of the total population of Nebraska. Most lived in Omaha. Some were unskilled laborers, but many found jobs in factories or with the railroads and others were skilled workers. Only a few, like Robert Anderson, lived on the land. According to the census of 1900, there were seventy-seven African-American farm families in Nebraska.

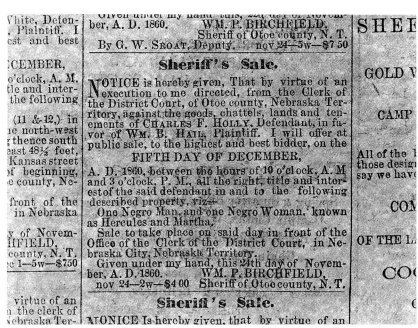

25.1. The uncomfortable fact that slavery existed in Nebraska is documented by this advertisement from the *Nebraska City News,* 24 November 1860, for the sheriff's sale of a man and a woman, Hercules and Martha, in Nebraska City to satisfy a debt incurred by their owner, Charles Holly. Neither slave is listed in the census manuscripts of 1860. Courtesy NSHS.

25.2. Although certain individual African Americans experienced economic success and social acceptance in Nebraska, the majority continued to suffer discrimination in many forms, including employment. In this 1864 image, the earliest known photograph of blacks in Nebraska, several men load wagons in Brownville, which at that time was still an important center of transportation. Courtesy NSHS, B884:283.

25.3. The best-known black homesteaders in Nebraska were three brothers—Moses Speece, Jerry Shores, and Henry Webb—former slaves who kept their masters' names and homesteaded east of Broken Bow in Custer County. Here Moses Speece and his family pose before their dwelling for Solomon Butcher in 1888. The substantial sod house, the windmill, the horses and carriage, and their clothing compare favorably with what other homesteaders displayed in those difficult years. Courtesy NSHS Butcher Collection, B983:1345.

25.4. African-American soldiers were enormously important for the U.S. Army in the West and were a majority of troops stationed at Fort Robinson for more than two decades (1885–1907). Here soldiers of the Twenty-fifth Infantry, a black regiment, stands at attention at Fort Niobrara in 1904. Courtesy NSHS, N393:25S.

25.5. After the Civil War, Henry Burden, pictured here with his family, homesteaded in Saline County southwest of Crete, where he farmed until his death in 1913. Courtesy NSHS, B949:2.

26 The Little School House on the Prairie

By the time Nebraska was created as a territory in 1854, Americans were generally committed to the ideas that a democratic society required an educated citizenry and that free public schools supported by taxation were essential. Not surprisingly, Nebraska's first territorial legislature enacted a law in 1855 that called for the establishment of a supervised system of schools and school districts supported by a property tax. But the legislators were not spurred by democratic ideals of universal free education so much as by the desire to stimulate settlement.

Most schools founded in the first several decades of Nebraska's history fell far short of the ideal, even though the legislature overhauled the school laws in 1869 following Nebraska's admission to statehood. Pioneer Nebraskans were so occupied with establishing homes and farms and finding jobs—questions of survival—that schools were often considered luxuries. In 1860, some counties reported having no schools whatever.

The typical public school was a crude, one-room structure with one teacher. Some of the first schools were private affairs transformed into public institutions when they took on public support, which amounted to very little in those days. Books were scarce; equipment mostly imaginary. Grades as we know them today hardly existed. Most rural children left school after a few years, presumably having acquired a minimal ability to read and write and the essentials of arithmetic. Not until 1887 did the legislature enact a compulsory school attendance law; it required children between eight and fourteen to attend school at least twelve weeks per year. By that time about 75 percent of school-age children were in attendance.

Property was usually assessed at the lowest possible level and the tax rate was set so low that there was often no money for teacher salaries. At first some teachers were to be paid by voluntary subscriptions, a system guaranteed to fail. Their compensation also often included free room and board with families having children in school—another voluntary arrangement. Teachers would move from home to home for a week or two at a time when school was in session. But the terms were remarkably short, usually only three or four months a year as late as 1880.

Most teachers lacked formal preparation; many were recent graduates of the schools they taught. At first male teachers were common, but by 1875 women teachers slightly outnumbered the men. By 1900 women were favored by 3.6 to 1. Certification was generally required by the mid-1880s. Teachers took day-long examinations administered at the county courthouse, and if they attended summer teacher-training institutes conducted by the state superintendent of public instruction, they could achieve certification for several years without reexamination. The few teachers who had had the opportunity to attend one of the state normal schools (teachers colleges) for two years could receive certification without examination. Four-year graduates would receive lifetime certification.

The quality of schools in Nebraska was also affected by the physical environment, which in most parts of the state dictated a low population density. At the same time, children usually had to walk to school. In its attempt to reconcile these realities, the state legislature in 1883 enacted a law specifying that a school district could not be smaller than four square miles in size or enroll fewer than fifteen children of school age. Permitting such a small size had the effect of proliferating school districts until they numbered 5,664 in 1888. This prompted the state superintendent of public instruction to complain in his 1888 Annual Report that "there are too many small school districts, with the inevitable result of small schools, low standards, low wages and poor teachers, with poor local supervision or none at all." The superintendent also reported that some "school districts were formed for no other reason than to defeat the levying of taxes and the maintaining of a school." But such complaints and warnings went unheeded and the number of school districts continued to increase until 1910, when the number ballooned to 7,071. By the 1920s the automobile began to have its effect and the consolidation movement began.

The quality of education in Nebraska improved steadily, despite the excessive number of school districts, inadequate financial support, and minimally prepared teachers. The number of "graded schools"—multiteacher schools in which pupils were separated by age and achievement according to grades—increased from 70 in 1880 to 448 in 1900. In 1881 the legislature enacted a school code, and ten years later passed a law requiring school books to be distributed free to pupils—a major piece of reform. At the end of the century, the legislature extended free public education to the high-school level. By then, Nebraska claimed a literacy rate of 97.7 percent, one of the highest in the United States.

26.1. Schools constructed of sod were often built in central Nebraska during the 1880s. The interiors of structures like this one photographed by Solomon Butcher in Custer County in 1889 were dark, dank, and cramped. The young teacher appears to be only a few years older than her pupils. Courtesy NSHS Butcher Collection, B983:1774.

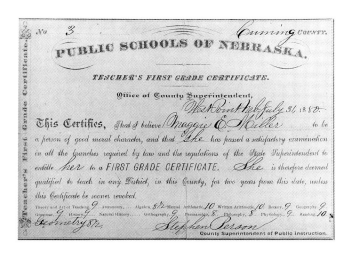

26.2. By the 1880s teacher certification was a nationwide concern. Because few teachers had attended a college or university, in-service training was especially important. This first-class certificate, issued to a teacher in Cuming County, qualified the teacher for two years. A score of ten on an individual test was the highest possible score. Courtesy NSHS Museum of Nebraska History.

26.3. One-teacher schools like this one in rural Buffalo County mushroomed during the 1880s due to permissive school district legislation and a compulsory attendance law. By 1900 there were about 6,700 schools in the state, but only 448 were organized by grades. Courtesy NSHS Butcher Collection, B983:2572.

26.4. Schools in the towns were often a source of community pride. Anselmo could boast of this structure, which apparently housed four classrooms. By 1890, when this picture was taken, the average salary for a male teacher was $43 per month, compared to $37.92 for females. Courtesy NSHS, s372:49.

26.5. Many classrooms in cities at the end of the nineteenth century looked like this one, a school in Fremont photographed in 1904. Two pupils are seated at each desk; the desks were screwed to the floor, with the writing surface of one desk attached to the back of another. This teacher was in charge of thirty-eight neatly dressed youngsters. Courtesy NSHS, s372:4.

26.6. Omaha High School, built on the site of the second territorial capital where the Joslyn Art Museum and Omaha Central High School now stand, was the grandest school building in Nebraska—and therefore the least typical. But it symbolized the burgeoning system of secondary schools in the state, and it set a standard to which other cities might aspire as free public education was extended by the legislature to include the secondary level. Courtesy NSHS, 054:980.

When Higher Education Was Lower 27

Boomers and town-site speculators in pioneer Nebraska who expected the establishment of a "common school" system to attract settlers with families also thought that the presence of a college or university would symbolize stability and culture in the frontier environment. Their hopes for institutions of higher learning to grace their ventures in town-building were augmented by the aspirations of many Protestant clergyman who perceived the local college as the agency to indoctrinate young people with the values associated with Christianity, home, and family. Colleges and universities could serve not only as guardians of popular sovereignty against aristocratic tyranny, but as agents to civilize the raw frontier and battlers against barbarism and the forces of sin and unbelief.

Such attitudes led to the founding of more than fifty so-called colleges, seminaries, and universities in territorial Nebraska. Most were "paper" institutions; only thirteen operated for more than a year and only two have survived to the present day, though in altered form. None was an institution of higher learning by present-day definitions. At best, they were preparatory schools of limited quality.

The pattern of establishing tiny private colleges, often by Protestant churches, was modified by the expectation that Nebraska would found a public university under the terms of the Morrill Act of 1862. This federal law promised thirty thousand acres of public land to any state for each senator or representative it had in Congress if, within five years, it would establish a college of agriculture and the mechanical arts. When Nebraska became a state and moved its capital from Omaha to Lincoln, the legislature specified that the state university should be located there and that it should be combined with the land-grant college. In this way the state's limited resources did not have to be distributed between two institutions, as was done in neighboring Iowa, Kansas, Colorado, and South Dakota.

In February 1869 the legislature founded the University of Nebraska by approving a charter that called for the establishment of six colleges and a military division. But classes were not held until two years later, as the deadline established by the Morrill Act forced the hasty construction of University Hall, a large, ornate building in the French Second Empire style. The campus, four square blocks in size, was placed directly north of Lincoln's infant commercial district. Future growth at this location was cramped by railroads that naturally followed the flood plain of Salt Creek on the west and north.

For two decades the tiny institution—a university only in aspiration—struggled to survive during dark years of drought, grasshopper plagues, and inadequate state funding. Enrollments ranged between 130 in 1871 to 384 in 1890, but many students were enrolled in the university's preparatory school, made necessary by the lack of high schools in the state. Contention between chancellor and faculty or between factions within the Board of Regents over the character of the institution was endemic, as reformers battled traditionalists in their efforts to introduce electives into the curriculum and professionalize the faculty.

Not until the late 1880s did the University of Nebraska emerge from its troubled and impoverished infancy to assume the functions of a genuine state university, with teaching on both the undergraduate and graduate levels, research and publication, and service to the public. Although this transformation was a part of a national trend, the form it took may be attributed largely to the leadership of Chancellor James Canfield, a richly talented man who served a brief tenure from 1891 to 1895. Recognizing that the university could never assume its proper role in the state without a system of accredited high schools that could prepare students for admission to study on the collegiate level, he gave that movement leadership. At the same time he traveled tirelessly across the state, recruiting students and winning popular support for the university. Enrollments expanded dramatically, reaching nearly two thousand students by the end of the century. Meanwhile the university organized its Graduate College, established the College of Agriculture on a separate campus, and started the College of Law and the Department of Pedagogy, the forerunner of Teachers College.

Data gathered in 1897 suggested that the University of Nebraska had become one of the leading state universities in the country. It ranked fifteenth in the nation in terms of enrollment; it exceeded the universities of Ohio, Indiana, Illinois, and Iowa, as well as Princeton, Stanford, and Brown. Although its library of about twenty-five thousand volumes could not match the resources of Harvard, Yale, Chicago, or Columbia, it compared well with its Midwestern peers.

Meanwhile, other colleges had been established in Nebraska in the nineteenth century, most with religious connections. Among those that survive, Doane College is the oldest, having been founded by Congregationalists in 1872. Presbyterians founded Hastings College in 1882. Creighton University, a product of Catholic philanthropy, opened its doors in 1887. The religious controversies at the University of Nebraska stimulated the birth of Nebraska Wesleyan by the Methodists in 1888. Seventh-Day Adventists founded Union College in 1891. Danish Lutherans, concerned about the preservation of their faith and culture in America, opened the predecessor of Dana College in 1884, and German Lutherans founded Concordia College in 1894 as a way to train teachers for their system of parochial schools.

27.1. Nebraska University, a private, church-related school founded in Fontanelle, was one of the few institutions of the territorial period that actually offered instruction, though never on the collegiate level. It was chartered by the legislature in its first session in 1855 and existed until 1872. Courtesy NSHS, F679:4.

27.2. The oldest college in Nebraska is Peru State. Opened in 1866 by Methodists, its founders gave it to the state in the following year. As Peru Normal School, it was the leading teachers college in Nebraska for many years. Pictured here is the old main building of the college as it appeared in 1909. Courtesy NSHS, P471:1.

27.3. Like the new state capitol, from which this photograph was taken in 1871, the first building of the University of Nebraska dominated the treeless landscape of Lincoln. The lumber was brought by wagon from Nebraska City and the stone from nearby limestone quarries, but bricks were manufactured locally. For its time, this building was a splendid facility, but its imposing appearance masked serious structural weaknesses. Courtesy NSHS, L741:23.

27.4. This image of Chancellor James H. Canfield was made shortly after he took office in 1891. Although he held office for only four years, Chancellor Canfield influenced the university profoundly and cemented its relationship to the state and its people. Courtesy NSHS, P853.

27.5. This photograph of a laboratory at the University of Nebraska, published in the *Sombrero* in 1892, suggests that enormous improvements had been made in two decades since its founding. In 1895 Chancellor Canfield claimed that Nebraska was one of the "big four" state universities of the time. Courtesy University of Nebraska–Lincoln Archives.

27.6. Creighton University, for many years the only college in Omaha, was started as a preparatory school in this building, erected in 1878 on what was then the western edge of town. The first college-level class was admitted in 1887. Gifts from the Creighton family made it a successful venture in free Catholic education. Courtesy NSHS, 054:317.

28 Churches and Politics in 1890

Religious belief was a sturdy strand in the social fabric of Nebraska in the late nineteenth century. Even though data gathered by the U.S. Census Bureau in 1890 indicated that only a minority claimed formal membership in a religious denomination, most Nebraskans shared some elements of the Christian value system.

As in the United States generally, the Roman Catholic church was the largest single denomination in 1890, attracting about one-quarter of all church members in Nebraska. The Methodists were the largest Protestant group, with more than one-fifth; several Lutheran bodies combined to represent about one-seventh. Other groups—Presbyterians, Baptists, Congregationalists, Disciples of Christ, and Episcopalians—were smaller, averaging about 5 percent each.

The latter part of the nineteenth century was a great church-building era in Nebraska. Most Nebraskans had come to the state from someplace else, whether from one of the eastern states or one of the European countries that were sending millions to America. Hence almost everyone in Nebraska was a first- or second-generation immigrant (or, more precisely, an in-migrant), and almost everyone was engaged in the process of re-creating familiar institutions in a physical environment that dictated a low-density population. Compared to other institutions, churches were relatively easy to establish in rural Nebraska, and they performed a wide range of social functions that in more heavily populated places would have been assumed by other agencies. Frequently, humble church buildings erected during the first years were replaced by grander edifices that reflected the importance people placed on them.

There were important differences among the several denominations. The suspicion, distrust, and even hatred with which Protestants viewed Catholics in the nineteenth century are well known, but it is useful to remember that most Catholics in Nebraska were German, Irish, Czech, and Polish immigrants. They, like Lutherans from Germany and Scandinavia and German-speaking Mennonites from Russia, seemed outlandish to many English or older American Protestants. Indeed, Catholics seemed to represent a special challenge to the values of typical English-speaking American Protestant denominations such as the Methodists, Baptists, Congregationalists, and Presbyterians, most of whom were strongly pietistic. Along with Episcopalians and the German Lutherans, Catholics emphasized ritual or liturgical practices in their worship services. Strongly creedal, they stressed theological orthodoxy and taught a morality that accentuated duty and submission to authority. And they often organized parochial schools to educate their children in their religious beliefs, languages, and ways of life.

In contrast, the American Protestant churches preached a morality of pious behavior—no drinking, no card playing, no dancing, no sex outside the bonds of marriage—and a strict observance of the sabbath day. Theirs was a theology of the heart rather than of the head that emphasized the importance of conversion as evidence of a person having been predestined by God for eternal salvation.

To people of such beliefs and attitudes, the flood of European immigrants threatened the primacy of established beliefs and behavior. Seeing themselves as guardians of tradition, the reformers, in their battle against sin, sought to use every weapon at hand, including politics, governmental authority, and law. They fought for what they perceived as reform legislation: prohibition of alcoholic drink, sabbatarian laws, public schools as agencies to socialize the children of immigrants, the regulation of parochial schools, and suffrage for women as means to ensure the enactment of pietistic legislation. Usually people with these sentiments saw the Republican party as the vehicle for the desired reforms.

To many Nebraska immigrants, especially Catholics and German Lutherans, such programs of political reform seemed to call for unwarranted extensions of governmental power into the realm of personal rights. Prohibition, for example, seemed like an attack on liberty in the land of the free. In their view, it was not a sin to drink; it was a sin to get drunk. To legislate morality was to threaten the authority of the church in spiritual affairs. In politics they generally found the Democratic party to be congenial because since the days of Thomas Jefferson and Andrew Jackson it had advocated limited government and had championed the largest measure of personal liberty consistent with principles of law and order.

In rural areas, where immigrant farmers from Europe often occupied much of the land, immigrant churches were more numerous. Before the end of the century, Gothic spires in the hamlets and countryside often signaled at a distance the presence of not merely a church building but also a parsonage or rectory, a parochial school, and sometimes even a parish hall.

Protestant churches were more common in the cities than the countryside. Often attracting members from the local social and economic elite, they usually were stout defenders of the status quo. Churches in Nebraska were important, not only for moral or spiritual reasons but for social and political history as well.

28.1. At least seven church buildings can
be identified in this image of Lincoln,
looking northwest from the state capitol
in 1889 when the city was only two decades old. The concentration of substantial edifices was the consequence of
the state legislature having given away
ten lots for the building of churches.

The large church in the foreground,
then under construction, was built by
the Disciples of Christ. In 1904 it was
purchased by the Catholic Church as
its cathedral for the Lincoln diocese.
Heavily damaged by fire in 1906, it was
redesigned and rebuilt in its present
form. Courtesy NSHS, L741:43.

28.2. Cemeteries often flanked rural immigrant churches, a location that suggests the centrality of the church in the lives of the parishioners. St. John's Lutheran Church in Burt County, erected in 1902, is an elegant example of rural liturgical architecture. Photograph by Roger Bruhn.

28.3. The elaborate altar of the Salem Swedish Lutheran Church, built in Wakefield in 1905, is an American version of the neo-Gothic style. Such an altar would ordinarily be found only in liturgical churches such as the Catholic or Lutheran. The liturgical style also called for a long nave with a central aisle, communion rail, lectern, pulpit, and baptismal font, here oddly centered before the altar. Photograph by Roger Bruhn.

28.4. This Presbyterian church in Hastings, photographed by Roger Bruhn, is an example of architecture in the pietistic tradition, which was in reaction against liturgical practice. Often built in a square auditorium style without an altar, pulpit, or central aisle, such churches focused attention on a lectern from which the clergy, normally not robed, prayed and preached.

28.5. Few ethnoreligious communities could boast of facilities more impressive than those of Polish Catholics who, beginning in 1873, had settled in rural Tarnov, a village north of Columbus. This photograph of St. Michael's Church and school was taken in 1910. Such rural clusters of church, school, and rectory or parsonage were also common among German Lutherans. Courtesy NSHS, S262:7.

Nebraska Politics, Nineteenth-Century Style 29

Politics has been at the core of American history. This is as it should be for certain times and places, especially such as the early history of Nebraska. Then, if ever, politics was lifeblood. Town-site speculators, railroad companies, lawyers, builders, printers, newspaper publishers, and hotel operators were all directly affected by state politics.

Politics was a hard game everywhere in nineteenth-century America, and its players found the rule book both imprecise and permissive. Many politicians pursued personal interests avidly, and often worked just as hard for the political demise of their rivals. They did not hesitate to charge each other with electoral fraud. Political appointments often went to friends and relatives who matched inexperience with ineptitude. Party loyalties ran deep, and in that post-Civil War era, a certain military style infused political behavior as well as its vocabulary.

So it was in Nebraska. The politicians who managed the removal of the capital from Omaha to Lincoln knew that if the new capital city did not succeed they would be finished. So they stretched the limits of acceptable behavior, even for that permissive era: the capital commissioners selected a site that technically was not on public land, as the law had specified; they rigged the bidding when city lots in Lincoln went on sale in 1867; and they refused to transfer money from the sale of lots to the state treasurer on the grounds that as an Omahan he was not likely to release it for the construction of the new capitol. When the capitol was built, it cost twice as much as the legislature had appropriated.

At the center of these irregularities was David Butler, Nebraska's first state governor. That his administration contributed impressively to the early success of Lincoln and the rapid growth of the state was indisputable. That he overstepped the law seemed not to matter much to the voters, and in 1868 and 1870 he and his allies were reelected. As quoted by James C. Olson in his *History of Nebraska,* one of the capital commissioners said they had "been governed by an honest purpose to subserve the best interests of the state."

But there were limits, and sentiment for Butler's impeachment grew. In 1871 new charges were made that Butler had failed to deposit funds received from the federal government for certain school lands and had "borrowed" them temporarily for his own speculative purposes. Impeachment proceedings followed. Butler was found guilty of misappropriating state funds and was removed from office.

The 1870s and 1880s were years of Republican dominance in Nebraska politics. Democrats were rarely elected to Congress or to statewide offices. This was partly a legacy of the Civil War; many Nebraska voters still perceived the Democratic party as the party of rebellion. Political parties were highly symbolic: a party stood for a set of beliefs and attitudes, and specific issues and candidates were comparatively unimportant. Debate focused on such questions as the location of state institutions and the distribution of subsidies for railroad construction and the exploitation of natural resources. The qualifications of individual candidates meant relatively little because one candidate would do as well as the next. It was the party label that counted.

In the 1870s and 1880s the Republican party saw itself as the champion of progress, reform, and morality. So as to assure prosperity, Republicans believed that governments should stimulate the economy by subsidizing railroads and by regulating commerce primarily through tariff legislation. Reformers in the party also believed that it was the province of government to attack moral problems. That usually meant favoring women's suffrage, prohibition of alcoholic beverages, and Sabbatarian legislation, and on the federal level, civil service reform. Republicans liked to think in terms of the national economy, which often resulted in the centralization of political power at the expense of the states. The party's base was strongly founded on big-business interests, small-town respectability, pietistic Protestantism, and the interests of farmers and Civil War veterans. Republican leaders were usually drawn from small-town elites.

The Democratic party offered a different vision. Standing firm on laissez-faire principles, it advocated the fullest measure of personal liberty and freedom consistent with law and order. True to its Jeffersonian roots, it believed that the best government was the one that governed least—and that included not only moral issues but also economic matters. It opposed, for example, both prohibition and high tariffs. Nebraska Democrats frequently attacked the great corporations for their power and called for their regulation. They believed that subsidies of all kinds, including those to railroads, should end. Deeply conservative, the Democratic party attracted the support of Jeffersonian idealists, most Catholics, many German Lutherans, and migrants from the South, as well as some people of considerable wealth and others, both immigrant and native-born, who saw advantages in minimal government.

In the first two decades of Nebraska state history, political parties were tightly bound by ethnicity, religion, and political idealism. This bond would loosen in Nebraska's third decade—the Populist era—when politics experienced a notable transformation.

"That political hermaphrodite, tom wolfe [sic], who pretends to publish a Republican paper here in Seward, last week prostituted the columns of his paper to the base use of carricaturing [sic] citizens of Seward . . . who were loyal to the Republican party. . . . He allied himself with Democrats for the sole purpose of defeating the party that has supported him for years, and to gratify the petty malice and hatred which forms a large portion of his selfish nature. . . . While pretending to be a Republican, this vile and hideous wart on the body politic descends to the vilest slanders and most atrocious lies to defeat Republicans and elect Democrats. . . . Thoroughly despised by nine-tenths of all who know him, not only in Seward county, but throughout the State, as a miserable skinflint, a base ingrate, a poltroon of the first water, and a liar without peer, his utterances are denounced by every decent man as a dirty, mean libel, conceived in a knave's heart and uttered by a scoundrel's tongue. . . . Of all the hideous, hybrid, pompous, purse-proud nonentities that ever infested creation he beats them all. . . . If all the sin-laden imps of perdition were concentrated, simmered down into one seething mass of pollution, it would smell as sweet as a rose compared with this foul renegade who has proven himself to be cringing, lying, oily scoundrel."

29.1. In the nineteenth century, politics could be cutthroat with vehement, unrestrained rhetoric, as excerpts from this diatribe illustrate. Entitled "Slightly Personal," it was printed in the Seward *Blue Valley Blade* on 3 November 1880.

29.2. David Butler of Pawnee City was Nebraska's first state governor. He served from 1867 to 1871, when the legislature removed him from office for financial irregularities. Unlike Butler, who was elected three times, most governors and legislators in those years served no more than two two-year terms. Leadership on the state level was therefore temporary and usually ineffective. Courtesy NSHS, B985:2.

29.3. A citizen ordinarily voted a straight ticket in the nineteenth century. It was difficult to split one's vote among the several parties, as this example of a Republican ballot from Gage County in 1886 suggests. The voter had to scratch out a name and write in the name of the candidate of the rival party. The use of the secret "Australian" ballot, which lists both slates of candidates, was adopted in Nebraska in 1891. Courtesy NSHS Museum of Nebraska History: 881-P-2.

29.4. Small-town newspapers were emphatically partisan in the nineteenth century, and strutting, crowing roosters were often used as symbols to proclaim party victories. Here the *Columbus Democrat* of 15 November 1884 happily announces the election of Grover Cleveland as the first Democratic president in twenty-four years. Courtesy NSHS, 071:C72T.

29.5. Antecedents of modern political campaigns can be found in this image of two Democrats campaigning in Alliance for the election of Grover Cleveland for president and Adlai Stevenson for vice-president in 1892. One campaigner arrayed in a white coat and top hat sits in a wheelbarrow to be pushed by his coworker as curious boys cluster around. Courtesy NSHS, A436:23.

The Emergence of *Part 3*
Modern Nebraska, 1890–1930

The last decade of the nineteenth century was a time of transition in which Nebraska moved out of its frontier phase and began to assume modern characteristics. During the boom years of the 1880s, the population of the state more than doubled to about one million. But growth faltered as a variety of adjustments had to be made to the realities of the Great Plains environment, especially to its climate.

In contrast to the wet 1880s, the 1890s were droughty years when Nebraskans experienced some of the driest years on record. Grasshoppers also returned, and matters were made worse by a severe economic depression. Devastating drops in farm prices came just when technological advances in agriculture and transportation were stimulating enormous increases in the productivity of Nebraska's farms. Economically distressed farmers turned to politics as a solution to their problems. They rallied especially to the Populist Party, a new organization that represented agrarian discontent.

The state's large cities also assumed some of their modern characteristics during the 1890s. Electricity transformed urban life; homes were lit, streets were illuminated, and efficient local transportation systems were developed. City dwellers acquired the amenities of paved streets and municipal water and sewage systems. Omaha became an important center of commerce, industry, and transportation in the Midwest, and Lincoln matured as a center of government and education.

Nothing symbolized the emergence of modern Nebraska more than Omaha's Trans-Mississippi Exposition of 1898. Attracting more than 2.5 million visitors, this "world's fair" was organized by businessmen and trumpeted by politicians to present Omaha as a mature city that had overcome the depression of the 1890s. But the real message was that Nebraska's frontier phase, still remembered by most adults, was over. The exposition's architecture, for example, drew nothing from western or pioneer experience; instead, it represented the triumph of Beaux-Arts classicism in an unlikely place. Omaha, the fair proclaimed, was a mainstream Midwestern metropolis, and what could happen in Chicago or other eastern cities could also happen here. Brilliantly conceived and executed, the exposition was a smashing success at the time, but it was soon forgotten. Nonetheless, it did wonders for Omaha's self-image as the city entered the twentieth century.

Like most Midwestern states, Nebraska then experienced a period of political reform, often called the Progressive era, in which the legislature enacted various electoral changes and regulatory measures. At the end of World War I, prohibition and women's suffrage became provisions of both the federal and state constitutions, and the state began construction of its splendid new capitol as a memorial to soldiers who had died in the war.

The 1920s, however, witnessed far-reaching changes in the way people lived. A revolution in transportation and communication was under way. Most important was the advent of the automobile, which transformed spatial relationships for rural people, but also meant spending millions of dollars on the construction of roads and bridges and reorganizing rural institutions, including churches and schools. Telephones seemed to be everywhere. Movies, still silent, were patronized in cities and towns all over the state. Electricity invaded urban homes in new ways in the twenties: appliances such as refrigerators, stoves, washing machines, vacuum cleaners, and irons were readily available to anyone who could afford them, and by the end of the decade radios could be found in most homes. The lives of ordinary Nebraskans had been profoundly transformed in only forty years.

Omaha's Trans-Mississippi Exposition of 1898 proclaimed that the West had come of age. Elegantly dressed visitors strolled along the Grand Court and its lagoon, the architectural centerpiece of the exposition. Constructed of wood and plaster, the buildings revealed the Beaux-Arts harmony and splendor prescribed by the planners. Omaha's fair, an imitation of Chicago's famous Columbian Exposition of 1893, was located at 24th and Pratt Streets on the bluff overlooking the floodplains of the Missouri River. Courtesy NSHS, T772:S1F1.

Facing Environmental Realities *30*

If they ever harbored false notions about the environment of the Great Plains, Nebraskans were brought closer to reality during the 1890s. In that decade the people of the plains finally understood that the region was subhumid—too dry for conventional agriculture as practiced farther east, yet not a desert. They accepted the fact that Nebraska is a grassland subject to periodic drought and that both farming methods and governmental policies had to be adapted accordingly.

It was a hard lesson to learn. During the 1880s, twenty-five counties had been organized west of the 100th meridian. By 1890 they boasted a total population of more than one hundred thousand and nearly 20,000 farms averaging 220 acres in size. Ten years later, after a decade of drought and depression, the population of these western counties had dropped to 88,000 and the number of farms to 13,300 averaging 660 acres. Hardest hit was the southwestern corner of the state, where Perkins County lost 61 percent of its population. Not far behind in the Panhandle was Banner County, which lost 54 percent. Thousands of farm families were ruined; they had no choice but to leave.

In their desperation, some people turned to rain-making schemes. One effort was based on the assumption that a loud noise like thunder could produce rain. Another assumed that volatile gasses released into the air would lower the temperature of the atmosphere sufficiently to condense the moisture in the clouds into rain. All such schemes were ineffective and a few led straight to the courtroom.

Other solutions to the problem of semiaridity were more promising. It was obvious, for example, that changes had to be made in how people farmed in central and western Nebraska. The most important of the new techniques was called "dry farming," whose leading advocate was Hardy Webster Campbell of Lincoln. He advised farmers to plow deeply, sow fewer seeds, space rows of crops widely, compact the soil, and mulch it after rainfall. They should select only crops that do well in semiarid climates, he argued, and drought-resistant strains should be grown when possible. Above all, farmers should grow a crop on a field only once in two or three years; in the fallow years moisture could be conserved by cutting weeds and dust mulching.

Irrigation was another solution. In Nebraska, fewer than twelve thousand acres were under irrigation in 1890, but during the next ten years there was a twelve-fold expansion as westerners were finally convinced that they could not rely on the celestial waterworks. But irrigation systems were very expensive, usually beyond the means of individual farmers. Cooperative measures had to be taken under either public or private initiatives. Irrigation as the key to the agricultural development of the Great Plains received an enormous amount of publicity in the early twentieth century, much of it extreme in its claims for what it could do for the region.

Government policies also had to be modified. The distinguished explorer and surveyor of the American West, Major John Wesley Powell, pointed out as early as 1878 that 160 acres per farm as specified by the Homestead Act of 1862 was impractical in the arid West and invited fraud. Congress amended and supplemented the Homestead Act several times, sometimes unwisely. For example, the Timber Culture Act, which had been introduced in Congress in 1873 by Senator Phineas

Hitchcock of Nebraska, unrealistically granted 160 acres to home-steaders who would plant a quarter of their grant in trees. People who believed that "rain follows the plow" expected the act to have a long-range impact on climate. Abuses led to its repeal in 1891, along with the Pre-emption Act of 1841.

Stockmen in western Nebraska also made successful adaptations. The open range had long since disappeared as cattlemen became ranch farmers who raised hay, alfalfa, and sorghums for winter feeding of cattle. Fences were essential, not only to protect fields, but to control breeding of stock. Ranchers also began to treat animal diseases system-atically.

Trees were a different matter. Most Nebraskans came to the plains from forested regions of Europe and the eastern United States, and they were determined to alter the appearance of the environment by planting trees in huge numbers. Political rhetoric often equated tree planting with civic righteousness. The legislature passed laws to en-courage it, and prominent political leaders, such as J. Sterling Morton and Robert W. Furnas, set public examples by planting highly suc-cessful private fruit orchards. By 1890 Nebraskans had planted several hundred million trees in cities and towns and in farm groves and wind-breaks. Despite these herculean labors, the effort to alter the appear-ance of the treeless landscape was scarcely noticeable to eastern visitors scanning the great spaces of Nebraska.

Perhaps the most romantic effort to revise the grassland environ-ment was spearheaded by Professor Charles Bessey of the University of Nebraska. Shortly after his arrival in Nebraska in 1884, Bessey, remem-bering pine forests on sandy soil in Michigan, began a campaign to plant a forest of pine trees in the Sand Hills. He cleverly marshaled sup-port from every possible source until in 1902 President Theodore Roo-sevelt established two national reserves, one in the heart of the Sand Hills west of Halsey and another southwest of Valentine south of the Niobrara River. Here horticulturalists created the only man-made na-tional forests in the United States. A large nursery was developed at Halsey that through the years has produced millions of seedlings.

Any enterprise of such magnitude will encounter great difficulties. Strong opposition came from Sand Hills ranchers and farmers, but drought, infertile soil, insect pests, and fungal diseases were more formidable. Today, after seventy-five years, extensive tracts of ponderosa pine and red cedar survive despite recurrent drought and devastating forest fires.

30.1. In both the 1870s and the 1890s,
drought devastated much of the Great
Plains. Pioneers suffered severely in
both decades, but in the latter relief
efforts were more general and systematic. Here destitute farmers line up to
receive aid at a Union Pacific siding at
Elm Creek, west of Kearney, in 1894, one
of the driest years on record. Courtesy
NSHS, E48.1.

30.2. Rainmaking schemes of the droughty 1890s included the use of this equipment devised by Charles Wright, which he called the "Drought Breaker." Railroads in Nebraska sometimes furnished transportation to rainmakers as a public service. Courtesy NSHS, s554:5.

30.3. By the late 1880s, Nebraskans recognized the need for large-scale irrigation projects in the west. In this 1889 image, workers construct a flume that was part of a system carrying water forty-two miles from the North Platte River to lands west of the city of North Platte. Courtesy NSHS, 171.6:32.

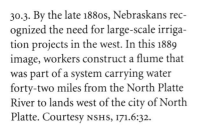

30.4. The Kinkaid Act, promoted by Congressman Moses P. Kinkaid of O'Neill, was an experimental law passed by Congress in 1904 that enlarged the size of a homestead in western Nebraska from 160 to 640 acres. It led to a land rush in the Sand Hills, as suggested by this crowd gathered outside the land office in Broken Bow on 28 June 1904. Within a decade, most of the "Kinkaiders" had pulled out, defeated in their attempts to pursue a way of life that the environment did not permit. Courtesy NSHS, c984:16–44.

30.5. Although J. Sterling Morton founded Arbor Day in the United States in 1872, Robert Furnas (1824–1905) was the first Nebraska governor to issue an Arbor Day proclamation. In 1885 the legislature designated Morton's birthday, 22 April, as Arbor Day, and soon virtually every state followed suit. An active horticulturalist, Furnas is depicted here in retirement among his cherry trees near Brownville. Courtesy NSHS, F987:16.

30.6. Although the photographic record shows that many homesteaders made no effort to plant trees, other homesteaders, like this family in Custer County in 1887, carefully nursed both orchards and windbreaks. Courtesy NSHS Butcher Collection, B983:1219.

30.7. Arbor Lodge, the Morton estate at Nebraska City, became a showcase for the possibilities of tree planting. The unidentified man in this photograph reveals the size of a magnificent American elm that had been planted in 1871. Courtesy NSHS, A666:166.

31 The Populist Response to Hard Times

Populism was a grass-roots political movement that fired the imagination of many Nebraska farmers in the 1890s, a decade of drought and economic depression. By no means limited to Nebraska, Populism restructured politics in the Great Plains. The Populist era was the first time Nebraskans were forced to cope politically with the long-range consequences of technological change in agriculture.

During the 1880s, settlement on the farmlands of the Great Plains and improvements in machinery stimulated a spectacular expansion of agricultural production. At the same time, steam-powered transportation on land and sea enabled the United States to move into international markets, especially for wheat and corn. By the end of the decade, however, farmers were producing more than they could sell. Overproduction and new competition for world markets from other countries, such as Canada, Argentina, and Australia, lowered the price of farm products.

Matters were made worse by deflation. The population of the United States was increasing rapidly at a time when the supply of money in circulation remained constant. Because the number of dollars per person was decreasing, the value of a dollar increased. Farmers got fewer dollars for their crops, which affected their ability to pay off their debts, many of which had been negotiated in more favorable times. Their farms were usually mortgaged, and most farmers had to borrow money each year to buy seed and implements. Farmers were eager to reform the monetary system so that it might work in their favor rather than to the advantage of bankers. And they were equally determined to regulate the transportation system to end unfair discriminatory practices in passenger fares and freight rates.

Even the weather seemed to conspire against them. By 1890, as corn prices were spiraling downward, the Great Plains began another series of dry, hot summers and grasshopper plagues. Mindful of the legendary injunction of the Kansas firebrand, Mary Elizabeth Lease, to "raise less corn and more hell," they entered politics, using the Farmers Alliance to find relief.

At first known as Alliancemen or Independents and later as Populists, these agrarian radicals experienced remarkable success in the election of 1890, winning a majority in the state legislature and four of five seats in Congress. Populists advocated regulation of railroad freight rates and the abolition of free passes on passenger trains; they also wanted to reform the political process by introducing the secret ballot, the initiative and referendum, and the direct election of U.S. senators. They courted the support of urban laborers by urging an eight-hour workday and wooed Civil War veterans by advocating more generous military pensions. The most radical Populists demanded government ownership of banks, railroads, and grain elevators. After a few years they also sought to increase the amount of money in circulation nationally by advocating the coinage of silver at the ratio of sixteen ounces of silver to one of gold, an artificial rate that would have had an inflationary effect.

Electoral support in Nebraska for the People's Party (the Populists' official name) was strongest in a wide band of counties stretching from the southwestern corner of the state to the northeast, a large area where traditional agricultural practices, especially corn and hog operations, were often unsuccessful due to lack of rain. Populist votes were cast mostly by marginal farmers, regardless of religion or ethnicity, who were united by economic distress. Ethnocultural conflict continued in the Populist era, but it no longer dominated political discourse on the state level as it had in the 1880s. Populist votes were drawn from both major parties, but because there had been more Republicans than Democrats in the state, the former were hurt more by the new agrarian radicalism.

Despite their phenomenal electoral successes, the Populists were unable to enact their program. This led them in 1894 to form a coalition with the Democratic party, which, under the leadership of William Jennings Bryan, had moved closer to the Populist position on many issues. This "fusion," as it was inaccurately called, led to the election of Populist governors during the remainder of the decade.

In 1896, Bryan, a brilliant orator from Lincoln who had represented Nebraska for two terms in Congress, won the Democratic nomination for president of the United States. Just thirty-six years old, Bryan campaigned tirelessly for the poor and dispossessed in American life. The Populist party in its national convention also nominated Bryan, but his image as a radical doomed him at the polls as the more conservative William McKinley won the presidency for the Republicans. After 1896, the Populist party waned nationally as prosperity returned.

In Nebraska, however, the Populist revolt altered the practice of state politics, even though its record of legislative accomplishment was not great. The old single-issue politics, which was symbolized by fights over prohibition, was replaced by a complex of issues in which economic concerns assumed greater importance, and the adoption in 1891 of the secret ballot weakened party loyalties as the personalities of candidates assumed new importance.

31.1. In 1890, when Populists were often called Alliancemen, these Platte County agrarians convened in Columbus to choose their candidates for election to county offices. Their clothes suggest common origins and their dour expressions reveal the determination that infused their venture into politics. Courtesy NSHS Butcher Collection, B983:2184.

31.2. Populists swept Republicans from two of Nebraska's three congressional districts in the election of 1890. The Populist winner in the Third District was Omer M. Kem, the only person ever elected to Congress while living in a sod house. He is pictured here with his family on his farm near Broken Bow. Courtesy NSHS Butcher Collection, B983:200.

PEOPLES PARTY
NATIONAL CONVENTION
OMAHA,   JULY 2ND 1892.
ADMIT ONE
TO SEAT AND SECTION INDICATED ON MARGIN OF THIS TICKET.

ADMISSION AT ⟶ EAST ENTRANCE ⟵

Thos. Swobe
CHAIRMAN
OF GENERAL CITIZENS COMMITTEE OF ARRANGEMENTS.

SEAT NO. 461 Stage

31.3. No photographs exist of the Populist national convention, which met in Omaha in 1892. Thousands of observers clamored to attend the meeting, and frugal party managers sold high-priced tickets of admission, some for the entire convention and others for specific sessions. This special ticket admitted the bearer to an assigned seat on the stage for the opening session on 2 July. Courtesy Robert Gillan.

31.4. Although Nebraska's most famous Democratic politician, William Jennings Bryan, was never a Populist, he supported some of the measures advocated by the agrarian radicals. After winning the Democratic nomination for president in 1896, he was also nominated by the Populists and the splinter Silver Republican party. Bryan, here labeled as a Popocrat in a cartoon by G. Y. Coffin, found it impossible to reconcile the divergent ideologies of these rather different political organizations.

32 The Emergence of Omaha as Nebraska's Metropolis

While rural Nebraskans were establishing their farms and planting their trees, other Nebraskans were developing Omaha as a regional metropolis between Chicago and San Francisco. Because of Omaha's superior location on the banks of the Missouri River near the mouth of the Platte, it quickly became the largest city in the state, boasting 30,000 inhabitants by 1880. If the census of 1890 is to be believed, Omaha grew by 360 percent during the decade that followed and earned its sobriquet as "The Gate City to the West." By then Omaha claimed to have 140,452 inhabitants, more than either Kansas City or Denver. That this figure was inflated by at least 30,000 suggests the determination of Omaha's leaders to win great urban honors for their city.

Actually, Omaha's growth had been so spectacular during the 1880s that it needed no exaggeration. Railroad transportation was the key. In 1867 Omaha was connected to Chicago by rail and in 1873 the bridge across the Missouri River was completed. Other lines made their connections in rapid order. The railroads made possible Omaha's major economic function—to receive, process, and distribute agricultural products. That meant beef, butter, wheat, beer, and whiskey; it also meant railroad yards, stockyards and meatpacking plants, creameries, grain elevators, flour mills, breweries, and distilleries. In addition, Omaha processed lead, gold, and silver ores produced in western mines and by 1890 claimed to have the largest smelting and refining capacity in the world. Be that as it may, the railroad and meat-packing facilities were even more important. The Union Pacific machine and car shops employed sixteen hundred men, and South Omaha became the third-largest meat processor in the nation. Omaha's breweries challenged the preeminence of Milwaukee and Cincinnati. At the same time, its jobbing or wholesale distributing companies made Omaha a regional center for trade and commerce, and property values increased eight-fold.

Like all cities in the American West at that time, Omaha could offer few of the amenities we take for granted today. In 1880 almost no streets were paved, not even in the business district, and stinking garbage, carcasses, and manure glutted the streets. Because the city waterworks was a small and recent development, most water came from private wells; privies were in backyards everywhere, and a sewage system was still in the future. Disease was common, as was quackery. Hospitals were dangerous places and medical care as we know it was in its infancy.

Unlike the great cities of the East, Omaha was uncrowded and open, usually with one dwelling on each lot. But public utilities were rudimentary. Gas street lighting was introduced in the 1870s, soon to be replaced by electricity, which, like telephone service, was functioning reasonably well by the end of the century. Horse-drawn streetcars provided transportation; electricity soon replaced horsepower but a unified system was not in place until 1900. Fire protection evolved from volunteer to professional status in the 1880s, but the police department consisted of political appointees. No welfare system was in place—most of society's unfortunates had to fend for themselves, despite occasional private relief efforts. A considerable transient population of male vagrants or unemployed workers could always be found in Omaha. Regarded as potential thieves and a threat to the city's order, they were subject to routine sweeps by the police through an area south of Dodge Street in the vicinity of 10th through 13th Streets. There were homeless women also, some of whom were prostitutes. Omaha's "red-light" district operated nearby.

Still, Omaha was a center of wealth, power, and prestige in the plains region. It had its share of imposing mansions and dignified business buildings erected in the latest architectural style. Creighton College was serving the community, an art gallery had been founded, and Omaha's public library was soon to be housed in a structure of considerable distinction.

Like most American cities of the late nineteenth and early twentieth centuries, Omaha developed a political machine. The man behind the scenes was Tom Dennison, the "Grey Wolf." A professional gambler, Dennison arrived in Omaha in 1892 and soon dominated the saloons, brothels, and gambling dens of the vice district. Though he never held public office, he negotiated arrangements with the police and indirectly with the business community and emerged as the "Boss" of Omaha. Like all city bosses of that era, he provided services, food, and clothing in return for votes for his candidates. Dennison virtually controlled the city until the early 1930s.

During much of this time, the man in charge of city government was James Dahlman, a former Texas cowboy who arrived in Omaha in 1898 after a decade in Chadron and a brief stay in Lincoln. A Democrat known as "Cowboy Jim," he was strongly attracted to the populistic doctrines of William Jennings Bryan. Dahlman was first elected mayor of Omaha in 1906 and, except for one term, served continuously until his death in 1930. A spare and abstemious man of high integrity, he maintained a remarkable rapport with the people. He was impatient with administrative routine and delegated responsibility to others. Intentionally or not, he was an ideal front man for the Dennison machine, his personal integrity notwithstanding. He believed that Omaha benefited from being a wide-open city, and he was willing to accept support from anyone who gave it, including the Grey Wolf. But it has not been proven that Dennison directly influenced his actions as mayor. Rather, their relationship was symbiotic.

By 1915 Omaha was a major Midwestern metropolis. It had lost out to Kansas City as the economic pivot of the central plains, but it retained its muscle as a leading grain market and regional marketing center. Its strength in meat packing, smelting, and refining continued unabated. The brewing industry thrived until its prohibition by an amendment to the state constitution in 1916. The railroads, as always in a thinly populated agricultural region, were at the foundation of Omaha's economic structure. Not a center of culture, education, or government, Omaha was a city of commerce and industry, a smaller version of Chicago on the edge of the Great Plains.

32.1. The completion by the Union Pacific of the 2,700-foot railroad bridge across the Missouri River in 1872 was a major event in the evolution of Omaha as the state's metropolis. Omaha was at the mercy of the railroad and went deeply into debt to get the bridge, shown in this view southwest from 13th and Harney Streets. Courtesy Great Plains Art Collection, University of Nebraska–Lincoln, 94-299-6.

32.2. Omaha's growth as a major transportation and industrial center during the 1880s is suggested by this view northeast from Forest Hill, which shows the intersection of the river, the railroad and its Emigrant House, the lead smelting facility on the riverbank, and the residential district. The streets are unpaved, streetlights do not exist, and residences (with outbuildings) are placed on spacious lots. Courtesy Great Plains Studies Collection, University of Nebraska–Lincoln, 94-299-9.

32.3. When this picture was taken, Omaha's stockyards had become the second largest in the United States. The Union Stock Yard Company opened in 1884 under the leadership of William Paxton, but only with the cooperation and participation of the Union Pacific Railroad. A whole new city—South Omaha—was built nearby. Courtesy NSHS, O54:411.

32.4. A grand courthouse to symbolize the aspirations of an expanding metropolis was built during the period of Omaha's great expansion. This photograph of the second Douglas County Courthouse was taken about 1905. E. E. Myers of Detroit, one of the leading designers of state capitols in the nineteenth century, was the architect. Courtesy Bostwick-Frohardt Collection, owned by KMTV and on permanent loan to the Western Heritage Museum, Omaha, 15-328-328B.

32.5. By 1889, downtown Omaha was a thriving center of business activity. This view looking east on Farnam Street reveals horse-drawn buggies, street car tracks, telephone poles, and many substantial commercial buildings of masonry construction. Courtesy NSHS, 054:28.

32.6. Tom Dennison was the unofficial but nonetheless real boss of Omaha from the mid-1890s to the early 1930s. Omaha was a "wide-open" city during the Dennison era. Courtesy NSHS, P853.

32.7. First elected mayor of Omaha in 1906, James C. "Cowboy Jim" Dahlman was a Democratic ally of Dennison, a Republican. Dahlman died in office in 1930. Courtesy NSHS, D131.

33 Lincoln as the Athens of the Plains

In the eyes of its citizens at the turn of the century, Lincoln stood out like an Athens among other cities of importance in the West. Created to serve as the center of government, Lincoln attracted legislators, politicians, bureaucrats, and lawyers from across the state, some temporarily and others permanently. As the site of the state university, it drew young men and women in pursuit of higher education and professors and other professional people who were interested in culture and learning.

Lincoln is to Nebraska what Madison is to Wisconsin or Washington DC is to the nation. Founded as the capital out of jealousy and rivalry with Omaha, Lincoln had the qualities of a small town grown large. Compared to Omaha, Lincoln seemed Protestant, Anglo-Saxon, clean, and moral. Immigrants formed a significantly smaller proportion of its population. It had one of the highest concentrations of Methodists, Presbyterians, and Congregationalists in the country. In Omaha, drunkenness, gambling, and prostitution seemed more protected than protested; in Lincoln vice was much less apparent. On a per capita basis, Lincoln's arrest rates were only half of Omaha's. Because of a high-cost license law, there were few saloons in Lincoln, and the extra-legal protection of prostitution had ceased in the 1880s. Still, Lincoln shared many of Omaha's urban problems—unpaved streets, a lack of sewers and trash collection, and other unsanitary conditions. As in Omaha, there were railroad yards and shops, some industrial development, and noteworthy ethnic groups, such as Germans from Russia.

Lincoln was also a city of culture and education. By 1900 it was the site not only of the University of Nebraska—one of the nation's largest at that time—but also of Nebraska Wesleyan University, Union College, and several other institutions of higher learning now defunct.

The University of Nebraska enjoyed remarkable development in the 1890s, even though the decade generally was marked by political unrest and economic stagnation. It was a time when an unusually gifted group of faculty and students were clustered in Lincoln. Most students of the 1890s tended to be very serious about their studies. Some went on to notable careers in politics, science, and higher education. Roscoe Pound was brilliant in both botany and law at Nebraska before he achieved national eminence at Harvard as dean of its law school, and his sister Louise became a distinguished folklorist. George Sheldon became one of Nebraska's best governors in 1907; together with Roscoe Pound, Frederic Clements founded the science of environmental ecology at the University of Nebraska; Alvin Johnson rescued New York's New School of Social Research as its head in the 1920s; and George Dern became secretary of war in Franklin Roosevelt's first cabinet in 1933.

Another student at Nebraska during the 1890s was the formidably intelligent Willa Cather, who later became one of America's foremost novelists. Some of her best-known works, such as *O Pioneers!* and *My Ántonia,* were set in Nebraska and drew upon her youthful experiences in Red Cloud and Lincoln. By writing brilliantly about the state and its people, Cather immeasurably enhanced the awareness of its citizens as Nebraskans and helped to define their identity.

Among faculty luminaries were Charles Bessey, a scientist and administrator who brought distinction to Nebraska in botany and agricultural education, and August H. Edgren, a world-renowned scholar of ancient languages from Sweden who served as the first dean of the university's graduate school. John J. Pershing, the commander of American forces in Europe during World War I, served memorably as professor of military science.

Like the university, the city of Lincoln attracted ambitious and able lawyers, businessmen, and politicians. The best known was William Jennings Bryan, a young lawyer from Illinois who was elected to represent Nebraska in Congress in 1890 and was chosen as the Democratic candidate for president of the United States in 1896, 1900, and 1908. Charles Dawes, elected vice-president under Calvin Coolidge in 1924, began his entrepreneurial career in real estate and banking in Lincoln from 1891 to 1895. Others less famous in the world of business and politics remained to build the city into a center of learning and culture on the plains—a small Athens in an unlikely place.

All these distinguished men and women came to Lincoln from elsewhere. In that sense, Lincoln in the 1890s was still a frontier city to which families of education and wealth transplanted their culture. Soon Lincoln could boast of social clubs, literary societies, and discussion groups, as well as two large theaters where scores of touring dramatic companies brought famous stars to the stage. Lincoln's best hotels met the standards expected by the most discriminating travelers. All this in a city of about thirty-five thousand.

At the beginning of the twentieth century, the city and the university assumed the appearance that we recognize today. The state capitol, the second constructed on the same site, was visually prominent despite its modest proportions. The university, like the city, continued to grow, and by 1910 its student body numbered forty-six hundred. In 1900 Benjamin Andrews, a prominent educator of liberal views, became chancellor. Loved and respected by students, Andrews presided over significant expansion in the university, especially in the development of new departments, new colleges such as medicine and engineering, and extension work in agriculture.

33.1. Nebraska's second state capitol was built in stages during the 1880s on the same site as the first. Typical of many statehouses built in the late nineteenth century, it imitated the style of the national capitol. By the time this photograph was taken in 1909, there was general agreement that the building, already deteriorating, was too small for the many functions assigned to it. Courtesy NSHS, C244:59.

33.2. This photograph, taken in about 1892, suggests that University of Nebraska had an attractive, spacious campus when such political and cultural figures as William Jennings Bryan, John J. Pershing, Roscoe Pound, and Willa Cather lived in Lincoln. The impressive University Hall still dominated the scene. None of the buildings in this photograph are extant today. Courtesy University of Nebraska–Lincoln Archives.

33.3. The brilliant son of a pioneer Nebraska judge, Roscoe Pound posed for this picture in 1888 when he was graduated from the University of Nebraska. He was admitted to the bar in 1890, practiced law in Lincoln, and continued to study botany, earning a Ph.D. in 1897. After a stint on the Nebraska State Supreme Court, he became dean of the university's law college in 1903. Later, as dean of Harvard Law School, he became one of America's preeminent legal scholars. Courtesy NSHS, P876:57.

33.4. Two of Nebraska's most illustrious daughters, Louise Pound (left) and Willa Cather, posed for this photograph about 1890 when they were students at the University of Nebraska. Like her brother Roscoe, Louise Pound became a renowned scholar. A University of Nebraska faculty member by 1894, she earned a doctorate from Heidelberg University in 1900 and became a distinguished linguist and folklorist. Cather, Nebraska's distinguished novelist, was graduated from the university in 1895 while she worked as a reporter for Lincoln newspapers. Courtesy Willa Cather Pioneer Memorial and Educational Foundation Collection/NSHS, w689:1163.

33.5. Charles Bessey, shown here in his study in 1914, was arguably the most important scientist and educator at the University of Nebraska during its first half-century. A professor of botany, he served at various times as dean, acting chancellor, and developer of the university's agricultural experiment station. Courtesy NSHS, P876:6.

33.6. Two old political foes, former Democratic Governor Charles W. Bryan (left) and former Republican Vice President Charles G. Dawes, reminisced in Lincoln in 1940, nearly fifty years after they had been young rivals in Lincoln. In 1924, they ran against each other as candidates for vice-president of the United States. Charles Bryan was the younger brother of the more famous William Jennings Bryan. Courtesy NSHS, B914:95.

33.7. Every political dignitary in Nebraska and every academic eminence at the university who achieved fame was supported by the scores of ordinary citizens who built this Athens on the Plains. Here three African-American workers interrupt their construction work to pose for a Lincoln photographer about 1910. Courtesy NSHS, H926:375.

The Progressive Movement in Nebraska *34*

Progressivism was a national movement for political reform early in the twentieth century that is usually associated with national figures such as President Theodore Roosevelt and Senator Robert LaFollette of Wisconsin. They were among the statesmen who led the country to adopt antitrust legislation, the federal reserve banking system, and electoral reforms including the initiative, referendum, recall, primary elections, and the direct election of senators that were intended to improve and enlarge democracy. The Progressive movement, which infused both major political parties, was also aimed at eliminating corruption in urban politics and the improvement of municipal government.

Progressivism came late to Nebraska. Only after the election of 1906, when Nebraskans elected Governor George Sheldon, a bright, young, and vigorous Republican, did the state legislature enact progressive legislation. By running on a strong antirailroad platform, Sheldon and like-minded legislators wrested control of the Republican Party from ultraconservative business-oriented leaders. They promptly enacted a series of reforms designed to curb the power of the railroads and their lobbyists in the state legislature and passed legislation regulating child labor, creating a board of pardons, and establishing a pure food and drug act. Most important, they initiated a primary election measure that transformed Nebraska politics by placing the power of nomination into the hands of the voters instead of the party convention.

Two years later, despite Sheldon's excellent record as governor, Nebraskans rejected him for a second term and elected in his place Ashton Shallenberger, a Democrat and former Congressman from Alma who, though elected with the support of the railroads, was also interested in reform. Under Shallenberger's leadership, the legislature enacted a bank guaranty law, a forerunner of the Federal Deposit Insurance Corporation that was strenuously opposed by the bankers, and also enacted a score of other progressive measures in railroad regulation and municipal government. It passed laws for the inspection of food and restaurants and expanded the state's system of higher education. The lawmakers also made the election of judges nonpartisan; enacted the "Oregon pledge law" requiring candidates for election to the legislature to promise, if elected, to vote for the candidate for the U.S. Senate who won a preferential election; and changed the Nebraska primary from a closed to an open election that permitted cross-over voting, an arrangement deemed desirable by the Democratic majority.

Moralistic legislation concerning the prohibition of alcoholic beverages also returned to the political stage. After intricate political skirmishes at the end of the legislative session, the legislature, by a margin of one contested vote, enacted a law that forbade the sale of alcoholic drinks after 8 P.M. Governor Shallenberger, who was expected to veto the bill, signed it instead, to the consternation of the liquor lobby and many lawmakers, especially in the Democratic party.

Prohibition then became the central issue in the election of 1910. Mayor Jim Dahlman of Omaha, the best-known "wet" in the state and a symbol of urban corruption, won the Democratic nomination for governor over Shallenberger. In the Republican primary election, the vote went to Chester Aldrich, progressive but "dry." Aldrich won the election, but in the legislative session of 1911 a prohibition measure in the form of county option was defeated. The lawmakers instead introduced major reforms, most notably the approval of a proposed amendment to the state constitution that would provide for the initiative and referendum. These measures gave voters the right to veto legislative acts and enact laws independently of the legislature. The legislature also passed a long list of minor progressive regulatory measures, including the inspection of livestock, sanitation of hotels and stores, and a trust company act.

These changes transformed Nebraska politics. Two decades earlier the Republicans had been dominant; by 1910 the two major parties were nearly even in strength. Ethnocultural divisions continued in the Progressive era, but economic issues and the politics of regulation, which cut across the political spectrum in new ways, acquired new significance. Even the character of political leadership changed as both parties developed professional leaders who held power longer than before. The secret ballot, primary elections, and the introduction of initiative, referendum, and recall petitions increased voter participation in decision making and reduced bargaining in political conventions. Soon the First World War would transform Nebraska politics even further.

SUBLIME GALL.

34.1. Early in the century, the *Omaha World-Herald,* then strongly Democratic, was the only Nebraska newspaper to employ a political cartoonist. In this cartoon from 19 September 1906, Guy Spencer condemns the Republican party for its presumably hypocritical endorsement of Progressivism. "Antipass" refers to the attack on free passes, regarded as a form of bribery, that railroads regularly issued to state legislators. Hiding behind the trash can of defeated reform measures is a figure representing the power of the railroads in Nebraska politics. Courtesy *Omaha World-Herald.*

34.2. In 1908 Governor George Sheldon, accompanied by an entourage of Nebraska dignitaries, presented a silver service to the crew of the recently commissioned uss *Nebraska* in San Francisco. After serving two terms in the state senate, where he had advocated various progressive measures, Sheldon led a campaign against the political power of the railroads and was elected governor in 1906. He was the first governor born in Nebraska and educated at the University of Nebraska. Courtesy NSHS, B336X.

34.3. On 7 April 1907, at the end of the legislative session, *Omaha World-Herald* cartoonist Guy Spencer credited the legislature for having resisted the political pressures of lobbyists representing the "corporations," defined here as railroads, express companies, brewers, and "drug and food adulterers." Spencer ignored the strong leadership of the Republican governor, George Sheldon. Courtesy *Omaha World-Herald*.

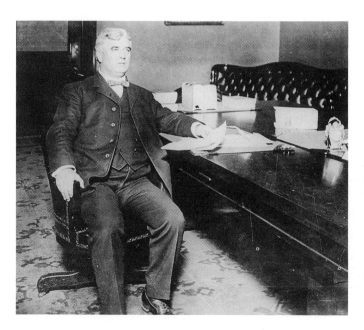

34.4. In 1908, when Nebraska's William Jennings Bryan was the Democratic candidate for president, the state elected Democrat Ashton Shallenberger as governor and gave his party a majority in the legislature. According to the *Omaha World-Herald*, Shallenberger and the legislature enacted the most remarkable list of progressive and reform laws in the history of Nebraska. Courtesy NSHS, P853.

34.5. This political rally in the streets of Beemer was photographed near the end of the Progressive era. A bald campaigner waves a pointed finger, and political bunting drapes the table, the platform, and the corner store. Musical instruments lying on the platform indicate that band music had been used to attract a crowd. Such gatherings were a form of public entertainment in the era before radio and television. Courtesy NSHS, C969:2–10.

Political Giants 35
Bryan and Norris

Two distinguished politicians, one an eloquent, populistic Democrat and the other a determined, idealistic Republican, are unequalled in Nebraska history for their impact on the nation. William Jennings Bryan of Lincoln, known as the Great Commoner, was the Democratic candidate for president in three national elections, 1896, 1900, and 1908. George W. Norris, a lawyer from McCook, made his mark in the U.S. Senate, where from 1913 to 1943 he was remarkably effective in advancing the interests of ordinary citizens through progressive legislation. Although Bryan and Norris were contemporaries, they were not personal friends. Both were progressives: one specialized in words, the other in deeds.

Bryan was a man of superb oratorical skills whose eloquence won him the Democratic nomination for president in 1896 when he was a mere thirty-six years old. As a two-term representative in Congress (1891–94) he identified himself with the interests of Western farmers and voiced their protests against changes in the economic system that worked against them. Although he was not a Populist, Bryan championed many populistic measures, especially currency reform—the coinage of silver at sixteen ounces of silver to one ounce of gold.

In the presidential election of 1900, Bryan was a fervent anti-imperialist. Always a popularizer and publicist of the causes he espoused, he advocated the progressive income tax, deposit insurance plans, and the federal reserve banking system. After 1908, when his presidential ambitions faded, he strongly endorsed prohibition and women's suffrage. In 1913, after the election of Woodrow Wilson to the presidency, Bryan served as secretary of state, a post in which he negotiated a series of conciliation treaties, mostly with Latin American countries, and fought unsuccessfully to sustain his view of American neutrality rights in the First World War. He died in 1925, just days after he had flared once more into national prominence, this time as the defender of fundamentalist Christian beliefs in the Scopes "monkey trial" in Tennessee.

A crusader to the end, Bryan was unshakable in his devotion to democratic ideals. Not an intellectual, never profound, but confident in his beliefs, Bryan used his rhetorical gifts to rally common citizens in favor of causes he thought righteous. Despite his failure to win the presidency, he was a remarkable man.

George Norris was a remarkable man for other reasons. He first achieved national prominence in 1910 when, as a Nebraska representative in Congress, he led a fight to clip the feathers of the tyrannical Speaker of the House, Joseph Cannon of Illinois. In the Senate, Norris built a reputation as "the gentle knight" of Progressivism, as Franklin Roosevelt called him years later.

A skilled parliamentarian, Norris opposed any legislation from any source he thought contrary to the public interest. Similarly, he blocked appointments of federal officials of either party if he thought them unworthy of public trust. Doggedly independent, Norris learned to be effective without the support of a solid political base. He believed that voters would value his honesty, integrity, and devotion to the public good and would therefore return him to office, as they did for thirty years. He fearlessly risked popular disapproval when his principles were at stake, as when he opposed the entry of the United States into World

War I. After the war he strengthened his reputation as a naysayer by opposing Wilson's Treaty of Versailles.

In the 1920s and 1930s, Norris achieved fame as the sponsor of the Twentieth ("Lame Duck") Amendment to the U.S. Constitution, but his most notable service was in conservation and the federal regulation of water power. Norris also gave crucial support to the construction of Kingsley Dam, which creates Lake McConaughy, a project on the North Platte River that combined the production of public hydroelectric power with irrigation and conservation. Always an independent thinker and political reformer, Norris was the father of Nebraska's nonpartisan unicameral legislature, which was approved by the voters in 1934. At the height of his personal prestige among ordinary Nebraskans, though not among Republican party regulars, Norris campaigned tirelessly for this unique structural change.

Bryan and Norris were born within a year of each other, one in Illinois, the other in Ohio. As young lawyers they resolved to seek their fortunes in Nebraska. Both entered politics as young men and left indelible marks on American history. Dramatically different in manner and personality, both served their nation and state with great distinction.

35.1. Following his nomination as the Democratic candidate for president in 1896, William Jennings Bryan (top row, right, with child) posed for this picture with his wife, children, and several newspaper reporters on the porch of his home at 1625 D Street in Lincoln. At thirty-six, he was the youngest candidate ever to be nominated for the presidency by a major political party. Courtesy NSHS, B915:140.

35.2. William Jennings Bryan was photographed in 1913 shortly after his appointment as secretary of state by President Woodrow Wilson. In 1915, after a German submarine torpedoed the *Lusitania* and 124 American citizens lost their lives, Bryan resigned in protest against Wilson's foreign policies. Courtesy NSHS, B915:48.

35.3. Fiercely independent, Republican Senator George W. Norris (shown here between the microphones) campaigned in 1936 for the re-election of President Franklin Roosevelt (second from right), whose New Deal he warmly supported. At the same time, Norris was elected as an independent to a fifth term in the United States Senate. Nebraska's Governor Roy Cochran is on the left behind the microphone. Courtesy NSHS, N855:43A.

35.4. In recognition of Senator Norris's central role in creating the Tennessee Valley Authority and its series of dams and hydroelectric plants, a dam in northeastern Tennessee, its reservoir, and a nearby town were named for him. In 1938 Norris inspected the dam, then the fourth largest in the world. Courtesy NSHS, N855:415.

35.5. In 1942, his last year in Washington as senator from Nebraska, Norris posed for a bust created by Jo Davidson, a prominent American sculptor. This work is now in the Hall of Fame in the Nebraska State Capitol. Courtesy NSHS, N855:25.

World War I in Nebraska 36

The First World War, which broke out in Europe in 1914, created difficult times for many Nebraskans. Sentiment throughout the nation tended to favor the Allied Powers—Great Britain, France, and Russia. But it was also clear that most Americans did not want to get involved directly in the war. They wanted the United States to remain neutral if it could.

For the United States, neutrality in the war was virtually impossible because such a policy could not affect both sides equally. Since there was no serious possibility of the United States helping Germany, Austria-Hungary, and Turkey (the Central Powers) because of their location in Europe, strict neutrality tended to work to their advantage. France and England were thereby deprived of a potential ally. The idea of neutrality was strongly supported by most Nebraskans of German birth or descent, by far the largest ethnic group in the state. Many of their leaders were convinced that the cause of Germany was just and that the United States should stay out of the war; some were stimulated to express their views intemperately, arousing the suspicions of those sympathetic to the Allies.

The dilemmas of neutrality were greatly intensified in May 1915 when a German submarine torpedoed the *Lusitania,* a British transatlantic passenger ship that was illegally transporting arms from the United States. The enormous loss of life, including 124 American citizens, led President Woodrow Wilson to insist on an aggressive defense of American neutrality rights. Wilson's policy, which caused Secretary of State William Jennings Bryan to resign in protest, strengthened pro-Allied sentiment, and a strong anti-German feeling developed in much of the United States. President Wilson subtly encouraged this trend, even though in his 1916 reelection campaign the Democratic Party stressed the slogan "He kept us out of War!" Early in 1917 Germany decided to risk war with the United States by resuming its submarine blockade of Europe. This meant that American merchant ships carrying supplies to England and France would be torpedoed. Germany's decision led directly to an American declaration of war in April.

There were few military installations in Nebraska in 1917, although a balloon school was conducted at Fort Omaha and a cavalry training center operated at Fort Robinson. Some young men were drafted into the armed forces, but many others volunteered for service. Omaha registered the second-highest ratio for American cities of enlistments relative to population. Nebraska also made a vital contribution to the war effort in the production of food. Prices for agricultural products rose dramatically, which led to unprecedented prosperity in the state. Nebraskans responded by purchasing war bonds at a rate that greatly exceeded the state's quota based on population.

The war on the home front was coordinated by the Nebraska State Council of Defense, an auxiliary to the National Council of Defense, whose members were appointed by the governor. In its effort to whip the citizenry into line behind the war effort, the council promoted the sale of war bonds and sought to enforce food and fuel rationing. The council also tried to stamp out all forms of what it perceived as dissent or disloyalty. In the name of patriotism it sought to restrict German-language instruction in the schools, to censor the extensive German-language press in Nebraska, and to erase the use of the German language in religious services and instruction.

These efforts contributed to rampant superpatriotism. Like many other states, Nebraska witnessed such excesses as the public burning of German-language books and supposedly patriotic ceremonies in which citizens of German birth or descent suspected of "disloyalty" were forced to kiss the American flag. Others were forced to buy war bonds. Yellow paint, designated as the color of disloyalty, was liberally applied to the property of persons suspected of being "slackers." As Bruce Nicoll described it in *Nebraska: A Pictorial History,* "While fighting to make the world safe for democracy, Nebraskans nearly lost it at home."

36.1. In World War I, hydrogen-filled balloons were often used to observe enemy troop movements. The nation's major center for training balloonists was at Fort Omaha, where about sixteen thousand soldiers were trained for service in France. In 1917 this German-made *Drachen* [dragon], shown here at Fort Omaha, was the only observation balloon owned by the U.S. Army. Courtesy Douglas County Historical Society.

36.2. World War I stimulated the growth of an industry to extract potash from alkali lakes in the western part of Nebraska's Sand Hills. Antioch, now a ghost town, became a city of twenty-five hundred in 1917 as five nearby factories, including the Nebraska Potash Company pictured here, operated around the clock. The boom collapsed at the end of the war, and soon only a few steel and concrete skeletons remained to remind Nebraskans of their participation in a war industry. Courtesy NSHS, P859:69.

36.3. During the course of World War I, 57,526 Nebraskans served in the armed forces of the United States. Of these, 1,655 were killed or wounded. Here soldiers of the Sixth Regiment parade westward on O Street in Lincoln on 14 September 1917 on their way to a military camp in New Mexico. Courtesy NSHS, L741:500.

36.4. Not all of Nebraska's soldiers came back alive. In this photograph, a military band from Camp Funston in Kansas leads a solemn escort to a cemetery in Ceresco. The flag-draped coffin contains the body of a soldier killed overseas. Although the number of American soldiers who died in World War I was small compared to the losses suffered by France, Great Britain, and Germany, that fact offered no comfort to Nebraska families who lost sons and brothers. Courtesy NSHS, A545:94.

36.5. The American Red Cross provided many important services on the home front. This group of Red Cross volunteers in Wahoo prepared thousands of surgical kits for use on battlefields in France. In Omaha, Red Cross workers provided assistance for soldiers passing through the city on troop trains. Courtesy NSHS, A545:186.

36.6. General John J. Pershing, commander of the American Expeditionary Forces in World War I, considered Lincoln his home even though he did not reside there after his service as commandant of cadets at the University of Nebraska in the 1890s. Here he inspects artillery in France in 1918 with Secretary of War Newton D. Baker. Courtesy NSHS, P465:183.

36.7. Two living caricatures—one as Kaiser Wilhelm of Germany, the other as Uncle Sam—stepped out of a war parade in 1918 for this photograph. During World War I the federal government, abetted eagerly by state and local agencies, encouraged overt displays of patriotism, sometimes with grotesque results. Courtesy NSHS, H926:319.

Race Riot in Omaha, 1919 *37*

On 28 September 1919, Nebraska lived through one of the most shameful episodes in its history. On that day in Omaha a frenzied mob, determined to lynch an African American named Will Brown who had been accused of assaulting a white woman, stormed the Douglas County jail on the top floor of the courthouse. They overwhelmed the police, set the courthouse afire, looted nearby stores for guns and ammunition, almost succeeded in hanging the mayor of the city, captured Will Brown, and murdered him. Order did not return to Omaha until the next morning, when sixteen hundred federal troops were ordered into the city to prevent any further outbreaks of racial violence.

Omahans were aghast at what had happened. In addition to the murder of Will Brown, two white men were killed by stray bullets, and others were injured. Property damage was extensive, especially to the Douglas County Courthouse, which had been erected only seven years earlier; irreplaceable county records were destroyed in the fire.

The causes of this tragic episode are interwoven with the aftereffects of World War I. In 1919, as Nebraska and the nation tried to adjust to a peacetime economy, prices for consumer goods spiraled as soldiers returning home swelled the ranks of the unemployed. Omaha also suffered a series of strikes that summer, especially among teamsters and in the stockyards. Businessmen hired nonunion laborers as strikebreakers, many of whom were African Americans brought in from Chicago and other cities. Feelings of dissatisfaction and resentment were intensified by sensationalist journalism. The *Omaha Bee* especially exacerbated racial tensions by playing up a series of incidents in which black workers allegedly attacked white women. When none of these incidents led to conviction, the *Bee* charged the police and the courts with incompetence.

Recent research has revealed that the newspaper reporting was part of a summer-long campaign to discredit the reformist mayor of Omaha, Edward Smith, and his police commissioner, Dean Ringer, by demonstrating that they were unable to maintain order. The implication was clear: Omahans should get rid of Mayor Smith and return the city to its erstwhile boss, Tom Dennison, and his ally, former Mayor James Dahlman.

In the aftermath of the riot, the Dennison machine was accused of orchestrating the demonstration. General Leonard Wood, who commanded the federal troops dispatched to Omaha, asserted that it was an organized effort that included the liberal distribution of alcoholic drink to potential rioters and free taxi service to the scene. Although these and other equally serious charges have never been proven, it is clear that Dennison and the *Omaha Bee* fomented racial strife for political purposes by creating a circumstance in which lawless rioters could with impunity destroy public property and take a human life.

Although the police arrested several suspects, no one was ever convicted of the murder of Will Brown. A grand jury impaneled to investigate the riot. One hundred twenty indictments were filed but the subsequent trials almost always resulted in acquittals or hung juries, as happened twice in the case of the man accused with assault to murder Mayor Smith. In the next election the voters of Omaha returned Jim Dahlman to the mayor's office, and Tom Dennison continued to wield power in the city for another decade.

37.1. Will Brown, an African-American
packinghouse worker, had allegedly as-
saulted a young white woman and
robbed her escort during the late hours
of 25 September 1919. The next day, following a disturbance near the woman's
home, the police took Brown into pro-
tective custody in the Douglas County
jail, located on the fifth floor of the
courthouse. On 28 September, an organized mob attacked the building and
demanded that Brown be surrendered
to them. Here rioters on the south side
of the courthouse have inflicted considerable damage to the building. One
hundred policemen confronted about
four thousand rioters. Courtesy NSHS,
M936:72.

37.2. This grisly scene depicts the terrifying consequence of the mob gone out of control. On 28 September 1919, the rioters broke into the jail and caught Will Brown, beat him unconscious, hanged him from a lamp pole, riddled his body with bullets, dragged his corpse through city streets, and finally burned him. Brown was almost surely a victim of false identification. Courtesy NSHS, M936:69.

37.3. As they stormed the courthouse, rioters set the building on fire. When firemen arrived to quell the blaze, rioters chopped their water hoses to pieces. Omaha's reformist mayor, Ed Smith, tried to control the riot and was nearly lynched for his efforts. Photographs taken the next day show the interior of the courthouse to be a shambles. Courtesy NSHS, 054:345.

37.4. City and state officials pleaded for the intervention of federal troops from Forts Crook and Omaha two hours before the riot began. They arrived too late to prevent the loss of life and property damage. One company-sized contingent was dispatched to protect people in the black neighborhood on the North Side. In this image, soldiers have set up a machine gun and a small cannon at 24th and Lake Streets. Troops remained in the city until 15 November. Courtesy NSHS, R586:17.

38 The Legacy of Samuel McKelvie

Not often in Nebraska history have governors exercised the powers of office in a way that had a long-range impact on the affairs of the state. Although partisanship was keen, political leadership was usually temporary. In more recent times, however, governors have wielded political power more effectively in their efforts to influence the legislature and define public issues.

Samuel R. McKelvie of Lincoln was a noteworthy example. First elected in 1918 at age thirty-seven, he served two terms as governor. During McKelvie's administrations, the state decided to build a new capitol and reorganize state government along the lines that remain in place today.

A native Nebraskan, McKelvie had a notable career as the publisher of the *Nebraska Farmer*. He was especially interested in helping farmers introduce business methods into their operations and take advantage of the latest technological developments. Later he became a rancher in the Sand Hills of Cherry County, where a national forest later was named in his honor. McKelvie was also active in the Republican Party and rose through the ranks from city councilman in Lincoln, state legislator, and lieutenant governor to the governorship.

World War I played an important role in McKelvie's success. His election as a Republican replacing a Democratic governor was partly fueled by the disillusionment many citizens felt about President Woodrow Wilson and the Democratic Party. Involvement in the war was an intensely emotional experience for many Nebraskans. When McKelvie and other public figures urged that the state erect a monumental capitol as a memorial to Nebraskans who had died in the war, the citizens agreed with little dissent.

McKelvie is best remembered for his reorganization of state government in accord with progressive principles by introducing the civil administrative code. Seeking to rid the state of inefficiencies imposed by the outmoded state constitution of 1875, McKelvie aimed to centralize governmental responsibility and to eliminate unnecessary and overlapping boards and commissions by reorganizing state administration in departments, each headed by a secretary appointed by the governor.

The overwhelmingly Republican state legislature responded to McKelvie's leadership by enacting his proposals. McKelvie wanted a new state constitution that would systematize this new legislation. A state constitutional convention was held in 1919–20, but instead of writing a new constitution, the delegates offered forty-one amendments, all of which were later approved by the voters.

38.1. In his inaugural address, Governor
Samuel McKelvie called for the construction of a new statehouse to replace
the one constructed in the 1880s, which
he described as unsafe and unsanitary.
A new capitol bill sailed through the
legislature was signed by the governor
on 20 February 1919. McKelvie is shown
here breaking ground with a horse-
drawn plow at ceremonies on 15 April
1922, the last year of his second term.
Courtesy NSHS, C244:125.

38.2. Surrounded by legislators, Governor Samuel McKelvie happily signed the "code bill," which reorganized the administration of state government. Born in Fairfield (Clay County) in 1881, McKelvie, a Republican, was well-known as the editor and publisher of the leading farm journal in the state. Courtesy NSHS, L514G:1919-9.

38.3. Governor McKelvie's chief goal was to reorganize state government by consolidating boards, commissions, and agencies under the central control of the governor. Reorganization was ultimately achieved by a constitutional convention of delegates chosen in a special election on 4 November 1919. They convened soon thereafter to begin their deliberations. But instead of writing a new state constitution, they patched up the old one with forty-one amendments. Courtesy NSHS, L514G:29-2.

39 Nebraskans Build a Monumental Capitol, 1920–1934

For more than half a century, Nebraska's monumental capitol has been the preeminent symbol of the state. Designed in 1920 by Bertram Grosvenor Goodhue of New York, a leading American architect, the structure is quite unlike its predecessors. A dignified, graceful, and carefully constructed building, it memorializes Nebraskans who gave their lives in World War I. But the capitol also symbolizes the values, hopes, and aspirations of its builders and the generations of Nebraskans who have followed them.

The winner of a national competition to design the capitol, Goodhue dispensed with columns, cornices, pediments, and the other customary elements of neoclassical architecture to produce a plan that seemed free of binding traditions. Designed in accordance with Beaux-Arts principles, but modified to suit pre-Modernist tastes, the capitol is a magnificent expression of civic pride, faith in democratic ideals, and the desire for responsive government. By uniting the skills of the architect, symbologist, sculptor, mosaicist, muralist, and landscapist, the Nebraska state capitol offers a harmony of the arts that has rarely been matched in the United States.

Construction of the new capitol began in 1922. It was designed to be built in stages around the old structure so that the latter could be used until most of the outer part of the new capitol was finished. The old capitol was then removed and the inner parts, including the legislative chambers, the foyer, and the tower, were erected. Constructed over a period of a dozen years on a "pay-as-you-build" basis, the new capitol was fully occupied by 1934, although some of the decorative work waited several decades for completion.

The capitol is everywhere infused with symbolism. This was due in part to the genius of Hartley Burr Alexander, a professor of philosophy and anthropology at the University of Nebraska. He was the author of most of the inscriptions, such as the somber declaration THE SALVATION OF THE STATE IS WATCHFULNESS IN THE CITIZEN, which greets visitors above the main entrance. He also prepared a detailed program specifying the subject matter of sculptures, mosaics, and other decorative elements. But the statue *The Sower* on top of the tower was Goodhue's idea. Although Goodhue had never visited the state before he designed the capitol, he, like Alexander, was eager to integrate manifestations of Nebraska's environment and culture into this building. It remains one of America's great architectural achievements.

39.1. The competition for the Nebraska state capitol included some of the most distinguished architectural firms in the United States. The brilliance of Bertram Goodhue's design is evident in this rendering of the front elevation. Goodhue's idea of integrating a tower into a monumental government building was a radical innovation in 1920. Courtesy NSHS, C244:83.

39.2. Each of Nebraska's three state-houses in Lincoln have been built on the same ground. This view of the second capitol, looking northwest from 16th and H Streets, shows trees being felled and the ground being cleared in preparation for the new construction, the outer parts of which were built around the old. Courtesy NSHS, C244:172.

39.3. By 1927, when this photograph was taken (also from 16th and H Streets), the old capitol had been torn down and government offices had moved into the completed parts of the new structure. With the central area cleared, construction of the tower could begin. Courtesy NSHS MacDonald Collection, M134:1927-01-07:1.

39.4 This aerial view shows the capitol under construction and southeast Lincoln in the background. Because access to the tower could not be impeded, construction of the legislative chamber on the west side (where the Unicameral presently meets) had not yet begun. Construction was completed in 1932. Courtesy NSHS, L741:2125.

39.5. When visitors enter the capitol through the main entrance on the north side, they encounter three magnificent interior spaces—the vestibule, the foyer, and the rotunda. Together they form the cathedral-like space shown here—richly ornamented with mosaics on the floor, arches, and ceiling. Photograph by Sidney Spelts. Courtesy Department of Administrative Services, Nebraska Capitol Collections.

Back Home on the Farm in the 1920s *40*

The 1920s were a promising but uncertain decade for Nebraska's farm families. The rural way of life was undergoing considerable change, due largely to the impact of gasoline-powered automobiles, trucks, and tractors. The victory of the automobile over rural isolation was virtually complete by 1930, when cars were owned by nearly all farm families and gasoline-powered tractors had been adopted by a third of Nebraska's farms.

The First World War's enormous appetite for agricultural products brought prosperity to many farmers as they expanded their operations, purchased additional land and new equipment, and encumbered themselves with new debts at high rates of interest. By 1921, however, the prices farm products could fetch had dropped more than 50 percent because of increases in production, curtailment of credit by the Federal Reserve Board, and contractions in the world market as Europe recovered from the war. Conditions improved somewhat during the late 1920s, only to be followed by the 1930s, long, hard years of drought and depression.

Unlike urban dwellers, most rural Nebraskans of the 1920s still lacked electricity and indoor plumbing in their homes. Even by the end of the decade, only one farm home in seven had electric power (usually generated privately) and one in five had running water. For most of Nebraska's farm families, every ounce of water for cooking, bathing, and laundering still had to be pumped by hand at the well and brought into the house in buckets. Kerosene lamps provided illumination for the majority, and stoves fueled by wood or coal were still commonly used for cooking and heating, although by 1930 one home in eight had furnaces or steam heat. Floors were bare in most rooms, except perhaps for the kitchen, where a linoleum covering might be found, and the parlor, which was seldom used except to entertain visitors.

Farm life continued to be lonely, even after the advent of the automobile. But the effects of isolation were greatly reduced by battery-powered radios. Nonexistent in 1920, they could be found in 40 percent of Nebraska's farm homes by 1930.

Farmhouses were usually surrounded by trees to provide shade and protection from the wind. Most farms in eastern Nebraska had a vegetable garden and some had a few fruit trees. A barn stood close by to provide shelter for horses and milk cows and storage for hay. Straw for bedding the animals was usually piled nearby. Silos for preserving and storing fodder were rare except in the eastern third of the state, where dairying was important. A windmill that pumped water for both man and beast was standard. Other buildings typically included machine sheds, corn cribs, a granary, a chicken coop, a hog barn, and the outhouse, unobtrusively set off to one side. Chickens ran about freely searching for food, cats challenged the rodent population, and a dog or two ostentatiously guarded the entire establishment.

Farming systems varied greatly across the state. In the northeast, an area of good soils and ample rainfall, production of hogs and beef cattle dominated; corn and oats were the chief crops, and wheat was unimportant. In 1930 a farm in the northeast averaged about 160 acres and had six horses, eight milk cows (often a beef breed), nine other cattle, ten sows, and over one hundred poultry, mostly chickens. In the southeast, general farming was also common, but wheat was the major cash crop, followed by corn. Livestock were fewer, but dairying for the butter market was important. Some acres in the southeast, as everywhere in Nebraska, were set aside as pastures for cattle and horses and fields of hay and oats. But this changed, too, as farmers replaced horses with automobiles and tractors. From 1915 to 1925 the number of horses in the state had decreased by 150,000, releasing about two million acres of pasture for commercial crops.

The size of farms generally increased across the state toward the west until they were three times as large as those in the east. In the upper reaches of the Elkhorn River valley, where much of the land adjacent to the Sand Hills is not suited to corn or wheat, wild hay was the most important crop. In the south-central part of the state, corn retained its importance, especially on large farms. Alfalfa was particularly important along the Platte. Farther south in the Republican River valley, hogs provided the largest source of income; wheat was an important cash crop, but more acres were sown in corn, which was used to feed the livestock. Dry-farming techniques were often used, the most important of which was summer fallowing. In much of western Nebraska, "suitcase" farmers who lived elsewhere came to the high plains once a year to plant their wheat and once again later to harvest it.

In the Sand Hills and much of the Panhandle, arable land is rare and cattle ranches dominated in the 1920s as they do today. In Scotts Bluff County, along the North Platte River, irrigated sugar beet and potato fields provided the major sources of income on relatively small farms that maintained horses, a few milk cows, poultry, and swine.

By the end of the 1920s the cumulative effect of agricultural technology had increased productivity and created larger but fewer farms, fewer farmworkers, the decline of small towns and villages, and the growth of regional market centers. The movement of farmers off the land, which had begun in the 1890s, increased in the 1920s and would accelerate in the decades to come.

40.1. Nothing liberated the farmer from the tyranny of space more than the automobile. Parking lots were invented to accommodate the needs of motorists attending special events such as the 1922 Adams County Fair in Hastings, pictured here. Participation in county fairs was an important activity for most farm families. Courtesy Adams County Historical Archives, Hastings.

40.2. Two International trucks wait their turn at a grain elevator in the late 1920s. By then, one farmer out of six in Nebraska operated a truck. The use of trucks dramatically reduced the number of horses in the state, and automobile repair shops gradually replaced blacksmiths and harnessmakers. Courtesy NSHS, F233:82.

40.3. Much more mobile and efficient than the heavy, cumbersome steam tractors they replaced, small general-purpose gasoline-powered tractors performed a variety of tasks, from grinding corn to mixing feed and silage. This model was introduced by the John Deere Company in 1928. Courtesy Deere & Company.

40.4. The cord hanging on the wall suggests that this farm woman, who lived near Kearney, had the advantage of electricity for her washing machine. During the 1920s many Nebraska farms acquired kerosene-powered generators that produced electricity for lighting, water pumps, and other labor-saving machines. Gasoline-powered washing machines were also available for homes without electricity. Courtesy NSHS, R433:50.

40.5. In western Nebraska, where environmental conditions stimulated the use of machines, combination harvesters cut swaths twenty-four feet wide. This rig harvested eighty to one hundred acres per day in 1926, a bountiful year that yielded seventy bushels of barley per acre on this farm near Dalton in Cheyenne County. Courtesy NSHS, F233:221.

40.6. Irrigation from the North Platte River made labor-intensive farming common in Scotts Bluff County, where sugar beets and potatoes were the main crops. German-speaking immigrants from the Volga region in Russia, seen in this image, did much of the back-breaking work, irrigating, hoeing, digging, topping, and hauling the beets to the local sugar refinery. Courtesy NSHS, W727:60.

The Big Change *41*
The 1920s as Transition

The character and quality of life changed dramatically in Nebraska during the 1920s. Compared to what was standard only forty years earlier in the 1880s, enormous changes in everyday life had occurred. The transforming effects of electricity, automobiles, and radios were felt the most keenly. In many respects, contemporary living is mere elaboration of what developed during this decade.

The effects of technological change were most obvious in the cities. By the 1920s most small cities had paved streets, municipal electricity and water systems, telephone systems, streetlights, and sewage systems (though raw sewage was still often dumped into rivers). The homes of most urban Nebraskans had running water and indoor plumbing. Wood-burning stoves, which had been used for both cooking and heating, were generally replaced by gas or electric stoves and coal- or oil-burning furnaces.

Electricity appeared in homes on a grand scale during the 1920s, at first for illumination but by the end of the decade for washing or sewing machines, irons, toasters, mixers, and vacuum cleaners, many of which could be bought on the installment plan. Refrigerators began to replace iceboxes for short-term food preservation, and electric fans began to cool hot summer days.

Change came more slowly for country people, who would wait another decade or two for electric appliances. Their lives were more profoundly transformed by the gasoline-powered automobile and truck, where effects were especially acute in sparsely populated agricultural states such as Nebraska. The number of automobiles in the state spiraled from 25,000 in 1913 to 367,000 in 1930, a ratio of 1 automobile for 3.2 people in Nebraska, compared to 4.6 for the nation. One-third of the automobiles in the state were owned by farmers. Most farm families were freed from their rural isolation between 1915 and 1930.

Urban landscapes changed dramatically as horse-drawn wagons and carriages began to disappear along with livery stables and blacksmith shops. The internal geography of towns evolved as the automobile reduced the need for a compact commercial district and encouraged businesses to string out along main highways, defacing the landscape with advertising billboards.

The advent of the automobile early in the twentieth century required that state or federal governments build hard-surfaced highways to connect farms to towns and link towns and cities with each other. Significant progress in road improvement began in the early 1920s. In 1923–24 Nebraska had 2,382 miles of earth-surfaced roads, 239 miles of "sand-clay," 615 miles of gravel, 50 miles of concrete, and 28 miles of roads that were bricked. The push for a transcontinental highway was advocated by the Lincoln Highway Association, a national organization, as early as 1912. Ten years later construction of the highway began, which eventually connected New York and San Francisco through Nebraska from Omaha to Kimball on a route close to the first transcontinental railroad line.

The network of federal arteries with its uniform system of signs was created by 1925, in the same year Nebraska instituted a gasoline tax to finance the construction and maintenance of roads. Soon five federal highways spanned the length and breadth of Nebraska.

Automobiles and hard-surfaced roads accelerated population shifts away from farms and many small towns created by the railroads. Even though Nebraska's total population increased during the 1920s, losses were registered in nearly half of its ninety-three counties, mostly those in the Sand Hills or other more isolated parts of the state. But in the other counties, county seats grew and other regional centers prospered. Many of Nebraska's seven thousand school districts, which were based on walking distances for children, were rendered obsolescent and the movement for consolidation began.

Automobiles and trucks increasingly dominated local transportation patterns. The state's railroad mileage decreased as local railroad passenger traffic and short-distance shipments of freight nearly disappeared.

41.1. Great changes in the style of women's clothing took place during the 1920s. These women met in Lincoln in December 1920 to organize the Nebraska chapter of the Daughters of Founders and Patriots of America. By the end of the decade dresses were shorter, hats smaller, and the tightly laced high-top shoes were gone forever. Courtesy NSHS, L741:1471.

41.2. Refrigerators, washing machines, stoves, water heaters, vacuum cleaners, and other small appliances—all operated by electricity—were offered for sale by the Lincoln Gas and Electric store in University Place in 1930. Courtesy NSHS MacDonald Collection, M134:1930-07-01:8.

41.3. Electricity was essential to two new forms of mass entertainment—movies and radio. Although motion pictures were still silent, they put small-town opera houses out of business. In 1926 the Sun, located on O Street in Lincoln, was typical of scores of movie theaters in Nebraska cities. Courtesy NSHS MacDonald Collection, M134:1926-03-19:1.

41.4. Radio got an early start in Nebraska when Dr. John Jensen, professor of physics at Nebraska Wesleyan University, began broadcasting over WCAJ in 1921–22. The photographer was attracted by the mysterious maze of wires, switches, transformers, and microphones. There were no commercial radio stations at the beginning of the decade; by its end they blanketed the state, and radios were standard equipment in most urban homes. Farm families without electricity often bought battery-operated radios. Courtesy NSHS, L741:1626.

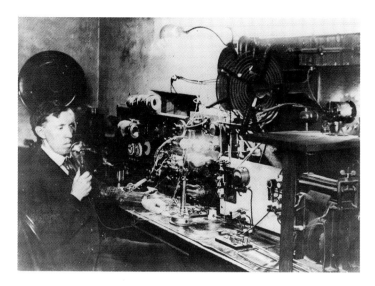

41.5. What kind of roads to build, how to pay for them, and whether to accept federal aid for their construction were major political issues in the 1920s. Farmers and ranchers were especially interested in country roads that could link them to nearby towns and cities. This photograph, taken about 1922, shows a road crossing West Muddy Creek in Frontier County. Courtesy Nebraska Department of Roads.

41.6. Urban dwellers of the time wanted paved highways connecting larger cities and towns, such as the Lincoln Highway, the nation's first transcontinental highway. This photograph shows a short segment of the original Lincoln Highway, regraded and improved in 1920, that is still in use today in Douglas County, east of Elkhorn on County Road 120. Photograph by Jay Bailey, courtesy Nebraska Department of Roads.

41.7. The tourism industry, in its infancy in the 1920s, was a product of the automobile age. Especially common on or near the Lincoln Highway, tourist camps such as this one at Ogallala welcomed travelers, offering rest rooms, a camp store, heated cabins, and free shower baths. The architecture of the gas station in this image is typical of the time. Courtesy NSHS, K65:5695.

41.8. Like most Midwestern states in the 1920s, Nebraska was not free of the Ku Klux Klan, a secret organization that fed on anxieties born of rapid technological and social change. It identified its "100 percent Americanism" with anti-Catholicism, anti-Semitism, and hatred of African Americans. Thousands of Nebraskans participated in cross-burning ceremonies, parades, and demonstrations before the Klan began to fade in 1926. Though local "klaverns" were formed throughout the state, the Klan was especially strong in Lincoln. This picture shows klansmen parading in Neligh. Courtesy NSHS, W855–2257.

Drought, Depression, War, and Recovery, 1930–1970

Part 4

The four decades between the onset of the Great Depression in 1929 and the national turmoil created by the Vietnam War in the late 1960s constitute a period of continuous change in the economic, political, and social lives of Nebraskans. Discoveries in science and technology, successes and failures in international affairs (including wars, both hot and cold), and the vagaries of weather and climate created circumstances out of which many contemporary attitudes and behaviors evolved.

The need to adjust to changing times was not something new in Nebraska history. Change and the adaptation to change is what history is all about. But there are unusual parallels between this period and the forty years that preceded it: both began with economic depression combined with severe drought; both experienced horrendous wars fought in distant lands; and some years of prosperity followed war in both periods. Furthermore, both saw examples of outstanding political leadership that resulted in far-reaching political reforms.

It is also true, however, that each time and place has its unique character and events. For Nebraska, like all the states of the Great Plains, the early 1930s were difficult years of distressing poverty with little hope for future prosperity. Thousands of families left their homes for more promising places either in Nebraska's cities or elsewhere, especially on the West Coast. But in 1932, when the weather and the economy seemed as bleak as they could be, Nebraskans were buoyed by the completion of their magnificent state capitol. It quickly became the symbol of the state's pride in its history, its diverse cultures, its ability to persevere in times of adversity, and its hopes and aspirations for the future.

Construction of the Nebraska state capitol was completed when this photograph was taken in 1934. The capitol became the preeminent symbol of the state in the decades that followed. The uniqueness of its design—dramatic innovations within traditional forms— symbolized the determination of the state to endure drought and depression, survive the stresses of war, and adapt to the problems of prosperity in the 1950s and 1960s. Sixty years were to pass before all the murals in the capitol were planned, executed, and installed. Although the structure cost twice as much as originally planned, it was paid for by biennial appropriations over a ten-year period. Courtesy NSHS McDonald Collection, M134:1934-04-18.

The Dirty Thirties 42
Drought and Depression

Like the 1890s, the 1930s was a time when twin threats of drought and economic depression combined to subject Nebraska to severe stress. What happened during the "dirty thirties" scarred the lives of many Nebraskans who experienced those difficult times. Farmers especially were hit hard, and many thousands abandoned the countryside for life in the towns and cities, some reluctantly, others gladly.

Although the 1920s had adequate rainfall, the 1930s were some of the driest years on record. Only two years in ten came close to average precipitation. Several summers, especially 1934, saw many consecutive days of dry, hot winds from the south that regularly pushed temperatures well over one hundred degrees, searing countless cornfields, and as usual in times of drought, many fields were stripped bare by grasshoppers. The people of the plains were especially frightened by the dust storms that swept across the state. Black blizzards of dirt rolled across the landscape, terrorizing man and beast with darkness at noon, penetrating the most tightly sealed homes, choking lungs, and cloaking fields and ditches with drifts of topsoil.

Nebraskans suffered even more from the Great Depression that crushed the national economy in the 1930s. Although few were directly affected by the Great Crash of November 1929, the subsequent collapse of prices for farm commodities was another matter. By 1932, for example, corn dropped to one-fifth of what it was worth in 1929, hogs and beef to one-fourth. Many farmers found it impossible to meet payments on their mortgages, which had been negotiated in the more prosperous 1920s.

Agricultural discontent boiled over in 1932 and 1933. Many farmers, especially in the northeastern counties, joined in the activities of the Farm Holiday Association, which attempted to raise prices by withholding farm products from the market. Even though their efforts—setting up road blocks and dumping milk into roadside ditches—were bound to fail, they called attention to the plight of the farmers and created momentum for political solutions. Farm Holiday leaders conferred with Midwestern governors and successfully sought moratoriums on farm mortgages. Another effective tactic was the "penny auction," in which sympathetic farmers prevented anyone from bidding more than a few cents for items sold at mortgage foreclosures.

News of agrarian discontent in the Great Plains attracted the attention of Communists in New York, a few of whom came west and infiltrated farmer protest organizations, urging more aggressive or confrontational tactics. The climax of this movement was a riot in the town square of Loup City, a small county seat in central Nebraska.

Hard times also had important political consequences in Nebraska. Democrats won enormous victories in 1932 as Franklin Delano Roosevelt captured the presidency. Among Republican politicians in the state, only Senator George Norris continued to command strong popular support, although his most bitter opposition came from within his own party. He won reelection in 1936, but as an independent running with Roosevelt's support. By 1938, as prosperity began to return to the plains, the period of Democratic dominance in Nebraska began to fade.

In the 1930s the federal government inaugurated unprecedented efforts to aid victims of drought and depression. Thousands of loans worth millions of dollars were made to Nebraska farmers by the Farm

Credit Administration. A million cattle and hogs were purchased for slaughter or shipment to distant markets. Programs were started to curtail the production of wheat and corn; by 1938 more than three hundred thousand crop adjustment contracts with Nebraska farmers were negotiated by the Agricultural Adjustment Administration. Jobs were created for thousands of Nebraskans in projects devised by the Public Works Administration, the Works Progress Administration, and many other agencies of the federal government. Meanwhile a variety of public assistance programs for the aged, the blind, and dependent children were undertaken. By the end of the decade, about one-fifth of the state's population had received some sort of direct governmental assistance, which meant that ultimately all Nebraskans were helped.

During the "dirty thirties" Nebraska lost nearly 5 percent of its population. Losses were heaviest in agricultural districts west of Lincoln and in the Republican and Loup River valleys. Five counties—Clay, Webster, Harlan, Frontier, and Arthur—actually lost more than 20 percent of their population between 1930 and 1940. Much of this loss would have occurred anyway, but the drought and depression accelerated the process.

Rural out-migration meant that Nebraska's cities grew larger. Some counties along the Platte River—Nebraska's life line of water and transportation—experienced growth. In Keith County, for example, the population surged by 24 percent because of jobs created by the construction of Kingsley Dam near Ogallala.

42.1. This dust storm, photographed in Naponee on 26 March 1935, was one of many that afflicted the Great Plains in the 1930's. At their worst from 1934 to 1936, dust storms were most common in late winter and early spring. They lifted millions of tons of powdery topsoil and deposited it hundreds of miles to the east. Dust storms were the natural consequences of farmers having plowed up thousands of acres of Great Plains grassland that should have been left undisturbed. Courtesy NSHS, F293:2966.

42.2. In this image, taken on 1 September 1932, striking members of the Farm Holiday Association block a road at the Omaha city limits to prevent the marketing of farm commodities. Although Farm Holiday leaders cautioned against violence, they could not always control their men. Fighting-mad pickets in Omaha battled sheriff's deputies for three nights from 30 August to 1 September 1932. Courtesy NSHS, F232:2.

42.3. On 6 October 1932, hundreds of farmers came to the Von Bonn farm near Elgin for the first of many "penny auctions" that year. Theresa von Bonn, a widow with several children, was unable to make payments on a $449 mortgage on her livestock and machinery. Her bank, also struggling to survive, decided to foreclose. An auction was announced. By prearrangement, the farmers permitted no one to raise the bid above five cents for any one of the mortgaged items. At the end of the day, the auction had brought the bank a grand total of $5.35. The successful bidders then returned all the rescued property to the widow in distress. The heartening success of this venture led to dozens more, especially in the eastern part of the state. Courtesy NSHS, F232:6.

42.4. In February 1933, the Farm Holiday Association organized a large but orderly march of farmers on Nebraska's new capitol in Lincoln. The Association successfully demanded that the legislature enact a two-year moratorium on all mortgage foreclosures. Massed on the monumental staircase on the north side of the capitol on 16 February, marchers hoisted banners with radical messages—ominous counterpoint to the pronouncement above the main entrance: THE SALVATION OF THE STATE IS WATCHFULNESS IN THE CITIZEN. Courtesy NSHS, F232:1.

42.5. An amateur photographer captured a moment of the violence that erupted in a small Nebraska town in June 1934. Truckloads of protesters, including local and out-of-town Communists, had entered Loup City, located in the worst drought-stricken area of Nebraska. They came to support a strike by women workers who dressed chickens in a local creamery. Town leaders, appalled by the invasion, organized a vigilance committee. On Flag Day (14 June), they confronted the protesters, and when the signal "Hey, Rube!" was called out, a riot ensued in the town square—ten minutes of fists and blackjacks. The conflict ended when one of the protesters was knocked unconscious and the other protesters fled. Nine of the protesters, including "Mother" Ella Bloor of New York City, were arrested and subsequently convicted for inciting riot, despite evidence that the fracas was planned by town leaders. Courtesy NSHS, S553:01-F4.

42.6. During the 1930s, relief offices like this one in Hastings were set up in many Nebraska cities to help people who were in immediate need of assistance. The well-dressed man and woman are government officials who came to inspect the efficiency of the office, as exemplified by the man at the desk and the woman at the table. The people in need stare at the photographer from the background. Courtesy NSHS, F293:535.

42.7. Some of the cattle purchased by the government to feed the poor in the cities were diseased or otherwise unfit for human consumption. Such animals were condemned and brought to an open pit or trench, such as this one photographed near Atkinson in 1934, where they were killed and buried. Courtesy NSHS, F293:327.

42.8. Nearly twenty-five thousand Nebraskans between the ages of seventeen and twenty-three found employment in the Civilian Conservation Corps, which emphasized the development of natural resources in rural areas. Camps consisting of barracks, such as this one under construction in Beatrice, suggested the quasi-military character of the corps, which many people, fearing involvement in another European war, found objectionable. Courtesy NSHS, F293:279.

42.9. Government projects, such as this bridge under construction on North 27th Street in Lincoln in 1934, provided employment for thousands of Nebraskans. By 1938 the Public Works Administration had built 52 schools, 41 waterworks systems, 13 bridge and street paving projects, and 11 sewage disposal plants in Nebraska—about 200 projects in all. During the same period, the Works Progress Administration erected 170 new buildings, including schools, auditoriums, recreational buildings, swimming pools, parks, and playgrounds, as well as courthouses, firehouses, and other administrative buildings. Courtesy NSHS, F293:252.

42.10. The federal government also tried to help unemployed people in the arts and humanities such as actors, artists, sculptors, writers, historians. Twelve Nebraska towns, for example, have post offices with murals painted as federal projects funded by the WPA. Here a group of women participate in a dramatics camp conducted in Crete. Courtesy NSHS, F293:299.

43 The Unicameral
Nebraska's Unique Legislature

In 1934, soon after Nebraskans had completed the construction of their new capitol, they rendered one of its chambers obsolete by adopting a one-house legislature. Usually called the unicameral, this unique body is a major departure from American political tradition in state government. Although unicameralism has been described appropriately as a liberal or progressive innovation designed to inject a new measure of accountability and responsibility in state government, it also has had many conservative supporters.

The idea of a unicameral legislature was not new to Nebraskans in 1934. It had been proposed in various ways since 1911 (when the British deprived their House of Lords of effective political power), but had not managed to find a place on the ballot. During the 1920s, the stalwart champion of unicameralism was John N. Norton of Polk County, a state legislator and two-term congressman. Others shared his enthusiasm, most notably Senator George Norris and Professor John Senning, a political scientist at the University of Nebraska. In 1934, its advocates got more than enough signatures for an initiative petition to place the measure on the ballot as an amendment to the state constitution.

Why did unicameralism succeed in 1934? That year offered a convergence of circumstances favorable to its acceptance. Because of the drought and depression, people were willing to consider radically different solutions to their problems. Unicameralism promised to reduce state expenditures—the number of legislators would be cut from 133 to a figure between thirty and fifty. That meant fewer salaries to pay. Also, the bicameral legislators who had been elected in 1932, mostly inexperienced Democrats elected in the Roosevelt sweep, were singularly inept, and any change in the state's political arrangements seemed to assure an improvement. Moreover, some of the proponents of unicameralism linked the measure with two others on the ballot that would stimulate economic recovery: one to repeal the prohibition in the state constitution on the manufacture, distribution, and sale of alcoholic drink, and another that would legitimize parimutuel betting on horse racing. More significantly, Senator Norris was not running for reelection in 1934 and was free to campaign tirelessly for the unicameral amendment. Bringing his immense prestige to bear in favor of the measure may have been decisive.

Opposition to the unicameral amendment was keen. Professional politicians in particular were against it because the legislature was to be nonpartisan. Others argued that it threatened the balance of powers by centralizing too much political power in the hands of a few legislators. Still others predicted that without one house checking the power of the other, too many laws would be passed. But Senator Norris insisted that nonpartisan unicameralism was necessary in order to curb the power of the lobbyists and to bring the legislative process out of closed meetings of conference committees into the light of public scrutiny.

Nebraska voters strongly endorsed unicameralism. The amendment won a majority in eighty-four of the state's ninety-three counties, even though both major parties and most daily newspapers (except the *Lincoln Star* and the *Hastings Tribune*) opposed it. In accordance with the law, the legislature decided that the unicameral should have forty-three members to be chosen in the next general election.

In the half-century since then, the unicameral has proved its worth, even though it has failed to curb the power of special interests in the way Senator Norris argued it would. Furthermore, its nonpartisan character has weakened rather than strengthened popular democracy: party responsibility has disappeared even though partisanship continues in a disguised and enervated form. Attempts have been made periodically to remove the nonpartisan feature, but all have failed. Yet as some of its early critics feared, the unicameral has tended to enact more laws than most state legislatures. In 1963 the number of legislative districts was increased from forty-three to forty-nine to comply with the "one-man, one-vote" ruling by the U.S. Supreme Court.

43.1. Members of the first unicameral took their oaths of office in January 1937. Although voters approved the unicameral in the general election of 1934, they could not elect the members of the first unicameral until 1936. The first legislative session of the unicameral then convened in the following January. About three-fourths of the legislators had served earlier in one of the bicameral chambers. Senators served two-year terms until 1966, when terms were extended to four years. Courtesy NSHS MacDonald Collection, M134:1937-01-05:1.

43.2. This photograph captured the same moment as the previous picture. United States Senator George Norris, who had been crucially important in convincing Nebraska voters to adopt the unicameral legislature and was invited to attend the opening session as a guest, stands beneath the vote-recording machine on the left side. The most persistent criticism of the unicameral is its nonpartisan feature, which was originally added to the unicameral proposal in 1934 at the insistence of Senator NORRIS. COURTESY NSHS, C244:435a.

44 Public Power Comes to Nebraska

Of all the states in the nation, Nebraska is the only one served entirely by an electric power system that is publicly owned and operated. Public power came to Nebraska through the confluence of several factors, including favorable experiences with municipal hydroelectric power production in the 1920s, the drought and depression of the 1930s, and the desire of farmers to use irrigation to increase their income. Additionally, the federal government was ready to do what private enterprise was unwilling or unable to do. A final variable was the energy and imagination of Senator George Norris. His ability to win both popular and governmental support for public power was a crucial element in its adoption.

As has happened so often in Nebraska history, water and the Platte River were at the heart of the matter. Since the mid-1920s, Senator Norris had been promoting federal financing of irrigation and hydroelectric power, arguing that the profit motive would never bring electricity to the state's sparsely populated rural areas. In 1932, when the Great Depression was in full swing, Congress passed a law that permitted the Reconstruction Finance Corporation to loan funds to public groups for irrigation and hydroelectric projects. The next year, despite fierce opposition from private power companies that denounced the scheme as socialism, the Nebraska legislature authorized the formation of public power and irrigation districts as governmental agencies with power to borrow money backed by revenue bonds.

Soon Nebraskans formed public power districts in Columbus, North Platte, and Hastings, and by the end of the decade an interconnected complex of dams, canals, reservoirs, hydroelectric plants, and power lines spread across the state. In 1940 the three power-generating districts organized the Nebraska Public Power System to sell the power they generated.

The most dramatic of the hydroelectric/irrigation projects of the 1930s is Kingsley Dam, located on the North Platte River north of Ogalalla. Completed in 1942, it created Lake McConaughy, a leading recreational attraction in the state.

By the late thirties it became clear, that in order to rationalize the production and marketing of electric power in Nebraska, the system must buy out competing public utilities that were privately owned. In 1939, a Consumers Public Power authority that was independent of the power-generating districts was created for this purpose. During the next two years it bought out most of the remaining private power companies with finances made available by revenue bonds. The last step in converting Nebraska entirely to publicly owned power utilities came in 1946 when the newly organized Omaha Public Power District purchased the Nebraska Power Company, which served Omaha and nearby communities.

A series of rural public-power districts were formed to distribute electricity to the farms of the state. Here again Senator Norris's leadership was decisive. Only the federal government, he insisted, could provide the seed money for rural electrification systems. He argued that such units were essential to encourage farmers to stay in agriculture and prevent their migration to the cities, where they might end up on the relief rolls. In 1935, President Roosevelt issued an executive order to create the Rural Electrification Administration. Soon there were more than thirty rural public power districts in Nebraska, and by 1950 most of Nebraska's farms had electricity.

Since then, new demands have been made on the supply of electric power because of growth in industry and agriculture. The administrative distinction between power production and distribution, strictly adhered to in the 1930s, had become insignificant. In 1970 the Nebraska Public Power System merged with the Platte Valley and Consumers districts to form the Nebraska Public Power District. Important changes have also taken place in power sources. Although the proportion for each source varies considerably from year to year, hydroelectric plants supplied only about 5 percent of Nebraska's needs in 1990; conventional steam plants that burn fossil fuels (mostly coal from Wyoming) accounted for 60 percent. Two nuclear-powered steam plants, in operation since the mid-1970s, produce the remainder, which in 1990 was 35 percent.

The history of public power in Nebraska is enormously complicated. When the process started in 1932 no one dreamed of a statewide publicly-owned power system. Though its evolution has been marked by much controversy, it has provided electricity at low rates and has won the support of most Nebraskans.

44.1. The success of public power in Nebraska is partly due to the many power plants that municipal governments built early in the century. Some burned coal to generate electricity, and others, like this dam on the Blue River at Milford, harnessed water power. Such municipally owned plants were attractive to city governments because they could get cheap electricity to light the streets, city hall, schools, library, jails, and other city-owned buildings, and sell the rest to citizens at favorable rates. Courtesy NSHS, C746:1411.

44.2. The most dramatic of the combined hydroelectric and irrigation projects was Kingsley Dam, located on the North Platte River north of Ogallala. The second-largest earthen dam in the United States when completed in 1941, it is three miles long, 162 feet high, 1,100 feet wide at the bottom, and 28 feet wide at the top. The Morning Glory Spillway and outlet tower, shown here under construction, were built first to allow the river to flow through as construction progressed. Courtesy NSHS, K55:229.

44.3. Kingsley Dam creates Lake McConaughy, which is 22 miles long with a 105-mile shoreline. Now a leading recreational attraction in the state, the lake at full capacity impounds enough water to irrigate 131,000 acres downstream in Gosper, Phelps, and Kearney Counties. Water discharged through the control tower is capable of generating eight hundred thousand horsepower of electricity. The tremendous energy of the falling water is dissipated in the stilling basin below the dam. Courtesy NEBRASKAland Magazine/Nebraska Game and Parks Commission.

44.4. The Loup River public hydro-electric plant, built in 1937 in the rich farmland northeast of Columbus in Platte County, harnesses power from water stored in Lake Babcock. In 1990 it was the largest generator of hydro-electricity in the state, except for the U.S. Corps of Engineers facility at Gavins Point Dam on the Missouri River near Yankton, South Dakota. This photograph shows the plant as it appeared in 1950. Courtesy Loup Power District.

44.5. Steam created by nuclear energy is the source of electricity produced in this plant located near Fort Calhoun and in another near Brownville. Both are located on the banks of the Missouri River, which supplies the coolant water, and both are near the concentrations of population in the eastern quarter of the state where the demand is greatest. Courtesy Omaha Public Power District.

45 World War II in Nebraska

World War II brought Nebraska into an era in which attitudes and expectations became much like they are today. The immediate effects of the war were no different for most Nebraskans than they were for people in other states—rationing of gasoline, automobile tires, shoes, coffee, sugar, and meat; shortages of other goods; and coordinated drives to sell government war bonds and collect scrap metals, especially aluminum. And there was the draft—sons and brothers who went off to war, some never to return. Approximately 120,000 men and women from Nebraska served in the armed forces of the United States during World War II, and 3,839 lost their lives. As with all other states, the Nebraska National Guard was federalized.

Because Nebraska is an agricultural state, its greatest contribution to the war effort was in the production of food. Despite worn-out farm implements and a shortage of labor partly caused by the draft, crop production increased greatly during the war years.

Nebraska's role as the highway to the West was intensified in World War II. The Union Pacific railroad, with its transcontinental connections, shuttled enormous freight loads through the state. Hundreds of thousands of soldiers passed through Nebraska on lumbering troop trains as they were shifted from one assignment to another. Many soldiers and sailors remembered especially the gracious hospitality of the North Platte canteen—a place that acquired a nationwide reputation for food and friendliness for troops on their way to combat in the Pacific.

But the war affected the state in other important ways, too. It brought wartime industries, army airfields for the training of pilots, and prisoner-of-war camps. In each case, the midcontinental location of Nebraska, far from both the Atlantic and Pacific coasts, was deemed an advantage.

The direct impact of World War II began to be felt in December 1940, a year before the United States entered the war after the Japanese attack on Pearl Harbor. The Department of War announced that a bomber-assembly plant would be built on the Fort Crook military reservation near Bellevue. Soon hundreds of construction workers and thousands of factory workers moved into the area, though most commuted from Omaha and other nearby towns.

The creation of a series of army airfields stimulated other communities. Eleven bases, most for training pilots, bombardiers, and maintenance crews, were built in the state: Alliance, Ainsworth, Bruning, Fairmont, Grand Island, Harvard, Kearney, Lincoln, McCook, Scottsbluff, and Scribner. The Kearney base was especially important for an inspection procedure for airplanes and crews before proceeding overseas. In each case, construction workers and their families temporarily swelled the size of nearby towns, often doubling the population. Government officials also regarded Nebraska to be an excellent location for prisoner-of-war camps. Most were located in the western half of the state where the chances for escape were minimal. Main bases were at Scottsbluff, Fort Robinson, Atlanta, and Indianola, and each had branch camps at other nearby communities.

War-related activity stimulated local economies, and many Nebraska towns were eager for the infusion of federal funds. But the strain on local infrastructures was enormous. Adequate housing did not exist;

trailer courts had to be planned and regulated; fire and police protection was inadequate; and schools were jammed with the children of transient workers. In Alliance, for example, 5,000 construction workers descended on a city of less than 7,000 inhabitants. In Hastings, the population leaped from 15,000 in 1940 to 23,000 in 1943. But no community was transformed more profoundly than Bellevue, which in 1940 was a village of 1,184, lacking paved streets, adequate sewers, and street lighting. Today Bellevue, with a population nearing 40,000, is a major urban adjunct to the Omaha metropolitan area.

The social effects of war reached even further. As young men were called to service, the enrollments at Nebraska colleges and universities plummeted, and some schools barely survived. Manpower shortages were experienced everywhere, on farms and in cities. Wages and salaries spiraled; debts were paid off. War industries attracted workers from other states and cities. The population of African Americans, especially in Omaha, swelled as the war effort promoted equality of opportunity in jobs and social relations. At the same time, however, racial tensions continued, especially in housing. Other social relationships were also put to the test: families suffered from the loss of young men drafted into the armed forces; many hastily arranged marriages foundered; transient workers often felt less than welcome; and problems of drunkenness and prostitution afflicted some communities.

World War II also had its long-term consequences. The prosperity it engendered reinforced the state's political conservatism. It led Nebraskans, like other Americans, to expect a standard of living that had been impossible before the war. It stimulated farm production enormously, which meant a return of agricultural surpluses; government price supports would be necessary if the deprivation that accompanied the agricultural depression after World War I was to be avoided. It also meant that migration out of the agricultural counties could continue in the postwar era.

45.1. In 1940 these Nebraskans lined up to register for the draft in Omaha in accordance with the first peacetime conscription law in American history. Passed by Congress in September 1940, more than a year before the United States entered the war, the law created draft boards to register and call more than a million young men to service in the armed forces. Courtesy John Savage Collection, owned by Western Heritage Museum, Omaha.

45.2. The 134th Infantry Regiment, commanded by Lieutenant Colonel Butler Miltonberger of North Platte, originally consisted mostly of Nebraskans, though most of the regiment's replacements came from other states. In this image, soldiers of the second battalion ford a river near Nancy as they participate in the liberation of northern France in 1944. Twelve hours later this unit suffered 80 percent casualties. Courtesy NSHS, M662:5992.

45.3. Nebraska women helped alleviate the labor shortage during the war by working on farms and in high-paying jobs in war industries. Food production was Nebraska's greatest contribution to the war effort. In 1942 Congress amended the conscription law to allow the temporary deferment of essential agricultural workers. Courtesy NSHS MacDonald Collection, M134:1943-07-28:2.

45.4. Everyone was expected to help win the war. Here three Boy Scouts from Lincoln, varying widely in age and rank, pose for a patriotic photograph. They contributed to the war effort by collecting and sorting scrap metal to be processed for the manufacture of guns, tanks, and other war materiel. Courtesy NSHS MacDonald Collection, M134:1943-08-11:5.

45.5. Although many African Americans benefited from the war effort, racial discrimination did not disappear. The armed forces were still segregated, as was this United Service Organization (USO) club in Lincoln. A similar USO club for blacks was opened in Kearney. Wartime conditions encouraged President Roosevelt to issue an executive order forbidding racial discrimination on all federal defense projects and contracts, opening many new jobs to African Americans in Nebraska and across the nation. Courtesy NSHS MacDonald Collection, m134:1945-09-22:2.

45.6. Defense industries in Nebraska created thousands of jobs for women, who contributed mightily to the war effort. In this image, women work in the large ammunition manufacturing plant in Grand Island. Other ordnance plants were built in Mead and Hastings, and ammunition storage facilities were created near Sidney. War contracts also went to smaller manufacturing companies in various parts of the state. Courtesy NSHS, C817:7–45.

45.7. The U.S. Army created eleven air bases in Nebraska for training pilots and crews of fighters and bombers. The side of this hangar at the Scribner base was camouflaged with the outline of a barn and trees. The army regarded Nebraska as an ideal place to train fighter pilots and flight crews: the population was sparse, land was cheap, and wide-open spaces were available for gunnery and bombing practice. The army even liked Nebraska's weather, which presumably provided excellent year-round flying conditions. Courtesy NSHS, D645:6-6.

45.8. Here a group of German soldiers arrive at the prisoner-of-war camp at Fort Robinson. Altogether, about twelve thousand prisoners, mostly Germans, were held in Nebraska. At the end of the war in 1945, the Scottsbluff camp had the largest number with 3,294. Under the provisions of the Geneva Convention, the prisoners were allowed to work as field hands on nearby farms. Courtesy NSHS, T467:13.

45.9. In 1942 the U.S. Army established a dog-training center at Fort Robinson. Known as the K-9 Corps, the operation trained dogs for sentry, scout, and messenger duty. This image shows handlers feeding dogs after a heavy snowstorm. The installation included more than seventeen hundred kennels, set in rows with military precision. Soldiers training to be handlers lived in nearby barracks. Courtesy NSHS, R659:415.

45.10. Joy swept the country with the news of the war's end when the Japanese surrendered on 14 August 1945 (V-J Day). Here revelers dance and drink at 15th and Farnam Streets in Omaha to celebrate the end of the carnage. Courtesy John Savage Collection, owned by Western Heritage Museum, Omaha.

From Fort Crook to Strategic Air Command Headquarters   *46*

Among the legacies of World War II in Nebraska, the most permanent and far-reaching was the transformation of Fort Crook, located south of Omaha in Sarpy County, into what eventually became the headquarters of the Strategic Air Command (SAC) at Offutt Air Force Base.

The story begins with the development of military facilities in the Omaha area in the 1890s. Fort Omaha, established in 1868, was too cramped for further expansion, and the army decided to establish Fort Crook about ten miles south near Bellevue. After World War I, Fort Crook was designated as the headquarters of the Seventh Corps, and a small cadre of army pilots came to the installation. Their needs led in 1924 to the building (on land adjacent to Fort Crook) of Offutt Field, named for a pilot from Omaha killed in World War I.

The airfield continued, but in a nearly moribund state until December 1940, when the federal government announced that it was leasing all airport facilities at Fort Crook to the Glenn L. Martin Company to build a bomber assembly plant, three additional runways, and other necessary facilities. Construction proceeded immediately. Operations began in January 1942 and soon hundreds of B-26 Marauders rolled off the assembly lines. In 1944 the plant was retooled for the assembly of B-29 Superfortresses. At the height of production, the plant employed 14,572 workers, of whom about 5,000 were women. Production at the bomber plant ceased within a month following the Japanese surrender in August 1945.

In June 1946 Fort Crook was transferred to the Army Air Corps and served as a regional headquarters for reserve training operations. In January 1948 the facility was assigned to the newly formed U.S. Air Force and renamed as Offutt Air Force Base. Its continued existence, however, was by no means guaranteed. A new lease on life came later in 1948 when Secretary of the Air Force Stuart Symington, in response to powerful pressure applied by Nebraska's Senator Kenneth Wherry and Omaha businessman Arthur Storz, directed that the headquarters of the Strategic Air Command be transferred from Washington DC to Offutt Air Force Base, one of the few airfields far from the coasts with a runway capable of handling fully loaded B-29 bombers.

This decision was by no means universally applauded. Several top air force generals much preferred Colorado Springs to Omaha; among their objections was a lack of housing for air force personnel. More-over, the Omaha business community seemed reluctant to risk its financial resources on so large a building project unless assurances of the permanence of the facilities were forthcoming. Senator Wherry saved the day by sponsoring legislation to provide federal guarantees for the construction of more than 600 housing units. In 1951, after much negotiation, the living quarters were built and other construction undertaken.

Meanwhile a new underground SAC command post was built. Occupied in 1957 and expanded since then, this facility made Offutt AFB a major nerve center of American defense. Well protected in the middle of the continent, SAC headquarters was equipped to coordinate worldwide retaliation against a potential attack from the Soviet Union.

The impact of Offutt AFB and SAC headquarters on the state's economy has been incalculable. Millions of dollars were spent to build the facility, and the annual payroll of thousands of air force personnel and civilian employees has added hundreds of millions more. Each year huge sums have poured into the Nebraska economy through the payment of telephone, electricity, gas, and water bills, as well as through the purchase of equipment and supplies. Thousands of jobs have been created by local companies to serve the needs of those associated with SAC operations. Sarpy County is the third most populous county in the state and has the lowest median age. Douglas and Sarpy Counties have also been enriched by the many air force officers who retire from service and remain in the area. The University of Nebraska at Omaha benefited from thousands of air force personnel who have completed their collegiate education there.

In recent years Omaha has received an unexpected dividend from Offutt AFB. Partly because of SAC requirements, Omaha has a state-of-the-art, efficient communication system, enabling Omaha to become a national center for telephone marketing—one more step in the expansion of Omaha's economic base from industrial production, food processing, and transportation to include specialized services in commerce and communication.

In 1992 the U.S. Department of Defense reorganized its operations and ended SAC. Along with the Tactical Air Command and the Military Airlift Command, SAC was combined and restructured into two new organizations, the Air Combat Command and the Air Mobility Command. As a result, Offutt AFB lost its status as a major Air Force command headquarters, but a new joint command to oversee strategic planning was created there. The net result of these decisions, combined with an overall reduction in air force strength, reduced the number of military and civilian jobs at Offutt AFB by 20 percent—a $100 million reduction.

46.1. Ground was broken for the construction of the Glenn L. Martin bomber assembly plant near Bellevue in March 1941, nine months before the United States declared war on Japan and Germany. The plant was operational early in 1942, and the first B-26 rolled off the assembly line in June 1942. At peak production in 1945, the plant employed about 14,500 workers, of whom 5,300 were women. Official U.S. Air Force photograph.

46.2. In 1943 the Department of War selected the Martin-Nebraska plant as one of four to assemble the Boeing B-29 Superfortress. After extensive modifications in the plant, B-29 production began in April 1944. This image shows the first Superfortress near the end of a modification process. In June 1945 the plant produced the *Enola Gay*, which was selected to drop atomic bombs on Japan. The last bomber assembled in the Martin plant rolled off the line on 18 September 1945. Official U.S. Air Force photograph.

46.3. The nerve center of the Strategic Air Command Headquarters was this underground command post at Offutt Air Force Base, here much enlarged and remodeled from its original 1957 layout. SAC was responsible for the operations of bombers, intercontinental ballistic missiles, strategic reconnaissance aircraft, and airborne tankers that refueled other airplanes in flight. Official U.S. Air Force photograph.

46.4. This 1972 aerial view suggests the magnitude of the Offutt Air Force Base and its impact on the Bellevue area. The city of Bellevue lies northeast of the base, in the upper part of this image. By 1975 the payroll for the 12,800 military and civilian personnel at the base was about $200 million annually. In addition, the base poured about $15 million into the Nebraska economy each year for various supplies, utilities, and services. Official U.S. Air Force photograph.

46.5. This low-altitude aerial image suggests the size and complexity of the headquarters of the Strategic Air Command at Offutt Air Force Base. Shown here as it appeared soon after it was built, the headquarters building is located southwest of the main runway, which may be seen beyond the baseball diamonds in the distance. Official U.S. Air Force photograph.

Higher Education in the Postwar Decades, 1945–1970 47

World War II was both threat and salvation for colleges and universities in Nebraska during the 1940s and 1950s. In the early years of the war, the draft was devastating to enrollments, and some small colleges barely survived. At Dana College in Blair, for example, the enrollment fell to 72 students, mostly women. At the University of Nebraska regular enrollment dropped from 9,300 in 1939 to 5,400 students in 1943.

Some of Nebraska's colleges were quickly revived by government programs to train army and navy personnel. Peru State College, for example, trained several hundred naval cadets under the U.S. Navy's V-12 program. In Lincoln, the University of Nebraska contracted with the federal government to educate and train soldiers in several programs, including an Air Crew Training Detachment, a Special Training and Reassignment School, and an Army Specialized Training Program. Love Library and other buildings were temporarily converted into dormitories for the soldiers.

After the war most colleges and universities in Nebraska expanded. Facilities were strained beyond capacity in their efforts to educate veterans under the "GI Bill of Rights," which granted substantial subsidies to ex-servicemen who wished to get a higher education. By the fall semester of 1946 the University of Nebraska student body had mushroomed to thirteen thousand, nearly half of whom were ex-servicemen. By 1950 the war-induced boom had run its course in most Nebraska colleges, and enrollments declined to normal levels.

There was much rebuilding to be done. It was clear, for example, that the University of Nebraska has lost the position of eminence it had achieved early in the century. It had survived on a starvation diet during the 1930s, when institutional income (both state tax dollars and tuition) had been severely reduced. Faculty positions had been eliminated, salaries had been cut to the bone, and new building construction had virtually ceased.

In 1946 it was Nebraska's good fortune to attract Reuben Gustavson, a former president of the University of Colorado, to the chancellorship of the university. A distinguished scientist, Gustavson built popular support for the university and a broad program of service to the state. He won substantial increases in legislative appropriations and inaugurated a new era of construction. Gustavson's major achievements during his seven-year term were to revise curricula, recruit and retain high-quality faculty, and raise the level of scholarship during an enrollment boom.

Other universities and colleges in Nebraska faced similar tasks in the postwar years of accommodating enlarged student bodies in inadequate and deteriorating buildings. Enrollment almost doubled in 1945 at the Municipal University of Omaha, and the four state colleges showed similar patterns. Kearney State College, for example, increased from 425 full-time students in 1945 to 1,629 in 1949. Thereafter enrollments leveled off, but problems of upgrading physical plants remained.

The next period of growth in higher education came in Nebraska during the 1960s. At the University of Nebraska, full-time enrollment spiralled from 8,700 in 1960 to 19,600 at the end of the decade. Much of the growth was due to the "baby boom"—a population bulge consisting of people born in the immediate postwar period who were of college age in the 1960s. Federal programs enacted as part of President Lyndon

Johnson's "Great Society" made possible the construction of desperately needed dormitories, classroom buildings, and laboratories on most campuses.

Gustavson's successor as chancellor, Clifford Hardin, also provided strong leadership. Serving until 1969, he pushed the development of the university's television network, the UNL Center for Continuing Education, the University of Nebraska Press, and the extension of agricultural education in Turkey, Colombia, and Morocco. The Hardin era was also a time when more than two dozen new buildings were constructed or remodeled, including Sheldon Art Gallery, C. Y. Thompson Library, Behlen Laboratory, Hamilton and Oldfather Halls, and three dormitory complexes. Near the end of Hardin's tenure the state university was expanded to include the Municipal University of Omaha, which, renamed as the University of Nebraska at Omaha, subsequently experienced dramatic growth in the size of its student body, physical plant, and programs.

During the unpopular war in Vietnam, a large number of young men sought to avoid the draft by maintaining student status. Added to "baby boom" enrollments, they stimulated the creation of several new colleges in Nebraska that appealed to many out-of-state students: John Kennedy College in Wahoo, Pershing College in Beatrice, and Hiram Scott College in Scottsbluff. Each experienced a brief period of vitality; but soon after Congress ended the draft in 1973, these institutions had to close their doors.

During the late 1970s and the 1980s most Nebraska institutions of higher education, both public and private, have had stable enrollments and have sought to improve rather than expand their programs of teaching and service.

47.1. Hastily built temporary buildings crowded the University of Nebraska campus to accommodate new enrollments during the postwar boom. Burnett Hall, the new home for the College of Arts and Sciences, was under construction in August 1947 when this photograph was taken. Beyond it lies Avery Hall, Memorial Stadium, and Bessey Hall. Courtesy University of Nebraska–Lincoln Archives.

47.2. Acting President Kirk Naylor presided over ceremonies that brought the Municipal University of Omaha (MUO) into the University of Nebraska system on 30 June 1968. Dignitaries at the left are Governor Norbert Tiemann, Chairman of the MUO Board of Regents Robert Spire, and Chancellor Clifford Hardin of University of Nebraska–Lincoln. Courtesy University of Nebraska at Omaha.

47.3. Hiram Scott College was founded in 1965 on the northern outskirts of Scottsbluff. This aerial view of its new campus was taken soon after the college was acquired by the state of Nebraska in 1974. The two connected buildings on the west (left) became the headquarters of the University of Nebraska's Panhandle Research and Extension Center in 1974. The dormitory complex of four three-story buildings was subsequently razed; the former student center, which occupies the interior of the square, presently houses several state agencies. Courtesy University of Nebraska Panhandle Research and Extension Center, Scottsbluff.

48 Nebraska Agriculture in the Postwar World

The end of World War II introduced a new era in agriculture for Nebraska. The demands for agricultural production during the war had been extraordinary, and farmers, stimulated by war-induced prosperity, demonstrated that they could produce more food than ever before. After the war, however, farmers expected a depression, as the country had experienced after World War I; but none came, partly because agriculture had come to depend increasingly on decisions made by legislators and bureaucrats in Washington DC.

International affairs were crucial to this aspect of Nebraska's history. Immediately after the war, American fears of world domination by Germany and Japan shifted to fear of the Soviet Union and its satellite powers. Government leaders were convinced that people with empty stomachs found communist ideology alluring. Postwar relief efforts emphasized supplying food to war-ravaged populations, and Congress continued price supports for agricultural production. Similarly, the Marshall Plan provided an export subsidy on a grand scale for farm products. The Korean War, followed by threats of war in Lebanon,

Cuba, and elsewhere, stimulated demands for agricultural commodities and resulted in a particularly prosperous time for farmers, who had the ability to produce far more than could be consumed or distributed.

In the 1950s and 1960s, the federal government tried a variety of plans to reduce surpluses or take farmland out of production without hurting farmers or impairing their capacity to produce. These programs included both fixed and flexible price support systems, a soil bank scheme, the food stamp plan, hot lunch programs for schools, and generous donations of food to starving people overseas. Such strategies, however, also had the unintended result of stimulating new efficiencies in production. Higher production meant larger government subsidies and more rigorous attempts to control production.

Farm machinery improved spectacularly as work horses disappeared. Multiple-bottom plows and multiple-row drills for seeding were pulled by powerful tractors. By the 1960s Nebraska farmers were using self-propelled combines, hay balers, and combined cornpickers and shellers. At the same time farmers began to use (and soon became dependent upon) chemical fertilizers, insecticides, herbicides, and additives to animal feed, including synthetic growth hormones and antibiotics to fight disease. The number of animals lost to disease was cut in half during these years, and notable improvements were made in the varieties and hybrids of major grain crops.

The results of all this were astonishing. Corn production in Nebraska, which during the droughty years of the mid-1950s had dropped to an average of only about twenty bushels per acre, grew to ninety by the end of the 1960s. During the same years, the production of grain sorghums increased from twenty-five bushels per acre to seventy-three. Wheat production, which had its ups and downs during this period, about doubled. Cattle feeding became a major industry in Nebraska, as the number of fed cattle marketed for slaughter increased from about a million in the early 1950s to nearly four million in 1969.

The relentless impact of technology worked still other changes in postwar agriculture in Nebraska. The average size of farms and ranches increased by 48 percent (from 427 to 634 acres) between 1945 and 1969 as the number of farms decreased by 36 percent (from 112,000 in 1945 to 72,000 in 1969). The number of Nebraskans gainfully employed in agriculture dropped spectacularly, from 26 percent in 1960 to about 14 percent of the work force a decade later.

Out-migration from farm counties, especially those located some distance from the interstate highway and other arteries of transportation, continued. Young people, unable to find employment in rural areas, sought jobs in market centers such as Norfolk, Fremont, Grand Island, Kearney, and North Platte. Their exodus raised the average age of inhabitants of Nebraska's sparsely populated rural counties. These social and economic changes were the natural concomitant of improvements in agricultural technology.

48.1. Although Nebraska farmers had
been feeding cattle for the market for
many decades, the practice expanded
greatly after World War II. This 1948
image of feedyards on a farm in Wayne
County shows two herds (large heifers
on the left and steers on the right) being
finished for early marketing. A brome-
grass pasture appears in the background. Courtesy NSHS, s683:91-45.

48.2. Self-propelled combines became common in Nebraska's wheat fields in the postwar period. In this scene in northwestern Nebraska, four combines harvest wheat in tandem. The combine farthest to the left empties its harvest into a truck at its side. Such work is commonly done by harvesters who work the Great Plains from south to north as fields ripen through the summer months. Courtesy NSHS, F233:101.

48.3. The use of commercial fertilizers, especially anhydrous ammonia, in the place of manure became standard practice following World War II. By the 1960s tractors pulling tanks similar to the one pictured here were a familiar sight on Nebraska farms. Unfortunately this practice contributed to soil erosion and chemical contamination of soil and groundwater. Courtesy Institute of Agriculture and Natural Resources, University of Nebraska–Lincoln.

Interstate 80   *49*

Travel across the state from east to west has been a central element in Nebraska's history ever since the fur traders, trappers, and explorers followed the Platte River across the Great Plains to the Rocky Mountains 150 years ago. The Oregon Trail, the Union Pacific railroad, and the Lincoln Highway all emphasized the role of the Platte River valley as Nebraska's spinal cord and the major route to the West.

Today this role has been assumed by Interstate 80. Constructed mostly during the 1960s, this spectacular highway reinforces the historic relationship of Nebraska to the river for which the state is named. Interstate 80 reminds us that for thousands of travelers who use it every day, Nebraska remains a vast space to be crossed in order to get somewhere else.

Most towns situated along Interstate 80 prosper as they service the people in automobiles and trucks speeding east or west. The service stations, truck stops, restaurants, and motels that cluster around exits are collectively the modern equivalents of the road ranches that lined the Oregon Trail more than a century ago. Nebraska's cities and towns along the Interstate readily recognize this historical relationship. At North Platte travelers on the interstate notice the fake frontier fort that hugs the north side of the highway, and Ogallala advertises its cattle-town heritage by recreating various Front Street businesses.

The state government also recognizes the importance of the interstate. Excellent rest stops and recreation areas line the route. The promise of prosperity offered by servicing travelers also attracts Nebraskans displaced from less prosperous places in the state. Generally speaking, counties located on or near the interstate and the towns linked by it benefit from its presence and experience economic growth. At most exits, huge signs are thrust into the sky, beckoning travelers to stop and fill both their gas tanks and their stomachs, and fast-food restaurants and other businesses huddle around some exchanges and often line the highways to nearby towns.

The national interstate system was authorized by Congress in the 1950s, although the idea itself had emerged during World War II, partly as a matter of national defense. The general pattern of the national network was set by federal law, but precise locations were determined later by state highway departments. This led to many political controversies. In Nebraska debates raged about whether the route was to be on the north or south side of the Platte River and which cities were to be linked to the system. Because the law required state capitals to be included, Interstate 80 would have to deviate from the Platte as it cut southwest from Omaha to Lincoln. Similarly, the route leaves the river at Big Springs as it heads west through the Panhandle to Cheyenne, the capital of Wyoming.

Construction began long before all questions of routes and exchanges were resolved. The first segment of Interstate 80, which connects Lincoln and Omaha, was opened in 1961, and the system was not completed in Nebraska until 1974. Since then many communities have experienced its impact, which generally relates to the size of the traffic flow. Traffic is heaviest in Douglas County at the eastern end and lightest in the sparsely populated Panhandle.

49.1. This portion of Interstate 80 between York and Grand Island was under construction in the early 1960s. Although the federal government assumed 90 percent of the construction costs, sparsely populated Nebraska had difficulty paying its share. In 1968 the voters amended the constitution to allow the legislature to authorize bonds for highway construction backed by motor vehicle license fees and gasoline taxes. Courtesy Nebraska Department of Roads.

49.2. This aerial view of the interchange near downtown Omaha suggests the extent of urban space taken over by the interstate. Construction was still incomplete when this photograph was taken in the early 1960s. The Missouri River and Council Bluffs, Iowa, are in the distance. Courtesy Nebraska Department of Roads.

49.3. From Omaha in the east to Kimball in the west, Interstate 80 has had a profound impact on the economy and internal geography of nearby cities and towns. This view, photographed when construction was completed in 1961, looks northeast toward Omaha; state highway 370 crosses from west to east. Since 1961, commercial developments have transformed the area. Such configurations of exits, overpasses, and access roads may have inspired the sculpture in the next illustration. Courtesy Nebraska Department of Roads.

49.4. Hans van de Bovenkamp, *Roadway Confluence*. Eight rest stops along Nebraska's Interstate 80 are enhanced by sculptures erected in commemoration of the nation's bicentennial in 1976. *Roadway Confluence* occupies a prominence in the westbound rest area near Sidney. The sculpture project, funded mostly by private contributions with some help from the federal government, provoked much controversy within the state. But nationally, Nebraska's imaginative and enduring memorial to American independence has attracted much favorable publicity. Courtesy Nebraska Department of Roads.

49.5. At the Milford exit, a businessman seeks to attract customers to his gasoline station by converting his building into a huge replica of a covered wagon, thereby exploiting the historic relationship between the interstate highway and the Oregon Trail. Photograph by author.

50 The Tiemann Legacy

The 1960s was a decade of strong gubernatorial leadership in Nebraska. Democrat Frank Morrison, first elected in 1960, served three two-year terms. He provided leadership for many changes in state government, including the appointment rather than the election of state judges, the introduction of a retirement program for state employees, and the creation of the Nebraska Educational Television network, the Governor's Commission on the Status of Women, the Nebraska Arts Council, and an Advisory Commission on Aging.

In 1967, Nebraska's centennial year, Morrison was succeeded by Norbert Tiemann, a small-town banker and president of the Nebraska Bankers Association, who effectively used the powers of his office to cope with problems of taxation and state aid to public school districts. Tiemann, as someone declared with colorful exaggeration, dragged this state "kicking and screaming into the twentieth century."

This remark alluded to the serious taxation problems that beset the state by the 1960s. Throughout its history, Nebraska had depended on property taxes as the main source of revenue, an appropriate arrangement for a society that was overwhelmingly rural and agricultural. But by the time Nebraska entered its second century, land-owning farmers had become a small minority of gainfully employed persons and a majority of citizens lived in cities. In 1966 the problem became a crisis. In the general election of that year, voters repealed an income tax law passed the previous year and prohibited the state government from levying property taxes, restricting those levies to local units such as counties, cities, and school districts. State government was thus deprived of about two-thirds of the revenue it needed to provide the services citizens expected of it. The voters had created a circumstance in which the tax problem and resulting government deficits had to be confronted.

Norbert Tiemann provided the necessary leadership. A Republican with limited experience in politics and government, Tiemann led the legislature to enact a new revenue bill that balanced an income tax with a sales tax and also to repeal several outmoded taxes on persons, household goods, and intangible property. Inequities were resolved and the tax burden was redistributed among all areas of the state and classes of people.

This sales and income tax package was the keystone of a legislative arch that included many other reforms. Most importantly, it made possible state aid to school districts in desperate need of financial assistance. Other legislation brought the Municipal University of Omaha into the University of Nebraska system. The centennial legislature also established a department of economic development and a state personnel office, passed the state's first minimum wage act and the first fair housing act, and paved the way for bonded indebtedness for the construction of highways and sewage treatment plants. Still other laws provided for the improvement of state mental health facilities.

This impressive record of legislative accomplishment was the product of many forces, unique circumstances, and strong personalities. Powerful and gifted leaders in the legislature worked long and hard for reforms in education, social welfare, and economic development. Governor Tiemann took unprecedented risks: he was the first governor elected to a four-year term, giving him two additional years of insulation from the vote-generating wrath of his opposition. During Tiemann's term, the legislature still met biennially instead of annually, allowing fewer opportunities, compared to now, for his opponents to generate negative publicity.

Tiemann paid the price of dynamic leadership when he ran for re-election in 1970. Among his opponents were powerful guardians of tradition within his own Republican party. His place was taken by James Exon, a conservative Democrat who served two terms as governor before his election to the U.S. Senate in 1978.

50.1. Norbert Tiemann was sworn into office as governor by State Supreme Court Chief Justice Paul White on 5 January 1967. A native of Minden and a graduate of the University of Nebraska, Tiemann had been president of a family-owned bank in Wausa before running for governor. Courtesy Lincoln Journal-Star Printing Company.

50.2. Nebraska celebrated its centennial as a state on 1 March 1967 with a birthday cake in the Capitol Rotunda. Here Governor Tiemann, surrounded by various dignitaries and aides, cuts the cake with a sword that had belonged to General Robert W. Furnas, the third governor of the state. Courtesy NSHS, T563.5:4.

50.3. Governor Tiemann addresses participants in the dedication of the Nebraska State Capitol on 6 July 1967 as part of the state's centennial ceremonies. Because the building had been in use for several years before its completion in 1932, Nebraskans did not schedule formal dedication ceremonies at that time. Courtesy NSHS Archives, RG1:5639–Box 54.

African-American Unrest in Omaha *51*

While Governor Norbert Tiemann and the centennial legislature coped with changes in the state's services and tax structure, Omaha struggled with the intractable and threatening inequalities endured by blacks in American society.

The late 1960s were a turbulent time for the United States. Society was in ferment and violence was in the air as the undeclared war in Vietnam assumed astonishing proportions and the assassination of political leaders was appallingly common. Riots in American cities led to arson and looting as some black leaders, impatient with the slow pace of improvement in their social, political, and economic status, used confrontation and violence to express their discontent and rage.

To the surprise of many of its citizens, Omaha experienced urban disturbances in the 1960s. More than 80 percent of Nebraska's African Americans lived in Omaha, more than 90 percent of these in a ghetto called the Near North Side, a district centered on North 24th and Lake Streets. Though segregation was not supported by law, it remained a fact of life for virtually all of Omaha's black minority, which numbered more than thirty thousand. Unemployment among African Americans was about ten times higher than the state's average, and race relations were soured by long-standing animosity between many blacks and the mostly white Omaha police force.

Leadership in the African-American community was divided. Older conservatives such as state senator Edward Danner, a Democrat who rose through the ranks of the packing-house union and whose district encompassed the Near North Side, were regarded as weak and ineffective by many of the younger, more radical leaders such as Ernest Chambers. Other traditional leaders, especially clergymen, sought to retain their status through more moderate or accommodating strategies.

Racial strife first struck Omaha in 1966, several months before Norbert Tiemann was elected governor. For three hot and humid days early in July young African-Americans gathered nightly at 24th and Lake Streets. Each night the police tried to disperse the crowds, but they succeeded only after their cruisers were pelted with bottles and rocks, store windows smashed, and businesses looted. Three weeks later another wave of violence and looting swept the Near North Side, this time intensified by vandalism and the fire-bombing of several businesses. Compared to Chicago and other American cities in 1966, Omaha's urban riots were mild: no deaths, only a few people injured, and less than a million dollars in property damage.

The state and city governments tried to respond positively to the crisis. Special efforts were made to find employment for young blacks and new recreational facilities were established. Mayor A. V. Sorensen, responsive to charges that he had not consulted African-American leaders when he had called for the intervention of the National Guard, involved blacks in the maintenance of order and brought business and labor leaders of both races into the process of planning for the welfare of the community. Many African-American leaders in the city did much to reduce tension and to control rebellious young people, and the Omaha police department sought to promote sensitivity among its officers in their contacts with racial minorities.

Unfortunately, the 1966 disturbances were not the last to afflict Omaha. Although the next year was quiet except for one brief outburst, 1968 witnessed several eruptions of violence. The most significant occurred in March 1968 when George Wallace appeared in Omaha in his campaign for the presidency on a platform with racist implications. In April and July other incidents led to more looting and vandalism, though none were in reaction to the assassinations of Martin Luther King Jr. and Robert Kennedy. But the introduction of sniper fire at 24th and Lake Streets represented an escalation in violence. Moderates on both sides found it increasingly difficult to negotiate solutions to the problems of the urban poor.

The last of the Omaha riots occurred in 1969, when a fourteen-year-old African-American girl was shot and killed by a police officer. Three nights of violence and fire devastated the Near North Side. As in the earlier disturbances, local teenagers were much in evidence, but newspaper accounts also stress the influence of militants who, according to local black leaders, came from outside the state. Property damage, looting, and fire-bombing were more extensive than in 1966. About twenty businesses were damaged or destroyed and an equal number vandalized or looted.

The consequences of black protest in Omaha are not easily assessed. Five years of sporadic violence revealed the disparities in wealth and status that separate African Americans from other Americans. Mayor Sorensen made new efforts to improve communications and solve problems. In 1969 the Nebraska legislature enacted a civil rights code that forbade discrimination in employment and housing transactions and also created an equal opportunities commission.

But the accelerated flow of government money into blighted American cities did little to relieve the misery of the urban poor. White flight from the urban core was stimulated; white ethnic neighborhoods lost much of their flavor. Schools were profoundly affected by racial unrest, usually in undesirable ways, but Omaha adapted relatively well to busing as a way to integrate the schools. Although private antipathies among some people, both black and white, were intensified by the years of protest, public discourse on black problems improved. The majority of Nebraskans seemed to accept a new measure of respect and responsibility for minority rights, even though the problems of urban blacks continued as intractable as ever.

51.1. In response to a request by Omaha Mayor A. V. Sorensen in July 1966, the Nebraska National Guard established a temporary command post in a fire station at 22nd and Lake Streets. On 5 July at about 1:40 A.M., soldiers with bayonets fixed to unloaded guns formed a wedge and moved down 24th Street, as shown in this photograph. This action, accompanied by the cooling effect of a thunderstorm, quelled the violence and looting. Courtesy Omaha World-Herald Company.

51.2. Incidents of firebombing and window smashing were frequent in a ten-block stretch of North 24th Street on 25 June 1969. Police escorted firemen as they fought blazes such as this one that destroyed a grocery and a shoe repair shop at 24th and Clark Streets. The next night other stores were bombed and looted, including one on 30th Street. Courtesy Omaha World-Herald Company.

51.3. Efforts of local black leaders and officials of the National Association for the Advancement of Colored People to quiet young African Americans were weakened by the appearance of five armed men from California who claimed to be members of the Black Panther Party, shown here leaving police headquarters in Omaha on 25 June 1969. Their appearance intensified intransigence among both black radicals and white reactionaries. Courtesy Omaha World-Herald Company.

Change in Contemporary Nebraska, 1970–1995

Part 5

People have lived in that small part of our continent we call Nebraska for many thousands of years, but as a political entity that occupies a defined space, Nebraska has existed only since 1854. Since then, in less than a century and a half, the human impact on this place has been astounding.

The effects of human habitation are everywhere apparent. They are especially obvious to an observer in an airplane cruising at an elevation of several thousand feet, or perhaps from the viewpoint of a satellite above the globe. As we look down, the landscape often appears to be a pattern of rectangles—cultivated fields separated by lanes and fences. Section roads delineate every mile of space, north, south, east and west, with the regularity of a checkerboard. In eastern Nebraska, Omaha or Lincoln sprawl below us. We quickly pass over towns and villages not easily identified even though they are connected by ribbons of concrete. The interstate, visible even from a satellite high in the sky, runs the length of the state. Lake Mc-Conaughy and other reservoirs have been imposed on the Nebraska landscape, and even the Sand Hills, where the population density is often less than one person per square mile, show evidence of what our society has done.

Our advanced technology affects much else as well. Today life on an isolated farm or ranch is not much different from life in the cities: homes are equipped with electricity, running water, indoor plumbing, and central heating and cooling; telephones allow instant communication; radio and television provide information and entertainment; automobiles and airplanes annihilate distance; and computers are put to many different uses. Technology makes it possible for us to transcend the limits imposed by our Great Plains environment.

Gradually the distinctive traits of people who have emigrated to this place have been modified and blended into a composite culture. Ethnic variation has diminished, not at a uniform rate and not always happily. Today the descendants of European immigrants must be taught about their heritage—it is not in their bones—and English has long since replaced the ancestral tongues. Education has encouraged social interaction between ethnocultural groups, and intermarriage has become common, at least partly because ethnic differences are no longer easily discerned. All combine to blur cultural distinctions.

Thus Nebraska, like its neighboring states, is gradually losing its unique character. American culture, at least in Nebraska, has become increasingly homogenized, despite concerted efforts at cultural maintenance among some racial and ethnic groups. Of course, this is not a new trend; such social processes have been underway since Nebraska was created. In recent decades, however, technology has accelerated change.

If we Nebraskans wish to understand ourselves, we must have some comprehension of our trajectory through time. Like a bullet fired through space, whose direction is modified by wind, air friction, and gravity, a culture passes through time, its course modified by social, economic, and environmental variables. To have any sense of where we are going, we must know where we have been. In this final chapter, we follow the trajectories of agriculture, economics, and population shifts in Nebraska, and monitor their interaction with politics, education, leisure, and our quality of life.

The impact of human occupation on the land is striking when Nebraska is viewed from satellites high in the sky. Depending on their distance from the earth, satellites permit photography that reveals on a grand scale urban sprawl, man-made reservoirs, and Interstate 80, as well as changes in vegetation and land use. That such photographs can be taken at all reminds us of how deeply contemporary life has been conditioned by technology and how vulnerable our plains environment is to human manipulation. Courtesy Visual Image Presentations.

Agriculture in Contemporary Nebraska *52*

Today, Nebraskans debate the relative importance of agriculture in the economy of the state. Some observers point out that the number of farmers and ranchers in Nebraska has steadily decreased from 10 percent of the state's total work force in 1970 to about 6 percent in 1990 and emphasize that in the 1980s farm income never exceeded 10 percent of all personal income earned in the state. Others insist that agriculture remains basic to the state's economy and that much of the nonfarm income derives directly from agriculture. Both are right. Production agriculture is less important than it once was, but when related service, processing, marketing, and transportation industries are accounted for, agriculture continues to be basic to the state's economy.

During the past quarter century, Nebraska's agricultural producers have experienced the best and worst of times. During the 1970s they prospered as never before, partly due to the expansion of center-pivot irrigation. This electricity-powered system, which consumes enormous quantities of water pumped from the ground, sprinkles circular fields from self-propelled rigs a quarter-mile in length, like gigantic minute-hands on clocks. Other technological improvements, aided by a generous federal farm policy designed to bolster farm income, stimulated huge increases in production, much of which was absorbed by foreign markets. At the same time, however, high inflation and favorable interest rates encouraged Nebraska farmers and stockmen to assume heavy debts, and federal tax laws encouraged investment in the livestock industry by outside investors. Often encouraged by their bankers and other lenders, farmers and ranchers bought new machinery and enlarged their acreages, even though land prices were seriously inflated at the time.

The bubble burst early in the 1980s when the Reagan administration brought inflation under control. Interest rates went up; land values dropped and the volume of agricultural exports shrank. More than one-third of Nebraska's farmers found themselves in financial distress. Bankruptcies increased and the flight from the farm was stimulated, causing reverberations throughout the state's economy. Many small-town businesses, dependent on agricultural prosperity, were forced to close. Nebraska's rate for bank failures was one of the highest in the nation. Many producers found that they could not pay their property taxes, as delinquency increased nearly 400 percent between 1980 and 1985.

Thousands of Nebraska's farmers discontinued operations, while others decided they could remain in business only by expanding the size of their operations. In 1970 there were about seventy-three thousand farms in the state; by 1992 the number had dropped by 23 percent to fifty-six thousand. The flight from the farm became a stampede in the 1980s, especially in the western half of the state, where in some counties, such as Keith, Perkins, and Chase, the farm population decreased by more than half. Other farmers continued to live on their land but sought employment, either full- or part-time, in nearby towns. Although the amount of land in farms has decreased only slightly since 1970, the average size of farms has increased greatly. In 1970, Nebraska farms averaged 659 acres; by 1992 they had increased by 28 percent to an average of 841 acres.

Nebraska remains one of the leading agricultural states in the nation.

In terms of income from both crops and livestock in 1992, Nebraska ranked fourth, behind California, Texas, and Iowa. Production of corn, its leading crop, ranked third nationally behind Iowa and Illinois. In cattle production Nebraska was second only to Texas; in commercial cattle slaughter Nebraska ranked first.

Farming as practiced in Nebraska during the past several years will continue to change as government support programs decline. In their efforts to adjust, some farmers have experimented with new crops and new patterns of crop rotation, while others, concerned for the state of the environment, have emphasized the need to reduce the use of chemical fertilizers, herbicides, and pesticides.

52.1 Rarely does one drive more than a few miles in rural Nebraska without encountering an abandoned farmstead, such as this one photographed by Robert Kay. Saturated with memories of family life but too expensive to repair or remove, these bleak, useless structures slowly deteriorate in the Nebraska sun, wind, and rain. They offer eloquent testimony to dramatic technological and social change. Courtesy NSHS, 90/2/1:12.

52.2. The use of center-pivot irrigation systems spread gradually after they were invented by Frank Zybach, a Nebraska native, in 1949. But the number of installations rose dramatically from about three thousand in 1972 to fifteen thousand in 1977, partly in response to increases in corn prices and low rainfall. Fully automatic and very expensive, the systems use about one-tenth the labor required by gravity-feed irrigation. This Washington County system was photographed in 1971. Courtesy NSHS, F233:127.

52.3. As this 1973 infra-red image of Imperial (Chase County) suggests, center-pivot irrigation systems transformed much of the Nebraska landscape with spectacular geometric patterns. Center pivots also fostered the cultivation of light rangeland soils, the mining of underground water resources, the removal of wooded shelter belts, and the gouging of circular arcs into woodland borders. Photograph by Les Sheffield. Courtesy University of Nebraska–Lincoln Conservation and Survey Division.

52.4. Concern for "sustainable agriculture" has led to significant changes in farming methods in recent years. In this photograph by Elbert Dickey, a farmer in Platte County plants soybeans directly into corn stubble without tilling the field first. This practice saves time, reduces energy costs, conserves moisture, and brings fewer weed seeds to the surface where they would compete with the soybean crop. Courtesy University of Nebraska–Lincoln Cooperative Extension Administration.

52.5. In Hamilton County near Aurora, where this photograph was taken, irrigated cornfields stretch to the horizon in all directions. Stalks are uniformly between six and seven feet high; ears appear at a height convenient for corn harvesting machinery. Hamilton County is second only to Dawson County in the number of acres under irrigation, mostly in corn. Corn remains Nebraska's most important crop, as it has for more than a century, validating Nebraska's nickname, the Cornhusker State. Photograph by author.

Nebraska's Changing Economy *53*

Changes in agriculture during the past quarter century have had profound implications for Nebraska's economy. Although the value of agricultural goods produced in the state dropped nearly 5 percent during the late 1980s, agriculture still accounts for approximately 40 percent of the wealth produced in the state. Moreover, about 60 percent of the manufacturing in Nebraska is directly related to agriculture.

Of Nebraska's industries that are based directly on agriculture, meat packing is the most important. By 1970 the great stockyards and meat-packing plants in Chicago and Omaha were technologically obsolete and were replaced by new packing plants in small cities in Iowa, Kansas, and Nebraska. With this decentralization, animals could be transported for slaughter by truck over short distances instead of by railroad over long distances. Beginning in the 1970s, several large new beef and hog processing plants were created in Nebraska towns, including Grand Island, Dakota City, West Point, Madison, Schuyler, and Lexington.

By the end of the 1980s, more than one hundred meat processing plants in Nebraska slaughtered twelve million cattle, hogs, and sheep per year and employed nearly ten thousand workers. Relocation in small-town Nebraska has been attractive to large meat-packing companies because it offers a way to reduce labor costs. Rarely unionized, the work force in these plants often includes a high proportion of Hispanic and Southeast Asian people. The integration of people with different languages and customs into small-town life has been difficult for some communities. Housing problems have been severe and schools have strained to accommodate new and often temporary students from different cultures. But most towns have eagerly welcomed the new plants and their workers, recognizing that they promise a new measure of prosperity.

Relocation of meat-packing plants has also stimulated the proliferation of small and medium-sized cattle feedlots in Nebraska. Such operations, which feed fewer than ten thousand head each, are encouraged by state laws against corporate farming and are largely financed by individuals and partnerships already in the livestock business rather than by corporations and limited partnerships, as has been the case in states where huge feed lots are more common.

At the same time, many Nebraskans have been searching for ways to diversify the economy and decrease the state's dependence on agriculture. Some Nebraska communities used telecommunication and computer technologies, which transcend limitations imposed by the vast spaces of the plains, to develop telemarketing businesses. Considerable growth has also occurred in service industries, especially in health care, transportation, travel, and tourism. Although Nebraska is rarely regarded as a vacation spot, tourism presently ranks behind agriculture and manufacturing as the third largest generator of revenue from outside the state. Similarly, the insurance industry, which has been big business in Omaha and Lincoln for many years, has continued to grow. More than thirty insurance companies have their headquarters in Nebraska.

53.1. In 1989 Iowa Beef Processors bought this large structure in Lexington, originally built for the manufacture of farm equipment, and converted it into a meat-packing plant. Located close to many cattle feeding operations in the Platte River valley, it also has the advantage of an ample supply of water. Unemployment virtually disappeared in the Lexington area after the plant opened and business activity has been stimulated. Courtesy Iowa Beef Processors.

53.2. Providing retirement homes for senior citizens and caring for people suffering from the disabilities of old age have become important economic activities in many Nebraska towns. This home, located in Crete, specializes in the care of those afflicted with Alzheimer's disease. Photograph by author.

53.3. Although Mutual of Omaha, because of its nationwide advertising, is the best-known insurance company in Nebraska, there are more than thirty other companies headquartered in the state that provide life, health, accident, and property insurance. Together they constitute an important and growing sector of the Nebraska economy. With approximately six thousand employees, Mutual of Omaha is the largest private employer in the state. Courtesy Mutual of Omaha.

Changes in Nebraska's Population *54*

Changes in Nebraska's population are among the most important developments in the history of the state and create some of the thorniest problems that legislators must resolve.

Nebraska's total population has shown little growth during the last quarter century, hovering at about 1.5 million and increasing to 1.6 million in 1992. The number of births normally exceeds deaths, but more people move out of the state than in. Population changes within the state are even more important, as many Nebraskans leave rural areas and small towns for cities where they can find jobs. Data from the 1990 census show that eighty-three of Nebraska's ninety-three counties declined in population during the 1980s. Half lost 10 percent or more, and four lost 20 percent or more. The least-populated counties often register the highest rates of out-migration.

The eastward tilt of Nebraska's population is now so strong that about 60 percent of the population lives within 60 miles of the Missouri River between Dakota City and Falls City. Census data reveal that the metropolitan areas of Omaha (Douglas, Sarpy, and Washington

Counties) and Lincoln (Lancaster County) have experienced the greatest growth. In 1990 these four counties accounted for 47 percent of the state's population. Farther west, Kearney registered a significant increase, though Norfolk, Columbus, and Grand Island were not far behind. Population studies also show that among age groups, outmigration is greatest between the ages of twenty-five and forty-four, especially among people at the highest education levels and people who own their own businesses.

In 1990 the median age of Nebraska's population was 33, a sharp increase over 29.7 in 1980. But many of the elderly also migrate out of the state, often to less rigorous climates in the South and West. Those who leave are usually most able to afford it, while the elderly who are most economically dependent tend to stay.

Even location on Interstate Highway 80 or near the Platte River and its branches proved no guarantee that a community would sustain at least modest growth, as western cities on these arteries, such as North Platte, Ogalalla, Sidney, and Kimball, lost population in the 1980s.

In the 1990s, however, the population movement began to reverse as technological change blunted distinctions between towns and cities. Recent census data suggest that many counties whose population dwindled in the 1980s are now either growing or have stabilized. This trend has been stimulated by the use of fiber-optic cable, a central element in the telecommunications revolution. More than six thousand miles of cable have been laid in Nebraska, linking all but five county seats to the national network. Advanced communications technology has helped small towns to attract new jobs, improve health services, and expand educational opportunities.

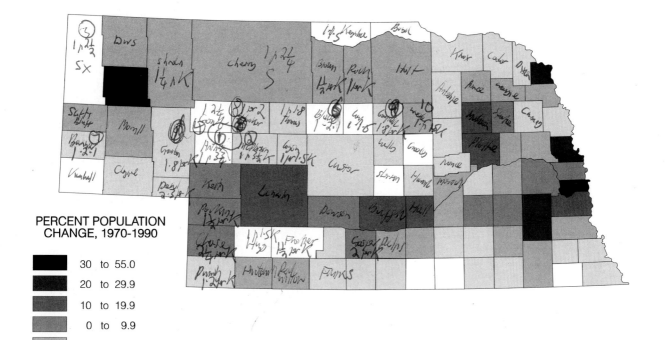

PERCENT POPULATION
CHANGE, 1970-1990

■	30 to 55.0
■	20 to 29.9
■	10 to 19.9
■	0 to 9.9
■	-10 to 0.1
■	-20 to -10.1
□	-32 to -20.1

54.1. This map suggests the extent of population loss in rural areas from 1970 to 1990 as revealed by census data. The greatest growth has occurred along the Missouri and Platte Rivers and Interstate 80. Growth in Box Butte County in the Panhandle is explained by the expansion of railroad yards in Alliance to transport coal from Wyoming. Generally, the most severe losses were registered by rural counties in the western half of the state (especially in the Panhandle and in or near the Sand Hills), but a few eastern counties, especially ones with poor soil, also lost population. Map by The Map Press, Lincoln.

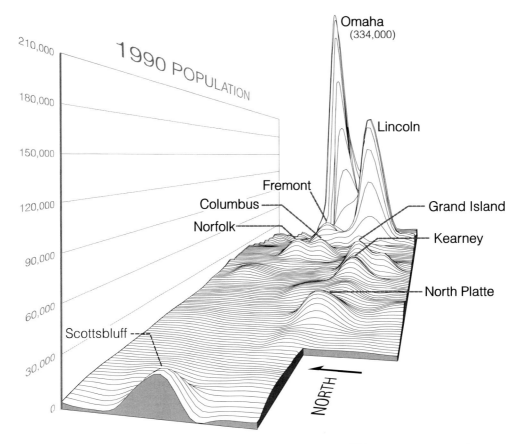

210,000

180,000

1990 POPULATION

150,000

120,000

90,000

60,000

30,000

0

Omaha
(334,000)

Lincoln

Fremont

Columbus

Grand Island

Norfolk

Kearney

North Platte

Scottsbluff

NORTH

54.2. This computer-generated map suggests how Nebraska's population is concentrated in the east. The view is from the west, with Scottsbluff represented at the left. North Platte, Kearney, Grand Island, Columbus, and Norfolk are easily identified. The two population peaks represent the Omaha and Lincoln metropolitan areas, which together contain nearly half the population of the state. Map by The Map Press, Lincoln.

Education in a Technological Era 55

Nebraskans have always considered public education to be essential to the state's development. Schools and the taxes levied to support them have been central issues in public debate since territorial days, and it is no different today. If anything, the pace of technological change has intensified the need for good schools and the cost of having them.

Before automobiles became common, one-teacher elementary schools were needed to serve a rural population. State law in the nineteenth century encouraged the creation of tiny school districts. But by the early 1990s they had dwindled in number to about eight hundred—a small fraction of the nearly 6800 in existence in 1950. Still, Nebraska has clung more tenaciously to tiny rural schools than any state in the union. Iowa, with twice Nebraska's inhabitants, has fewer than half the school districts. Nebraska's neighboring states have all consolidated at a more rapid rate.

As population declines in rural Nebraska, the tax base narrows. At the same time, administration has grown more complex and educational equipment and supplies more costly. But when small towns contemplate school consolidation, citizens complain about the inconvenience and expense of busing and worry about the impact of school closings on local economies.

Nebraskans thus have been reluctant to come to grips with educational problems, especially as they relate to taxes. In 1967 Governor Norbert Tiemann and the legislature confronted them by reorganizing the state's tax structure and introducing substantial state aid to local school districts. But thereafter matters were allowed to slide. By the end of the 1980s Nebraska once again was nearly at the bottom in state financial aid to local schools (26 percent compared to a national average of 54 percent). Conversely, Nebraska was among the highest in terms of local tax monies spent on local schools (70 percent compared to a national average of 44 percent). Not surprisingly, teachers' salaries were also far below the national norm.

In 1990 the unicameral courageously attacked the problem of public school financing. By overriding a gubernatorial veto, it enacted a measure to increase sales and state income taxes and dedicate increased receipts to equalize per pupil spending in the state. In this way the legislature sought to make it easier for poor school districts to improve the quality of education without raising local property taxes.

Problems of excellence, cost effectiveness, and taxation have also beset colleges and universities in the state. Nebraska's system of public universities and colleges came under special scrutiny as the costs of higher education spiralled in the 1980s and the need for an overall plan became obvious. The legislature placed on the ballot a constitutional amendment for the creation of an agency to coordinate planning, programs, budgets, and capital construction for the University of Nebraska system, the state colleges, and the community technical colleges. After approval in the general election of 1990, the new Coordinating Commission for Post-Secondary Education, whose members are appointed by the governor and approved by the unicameral, assumed its duties on 1 January 1992. Among its major decisions in 1993 was to approve a doctoral program in criminal justice at the University of Nebraska at Omaha.

55.1. The abandoned Bookwalter School in Pawnee County is representative of thousands of one-teacher schools that in a preautomobile era were maintained by rural school districts. Today most such schools and school districts have been consolidated. For example, the ninety-four districts in York County in 1950 have been reduced to six today. Photograph by David Murphy. Courtesy NSHS, 8003/6:10.

55.2. Children learn to use computers and word processors as part of the curriculum at Kahoa Elementary School in Lincoln. Buying and maintaining such instructional equipment has contributed to the spiraling costs of education. Many school districts are unable to offer computer education without state aid. Photograph by Jodie Fawl. Courtesy Lincoln Public Schools.

55.3. By 1990, Kearney State College, by far the largest of the state colleges, was eager to become a campus of the state's university system. This was accomplished on 1 July 1991 when it became the University of Nebraska at Kearney, with more than nine thousand students organized into five colleges. Courtesy University of Nebraska at Kearney.

55.4. Ground was broken in 1992 for the George W. Beadle Center for Genetics and Biomaterials Research at the University of Nebraska–Lincoln, shown here under construction in 1994. Named for a Nobel Prize–winning scientist and president of the University of Chicago who was born in Wahoo, the center will house laboratories for research and development in biotechnology. Most of the construction costs of this $31 million facility were covered by federal grants. Photograph by David Ochsner. Courtesy University of Nebraska–Lincoln Office of Public Relations.

56 Minorities in Contemporary Nebraska

Nebraska's population has always included ethnic and racial minority groups. In the early decades, relationships with various Indian peoples were most important. Feared and misunderstood by the dominant white population, the Indians were forced onto reservations, mostly in South Dakota and Oklahoma, where they languished, victims of poverty and neglect.

Today most of Nebraska's 12,500 Native Americans are members of five tribes—Omaha, Teton Sioux, Santee Sioux, Winnebago, and Ponca. Their largest concentration is in Thurston County, the location of the Omaha and Winnebago reservations, but others have moved to Omaha and Lincoln in search of work.

Although many people tend to perceive Native Americans as a single group, the several tribes have distinct histories and their cultures differ markedly from each other. But because many Indians share a view of the world and the place of human society in it that is different from mainstream Americans, they find it difficult to find a place in American life. Their forced economic, political, and social isolation on reservations has led to high rates of disease, unemployment, and alcoholism. In recent years, the Nebraska tribes have emphasized the importance of self-sufficiency for their reservations and have become adept at accessing capital for development. They also have worked hard to maintain and develop their cultural identity through traditional religion, native languages, and art, including story telling, ornamental clothing, and ceremonial dances.

Although African Americans were present in Nebraska in the territorial period, they began migrating in significant numbers to Nebraska during World War I, mostly to Omaha where jobs were created by the war effort. Since then their number has grown to nearly 4 percent of the state's population. Despite improvements in their economic and social status, African Americans as a group still lag behind state averages in health, wealth, and education.

Spanish-speaking people, of whom Mexicans constitute about 80 percent, are more widely distributed across the state. They are especially numerous in Scottsbluff, Grand Island, and North Platte, in addition to Omaha and Lincoln. Hispanic people form nearly 3 percent of the state's population, but in Scotts Bluff County, where many work in sugar beet production, they constitute 15 percent. In other parts of the state, many Mexican immigrants have been employed in meat-packing industries. Like Indians and African Americans, Spanish-speaking Nebraskans are almost always underenumerated by the census.

Nebraska also received many immigrants from overseas after World War II, though never in the numbers recorded in the nineteenth century. A few, such as the Latvians, most of whom settled in Lincoln, were refugees from war-devastated Europe, but others have come from Vietnam, Japan, China, Korea, and the Philippines. Like African Americans, they are concentrated in the Omaha metropolitan area, but others live in Lincoln, where they study or work at the University of Nebraska. Combined as one group, East Asians constitute less than 1 percent of Nebraska's people.

According to the 1990 census, 118,290 Nebraskans were members of minority groups, an increase of about 25 percent since 1980. The growth of minority-owned small businesses has been even greater. African Americans show the largest numerical increase in small businesses, and Asian Americans show the largest percentage increase. Nearly three-fourths of the minority-owned enterprises are located in the Omaha and Lincoln metropolitan areas. About half the firms are in services, with retail trade ranking second in importance.

56.1. The Peabody Museum of Harvard University encouraged respect for Native American customs, values, and beliefs when it returned the Sacred Pole of the Omaha Tribal Nation to Nebraska on 12 July 1989, a century after it had been taken. Here Joe Johns, a member of the Creek Nation of Oklahoma who was artist-in-residence at the museum, carries the pole through the powwow grounds in Macy before presenting it to Doran Morris, pictured on the right, chairman of the Omaha Tribal Council at the time. Photograph by Michael Farrell.

56.2. Although Senator Ernie Chambers has represented the largely African-American Eleventh District in the Nebraska legislature since 1970, he has eloquently defended the interests of all minority groups in the state. With a characteristic gesture, Senator Chambers here addresses his colleagues in the unicameral in 1994. Photograph by Kiley Timperley.

56.3. Children perform a folkdance at the 1990 Hispanic Heritage Festival in Lincoln. The festival is sponsored annually by the Hispanic Community Center, which offers educational, social, and cultural programs. Similar community centers located in Omaha, Kearney, and Lexington serve Spanish-speaking people regardless of race or origin. Courtesy Hispanic Community Center, Lincoln.

Two Decades of Politics, 1970–1990 *57*

In 1970, Republican Governor Norbert Tiemann was defeated in his re-election bid by Democrat J. James Exon. Analysis of voter behavior suggests that many conservative Republicans switched their votes, though not their allegiance, to Exon. This election revitalized the Democratic Party in Nebraska and stimulated a series of Democratic victories that has extented into the 1990s. From Tiemann's defeat until 1994, Democrats won an increasing share of the state's elective offices.

In 1970 Republicans held all statewide elective offices in government: both U.S. senators, all three congressional representatives, the governor, lieutenant governor, secretary of state, treasurer, auditor, and attorney general. By 1991 the picture had changed dramatically: Democrats held both seats in the U.S. Senate, one of the three congressional seats, the governorship and lieutenant governorship, auditor, and state treasurer. This in a state where, since 1967 when statewide voter registration was first mandated by the legislature, a substantial plurality of voters have repeatedly registered themselves as Republicans.

Democratic Party success in electoral politics despite minority status was brought about by a combination of national, local, and personal causes—but one cannot attribute it to imaginative or daring records of achievement. During the past two decades, the state's governors and legislators, regardless of political party affiliation, have generally sought ways to avoid tax increases without curtailing governmental services. James Exon served two terms as governor (1971–79) before his election to the U.S. Senate. He was succeeded by Republican Charles Thone (1979–83) and Democrat Robert Kerrey (1983–87), who, like Exon, later moved on to the U.S. Senate.

By the late 1980s unresolved problems in state government were too pressing to be postponed. Since 1967, when the legislature had last revised Nebraska's revenue structure, it had increased sales and income tax rates several times to reimburse local governments for property tax exemptions. Such taxes were indirectly linked to out-migration from rural areas and the inequities and inadequacies that weakened the state's program of aid to local school districts. Similarly, increased support for higher education was essential if Nebraska was to broaden its economic base and reduce the out-migration of young people to other states.

In 1986 Nebraskans nominated women as candidates for the governorship in both major parties—the first such instance in American history. Both Republican Kay Orr and Democrat Helen Boosalis were strong, competent, and experienced candidates. Given the Republican edge in voter registration, it came as no surprise that Kay Orr was elected.

Having pledged no increases in taxes, Governor Orr offered conservative solutions to the state's formidable problems, and the legislature responded positively to her leadership. Her task was complicated in 1987 when the Omaha-based conglomerate ConAgra announced that it would leave Nebraska for a new home in Tennessee if the legislature failed to revamp the state's tax laws in its favor. Even though Nebraska ranked low among the fifty states in the tax burden it imposed on corporations and personal incomes, the legislature, in response to Governor Orr's bidding, enacted by a two-to-one margin a law that provided substantial tax breaks for corporations, including credits for large investments in Nebraska, exemptions for selective property and equipment, and restriction of the taxable base for corporate earnings to in-state sales only. Another law reduced personal income tax rates on top earners.

By the general election of 1990, a majority of Nebraska voters were convinced that it was Governor Orr, not the legislature, who had raised taxes. Like Tiemann twenty years earlier, she narrowly lost her bid for reelection at least partly because the Republican party was not united in her support.

57.1. J. James Exon, a Lincoln businessman, was active in Democratic party
politics before his election as governor
in 1970. After serving two terms, he was
elected to the United States Senate in
1978. By emphasizing fiscal conservatism, Exon often attracted the support
of traditional Republicans. Courtesy
NSHS, E96.6:3.

57.2. Charles Thone, a Republican, had
a long and distinguished career in politics. He served four terms in Congress
as representative of the First District before his election as governor in 1978. In
this 1981 image, he cuts a ribbon to open
the renovated Frank House on the
campus of the University of Nebraska at
Kearney. Courtesy NSHS, T486.8:2–7.

57.3. J. Robert Kerrey, a native of Lincoln who presently resides in Omaha, served as Democratic governor of Nebraska from 1983 to 1987. A veteran of the Vietnam War who was awarded the Congressional Medal of Honor, Kerrey entered politics from the business world. He was elected U.S. Senator from Nebraska in 1988. Here he is shown as governor in September 1986. Courtesy Journal-Star Printing Co.

57.4. In 1986, Kay Orr of Lincoln became the first woman to be elected governor of Nebraska. Active in Republican Party politics, she had been appointed state treasurer in 1981 and was elected to that post in 1982. As governor she was especially strong in her support of higher education in the state. She is pictured here at her desk in December 1990. Courtesy Journal-Star Printing Co.

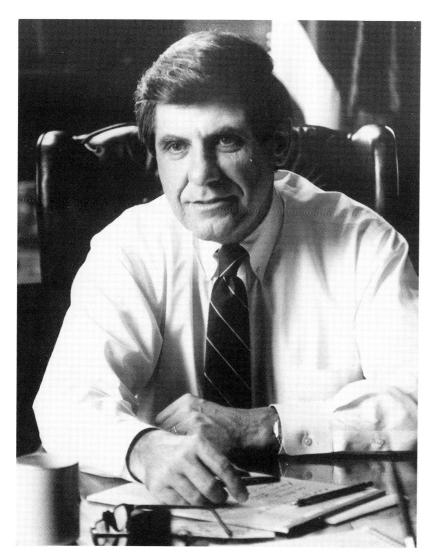

57.5. E. Benjamin Nelson, a lawyer and insurance executive, became the first resident of Omaha in a century to be elected governor of Nebraska. A native of McCook, Nelson, like his predecessors Exon and Kerrey, had been active in Democratic party affairs but had not previously held elective office. Courtesy Office of the Governor, Nebraska State Capitol.

The Quality of Life in Nebraska 58

Compared to other Americans, Nebraskans generally show high levels of satisfaction with the quality of their lives. This has not always been the case. Only since World War II have improvements in transportation and communication, the availability of water and electric power, and advances in agricultural technology led Nebraskans to express greater satisfaction with their lives than the people of the nation generally. The painful isolation and the difficulties of coping with a harsh climate that were typical of early times have virtually disappeared.

By most measures, Nebraskans seem to enjoy a quality of life that is superior to that found in the United States generally. They are pleased to occupy single-family dwellings, and they generally like the communities or neighborhoods in which they reside. Sociological studies indicate that they are more happily married than Americans in general. The proportion who consider themselves to be in excellent health is well above national norms. Their level of education is higher; their rate of unemployment is one of the lowest in the country. The crime rate for Nebraska is dramatically lower than that of most states. Quality of life is also related to the stress—or rather the lack of it—that people feel as they go about their daily tasks. Research suggests, happily, that Nebraska ranks near the bottom in terms of stress induced by business failures, unemployment, divorce, and bankruptcies.

Of course, modern Nebraska has its stubborn economic and social problems, mostly related to the decline of agriculture in the national economy and to the consequent exodus from rural areas. Adverse economic trends in Nebraska are likely to continue for some time. But rural people have a keen sense of community, and many plains communities consist of interrelated families who help each other in adversity. They volunteer more and respond to calls for help. Family ties also seem to be more powerful in lightly peopled places where solidarity is enhanced by ethnic and religious bonds.

Nebraskans, like most contemporary Americans, usually do not think of themselves as participants in a leisure society, but the fact is that they have both the time and wealth, compared to their nineteenth-century forebears, to engage in many recreational and cultural activities. One study of how Nebraskans spend their leisure time revealed that the most popular form of recreation is picnicking, followed by fishing, swimming, and visiting historical sites. Hunting, camping, hiking, rafting, and boating attract thousands more. One can scarcely estimate the number of persons who participate in baseball, softball, bowling, tennis, swimming, and other sports, both informal and organized.

The Nebraska Game and Parks Commission has developed over fifty recreational areas throughout the state with facilities for camping, fishing, swimming, and boating, which register millions of visitors annually. Lake McConaughy near Ogallala is the best known, but parks in the east such as the Fremont Lakes, Pawnee Lake, and Branched Oak Lake State Recreational Areas regularly serve the most people.

Attendance as spectators at football and basketball games is another matter. Nebraskans boast that University of Nebraska–Lincoln football games in the 76,000-seat Memorial Stadium have been sold out for every game since November 1962. Lacking major-league teams in any professional sport, Nebraskans attach great symbolic importance to the

Cornhuskers and their success in college football. Large crowds faithfully follow annual rodeos in North Platte, Burwell, and other communities. Horse racing is also well attended, though interest has declined in the 1990s since lottery gambling was legalized.

Nebraskans have also developed cultural resources. Omaha and Lincoln have supported symphony orchestras and theater groups for many years. The Joslyn Memorial in Omaha, a pink marble building that combines the Art Deco and Moderne styles, offers a fine collection of paintings and other artworks, including many that relate to history of the American West. The Sheldon Gallery at the University of Nebraska–Lincoln, which specializes in twentieth-century American art, occupies a classically proportioned building designed by Philip Johnson, a leading American architect. The Museum of Nebraska Art in Kearney emphasizes art on Nebraska themes and work by Nebraska artists. The opening of the Lied Center for the Performing Arts at the University of Nebraska–Lincoln in 1990 was a major event in the cultural history of the state.

Among the many museums in Nebraska is the State Museum (Morrill Hall) on the University of Nebraska–Lincoln campus, which features natural history. It houses one of the world's best collections of skeletons of prehistoric animals, all unearthed in the state and region. The Museum of Nebraska History in Lincoln and the Stuhr Museum of the Prairie Pioneer in Grand Island specialize in state history. The Western Heritage Museum in Omaha occupies the former Union railroad station, an important Art Deco structure built in 1931. The Nebraska State Historical Society, the Nebraska Game and Parks Commission, and the National Park Service maintain historic sites and visitor centers in the state.

By patronizing these and many other smaller historical museums in the state, Nebraskans gain a sense of identity—knowledge of who they are and where they came from. Because Nebraska occupies a unique space that has been populated by a unique mixture of cultural groups, its history is also unique—a product of the interaction of culture and environment.

Nebraskans have not always had an easy time of it in the past, nor will they in the future. Certain adverse economic and demographic trends are likely to continue. But that does not mean that Nebraskans will be less content. They will respond to new forces and new leaders who will identify new ways to solve old problems of community survival.

58.1. Each fall, as the football season gets underway, Memorial Stadium at the University of Nebraska–Lincoln becomes a mecca for thousands of spectators from all over the state. Its capacity far exceeds the population of any city in the state save Omaha and Lincoln. A source of great pride to the state, the Cornhuskers have often contended for the mythical national championship. Photo by Robert Becker. Courtesy Lincoln Journal-Star Printing Company.

58.2. The Lied Center for the Performing Arts at the University of Nebraska–Lincoln has greatly enriched the cultural life of Nebraska. Every year, world-famous orchestras, soloists, dance companies, and theater groups, as well as pop artists, perform in the 2,200-seat auditorium of this magnificent building, made possible by a multimillion dollar gift from the estate of Ernest Lied, a former Omaha businessman. Photograph by Tom Tidball. Courtesy UNL Office of Public Relations.

58.3. Grand Island is the home of the beautiful Stuhr Museum of the Prairie Pioneer. The main building, designed by the eminent American architect Edward Durrell Stone, occupies a dramatic location a few miles north of the Platte River. The museum also includes a reconstructed village with many buildings preserved from the pioneer period. Courtesy Stuhr Museum of the Prairie Pioneer.

Readings in the History of Nebraska

Even though Nebraska is a young state with a small population, thousands of documents, books, articles, doctoral dissertations, and masters theses touch on its history. One explanation for this abundance is the effectiveness of the Nebraska State Historical Society. Throughout its history, which is nearly as long as that of the state, it has gathered primary source materials in its archives, built a substantial library, and published extensively. Its most notable publication is the quarterly journal *Nebraska History*. The research presented in scores of articles that have appeared there provide the foundation for this book.

There are other major published sources, especially for the early decades. The most important are J. Sterling Morton and Albert Watkins, *Illustrated History of Nebraska*, 3 vols. (Lincoln: Jacob North & Co. and Western Publishing and Engraving, 1905–13); Addison E. Sheldon, *Nebraska: The Land and the People*, 3 vols. (Chicago: Lewis Publishing, 1931); and James C. Olson, *History of Nebraska*, 2d ed. (Lincoln: U of Nebraska P, 1966). Other valuable surveys include Dorothy Weyer Creigh, *Nebraska: A Bicentennial History* (New York: W. W. Norton; Nashville: American Association for State and Local History, 1977); Donald R. Hickey, *Nebraska Moments: Glimpses of Nebraska's Past* (Lincoln: U of Nebraska P, 1992); and Bradley H. Baltensperger, *Nebraska: A Geog-*

raphy (Boulder CO: Westview Press, 1985), which interprets Nebraska history from a geographical perspective. A volume useful for its illustrations is Bruce H. Nicoll, *Nebraska: A Pictorial History,* revised and enlarged by Gilbert M. Savery (Lincoln: U of Nebraska P, 1975). John Carter has celebrated frontier photography in his *Solomon D. Butcher: Photographing the American Dream* (Lincoln: U of Nebraska P, 1985).

Another essential source consists of data presented in the various publications of the U.S. Census Bureau. The many volumes of the *Nebraska Blue Book,* now published biennially by the Clerk of the Legislature, have been useful in countless ways. Similarly, the *Nebraska Statistical Handbook,* published by the Nebraska Department of Economic Development and now in its eleventh edition, offers a compendium of demographic, social, and economic data based on annual reports of governmental agencies. An example of the latter is *Nebraska Agricultural Statistics,* published biennially by the Nebraska Department of Agriculture. I have also used many statistically based articles that have been published through the years in *Business in Nebraska,* a publication of the Bureau of Business Research, College of Business Administration, University of Nebraska–Lincoln. Among newspaper sources, the most important were the *Omaha World-Herald,* the *Lincoln Journal,* and the *Lincoln Star.*

It would be inappropriate, in a book such as this, to list individually all the books and articles that I have depended on in preparing this volume. But some, because of their importance to me, deserve to be mentioned. Among them are several books produced by a generation of earlier historians, especially the well-known works of Everett N. Dick, such as *The Sod House Frontier, 1854–1890* (1937; reprint, Lincoln: U of Nebraska P, 1979) and *Conquering the Great American Desert: Nebraska* (Nebraska State Historical Society Publications, vol. 27 [Lincoln: Published by the Society, 1975]), as well as *The Populist Revolt* (1931; reprint, Lincoln: U of Nebraska P, 1961), by John D. Hicks.

More recent scholars have also left their marks on the bibliography of Nebraska history. Their books, often scholarly monographs not intended for a general readership, provide the building blocks for a more popular history. A brief selection follows.

Aucoin, James. *Water in Nebraska: Use, Politics, Policies.* Lincoln: U of Nebraska P, 1984.

Bleed, Ann, and Charles Flowerday, eds. *An Atlas of the Sand Hills.* 2d ed. Lincoln: Univ. of Nebraska Conservation and Survey Div., 1990.

Blouet, Bryan W., and Frederick C. Luebke, eds. *The Great Plains: Environment and Culture.* Lincoln: U of Nebraska P, 1979.

Bremer, Richard G. *Agricultural Change in an Urban Age: The Loup Country of Nebraska, 1910–1970.* University of Nebraska Studies, New Series no. 51. Lincoln: Univ. of Nebraska, 1976.

Broken Hoops and Plains People. [Lincoln]: Nebraska Curriculum Development Center, Univ. of Nebraska, 1976.

Cherny, Robert W. *Populism, Progressivism, and the Transformation of Nebraska Politics, 1885–1915.* Lincoln: U of Nebraska P, 1981.

Chudacoff, Howard P. *Mobile Americans: Residential and Social Mobility in Omaha, 1880–1920.* New York: Oxford UP, 1972.

Coletta, Paolo E. *William Jennings Bryan.* 3 vols. Lincoln: U of Nebraska P, 1964–69.

Emmons, David M. *Garden in the Grasslands: Boomer Literature of the Central Great Plains.* Lincoln: U of Nebraska P, 1971.

Fink, Deborah. *Agrarian Women: Wives and Mothers in Rural Nebraska, 1880–1940.* Chapel Hill: U of North Carolina P, 1992.

Jenkins, Allan, ed. *The Platte River: An Atlas of the Big Bend Region.* Kearney: Univ. of Nebraska at Kearney, 1993.

Larsen, Lawrence H., and Barbara J. Cottrell. *The Gate City: A History of Omaha.* [Boulder CO]: Pruett Publishing, 1982.

Lass, William E. *From the Missouri to the Great Salt Lake: An Account of Overland Freighting.* Lincoln: Nebraska State Hist. Soc., 1972.

Lonsdale, Richard, ed. *Economic Atlas of Nebraska.* Lincoln: U of Nebraska P, 1977.

Lowitt, Richard. *George W. Norris.* 3 vols. Vol. 1, Syracuse: Syracuse U P, 1963. Vols. 2 and 3, Urbana: U of Illinois P, 1971, 1978.

Luebke, Frederick C. *Immigrants and Politics: The Germans of Nebraska, 1880–1900.* Lincoln: U of Nebraska P, 1969.

Manley, Robert N. *Frontier University (1869–1910).* Vol. 1 of *Centennial History of the University of Nebraska.* Lincoln: U of Nebraska P, 1969.

Mattes, Merrill J. *The Great Platte River Road.* Lincoln: Nebraska State Hist. Soc., 1969.

McKee, James L. *Lincoln: The Prairie Capital.* Northridge CA: Windsor Publications, 1984.

Menard, Orville D. *Political Bossism in Mid-America: Tom Dennison, 1900–1933.* Lanham MD: University Press of America, 1989.

Miewald, Robert D., ed. *Nebraska Government and Politics.* Lincoln: U of Nebraska P, 1984.

Milner, Clyde A. *With Good Intentions: Quaker Work among the Pawnees, Otos, and Omahas in the 1870s.* Lincoln: U of Nebraska P, 1982.

Parsons, Stanley B. *The Populist Context: Rural versus Urban Power on a Great Plains Frontier.* Westport CT: Greenwood Press, 1973.

Pedersen, James F., and Kenneth D. Wald. *Shall the People Rule? A History of the Democratic Party in Nebraska Politics, 1854–1972.* Lincoln: Jacob North, 1972.

White, Richard. *The Roots of Dependency: Subsistence, Environment, and Social Change among Choctaws, Pawnees, and Navajos.* Lincoln: U of Nebraska P, 1983.

Williams, James H., and Doug Murfield, eds. *Agricultural Atlas of Nebraska.* Lincoln: U of Nebraska P, 1977.

Wishart, David J. *The Fur Trade of the American West, 1807–1840.* Lincoln: U of Nebraska P, 1979.

Index

airplanes: B-26 Marauders, 308, *310;* B-29 Superfortresses, 308, *310;* military, 299, *305, 311;* and the Platte River, 3; and transportation, 8; view from, *339*

alcohol, 218; breweries, 211, 213, *229;* drunkenness, 300; and Indians, 12, 17, 19, *33;* and the military, 28; and Protestant morality, 179, 180; and racial strife, 246; regulation of, 226; saloons, 60, 94, 212, 219. *See also* prohibition

Aldrich, Chester, 226

Alexander, Hartley Burr, 255

Alliance, *190,* 299, 300, *355*

Alliancemen. *See* Farmers Alliance

American Fur Company, 24, 31, *34*

American Red Cross, *243*

Anderson, Robert Ball, 158, 159

Andrews, Benjamin, 220

Anselmo, *169*

Ansley, *97*

Antioch, *241*

anti-Semitism, *274*

appliances, 192; in cities, 267–68, *271;* on farms, *265,* 268

Arapahos: buffalo hunting, *15;* massacre of, 143; migration, 11–12; raids by, 72, 143; reservation, 145

Arbor Day, *202*

Arbor Lodge, *203*

archaeology, 11

architecture: "business blocks," 95, *101;* churches, 182, *183, 184;* in Lincoln, 375; in Omaha, 192, *193,* 212, *216,* 375; school houses, *167, 168, 169;* Stuhr Museum, *378;* at the University of Nebraska, 172, *175, 375. See also* capitols; houses

Arikaras: and fur trading, 18, 28; migration, 11; and the military, 28

Armour, Philip, 118

Army, U.S.: black soldiers, *156, 162;* and the Civil War, 70; dog training, *306;* and Indians, 13, 143, 152; and freighting, 54, *56, 57;* military expeditions, 22, 23, 24, *26;* and overlanders, *40;* relief efforts by, 103; training, *240. See also names of individual forts*

Army Air Corps, 308

Army Specialized Training Program, 313

Arthur County, 281

the arts: during the Great Depression, *287;* in the capitol, 255, *258, 277;* by explorers, 23, 24; galleries, 212, 375; and Interstate 80, *326, 327;* Native American, *16,* 363; Nebraska Arts Council, 328; sculptures, 236, 255, *327;* symphonies, 375

Ash Hollow, 37

Astor, John Jacob, 18, 23

Atkinson, Henry, 27

Atkinson (town), *285*

Atlanta, 299

auctions, 280, *283*

Aughey, Samuel, 113

Austin, Sadie, *111*

automobiles: in cities, 268; and highways, 268; influence of, 8, 166, 192, 267; and rural life, 259, 261, *262–63,* 268. *See also* streets and highways

Dickey, Elbert, *348*

"Dirty Thirties," 279–81, *283, 284,* 293; relief efforts, 280–81, *284, 285, 286, 287*

diseases: of animals, 197; in cities, 95, 211; among Indians, 12–13, 19, 145, 152, 362; and overlanders, 38; among settlers, 131. *See also* medicine

Dismal River, *126*

dissent, political, 238–39

Doane College, 173

doctors. *See* medicine

Dodge, Col. Henry, 24

Dakota Territory, 44, 71

Dougherty, John, *20*

Daughters of Founders and Patriots of America, *270*

Department of Defense, U.S., 309

Department of War, *310*

Douglas, Stephen A., 42–43

Douglas County, *273,* 309, 324, 353; courthouse, *216, 245, 247*

draft, military, 298, *301, 302,* 315

drought, 3, 195, 198, *199, 200;* in the 1800s, 55, 102–3, 108, 114, 191, *199,* 205; in the 1900s, 275, 279

Dull Knife, 152

Dundy, Elmer, *148*

Durant, Thomas, *62, 64*

dust storms, 279, *282*

economics: and children, 131; and currency reform, 204–5, 232; deflation, 204–5; Department of Economic Development, 329; depression in the 1800s, 55; 102–3, 114, 191, 192, 195, *199;* economic

changes, 349; and immigrants, 138; and Interstate 80, 324, *326;* minimum wage act, 329; of modern Nebraska, 374–75; and Offutt Air Force Base, 212; of Omaha, 82, 210–11, 212; Panic of 1873, 102; and politics, 186–87, 205–6, 231–32; prosperity, 275, 280; and racial strife, 246, *333–34;* and railroads, 102; and SAC, 308–9; territorial, 54–55, *56, 57, 58;* and wars, 238, *241,* 259, 300. *See also* banks, Great Depression; *and under* agriculture

Edgren, August H., 219–20

education. *See* colleges and universities; schools; University of Nebraska

elections: ballots, *189,* 205, 206; campaigning, *190,* 238; electoral reforms, 205, 206, 225, 226, 227. *See also* politics

electricity: lack of, 93, 95, *215;* rural, 260, *265,* 268, 292, 293–94; urban, 191, 192, 211, 267–68, 295. *See also* public power

elevation, 2

Elkhorn River: and farming, 55, 102, 261; and Indians, 13; and log cabins, 124; and other rivers, 2

Emigrant House, *215*

emigrants. *See also* overlanders

Enola Gay (bomber), *310*

entertainment: football, 374–75, *377;* leisure activities, 374; movies, 192; political rallies, *230;* radio, 192, 260, *271, 272;* rodeos, 375; theaters, 220

Mormons, 37, *39, 40*
Morrill Act (1862), 172
Morris, Doran, *365*
Morrison, Frank, 328
Morton, J. Sterling, 197, *202, 203*
Morton, Nancy Jane Fletcher, *75*
Morton, Thomas, *75*
mountain men. *See* fur trading
movies. *See under* entertainment
Municipal University of Omaha,
    314, 315, *316,* 329. *See also* University of Nebraska at Omaha
Museum of Nebraska Art, 375
Museum of Nebraska History, 375
Mutual of Omaha, *352*
My Antonia (Cather), 219
Myers, E. E., *216*

Nance County, 137, 144, 151
Naponee, *282*
National Association for the Advancement of Colored People
    (NAACP), *337*
National Banking Act, *58*
National Guard, 298, 334, *336*
National Park Service, 375
Native Americans. *See* Indians
Navy, U.S., 313
Naylor, Kirk, *316*
Nebraska: aerial view of, 339, *341;* constitution, 78, 192; as the Cornhusker State, *348;* origin of name, 2; as a transit area, 7–8, 17. *See also* legislature
Nebraska: The Land and the People (Sheldon), 103
Nebraska: A Pictorial History (Nicoll), 239

Nebraska Arts Council, 328
Nebraska Bankers Association, 328
Nebraska City, 49, 82; during the Civil War, 71; and freighting, *56, 57,* 71; and overlanders, *39,* 54; as a river port, 93; slavery in, 157, *160;* and steamboats, 31, *35,* 36; and trees, *175, 203*
Nebraska City News, 160
Nebraska Educational Television, 329
Nebraska Farmer, 250
Nebraska Game and Parks Commission, 374, 375
Nebraska Palladium, 49
Nebraska Potash Company, *241*
Nebraska Power Company, 293
Nebraska Public Power District, 294
Nebraska Public Power System, 293, 294
Nebraska State Council of Defense, 238
Nebraska State Historical Society, *74,* 375
Nebraska State Horticultural Society, 114
Nebraska State Supreme Court, *222*
Nebraska Territory, 8, 31, 157; creation of, *35,* 42–44, *45, 46, 47,* 59; schools in, 164. *See also* legislature; government
Nebraska University, *174*
Nebraska Wesleyan University, 173, 219
Neligh, *274*
Nelson, E. Benjamin, *372*
New Deal, *235*
newspapers: foreign-language, 138,

238; on Indians, 38; Lincoln, *223;* on Omaha, 48; and politics, *188, 189, 234;* and racial strife, 246; territorial, 49; on the unicameral, 289. *See also names of specific newspapers*

New York Times, 48

Nicoll, Bruce, 239

Niobrara River, 103, 124, *133,* 142, 144, *156*

Norfolk, 320, 354, *356*

normal schools. *See* colleges and universities

Norris, George, *101,* 231, 232–33, 280; and public power, 233, *236,* 292, 293–94; and the unicameral, 233, *288,* 289, *291*

North Loup River, 151

North Platte (city): canteen, 299; as a cattle town, 324; Hispanics in, 363; as a market center, 320; population, 354, *356;* and railroads, 60, *65, 154,* 293; rodeos, 375

North Platte River, 18–19, *57,* 152; and farming, 261, *266;* and overlanders, 37; and Kingsley Dam, 233, 293, *296*

Northern Cheyennes, 152

Northwestern (railroad), 88

Norton, John N., *288*

nuclear power, 294, *297*

O'Brien, Maj. George M., *75*

occupations: cowboys, *110, 111,* 158; doctors, 131; railroad workers, 60, *90,* 136; "road ranchers," 106; teachers, 165, 166, *167, 168, 169;* of blacks, 158, 159, *160, 162, 163,* 164;

in cities, 48–49, 81; in Nebraska Territory, 54–55, *57;* of settlers, 8; in towns, 94, 185. *See also* businesses; cattle industry; farming; freighting; fur trading; ranching

Oconto, *129*

Offutt Air Force Base (Offutt Field), 308–9, *311, 312*

Ogallala, 107, *274,* 281, 293; population changes, 354

Oglala Sioux, 144, 152

Olson, James C., 186

Omaha (city), *306,* 339, *356;* and agrarian dissent, *282;* the arts in, 375; blacks in, 157, 159; business district, 211, *216;* census data, 353; character of, 83, 218–19; colleges and universities, *177;* conditions in, 95, 211, *215;* and freighting, 54, 71; hospitals, 211; immigrants in, 136, *140, 215;* Indians in, 362; as an industrial and transportation center, 44, 82, 192, *215;* and Interstate 80, 324, *325, 326;* labor strikes, 246; library, 212; meatpacking plants, 107, 211, 213; as a metropolis, 210–13, *214, 215, 216;* and the military, 71, 238, *243;* minorities in, 363, 364, *366;* museums, 375; and overlanders, 37; police, 211, 245, 246, *247,* 334–35; politics, 212, *217,* 246; and Populism, *208;* and railroads, 8, *58,* 60, 62, 211; relocating the capital, 81–82, *84, 85,* 102, 185–86; as a river port, 93; and SAC, 308, 309; schools, *170;* smelting, 211, 213, *215;* and steamboats, 31, 36, 71;